NEVER FORGET AGAIN

Master Your Imagination and **Develop a Legendary Memory**

MATTHEW CANNING

THIRD EDITION

Never Forget Again ©2013 Matthew Canning

Published by the Influxa Media Group

Edited by Erin Thorp

All rights reserved. No part of this publication may be reproduced, stored in a retrieval system, or transmitted in any form or by any means without the prior written permission of the author.

ISBN 978-0615844732

First Edition: October 2013 | Third Edition: August 2019

MATTHEWCANNING.COM

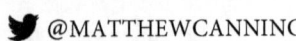 @MATTHEWCANNING

This book is dedicated to George Canning, who is living proof that you don't need a good role model, mentor, or fancy education in order to amass a stunning amount of worldly knowledge. He taught me that the best education is the one that you bestow upon yourself.

Contents

Introduction 1

Section 1: Basic Memory Development 18

    Lesson 1: Memorizing Small Numbers and the Journey Method (Part 1).......... 19
    Lesson 2: Memorizing Small Numbers and the Journey Method (Part 2).......... 30
    Lesson 3: Memorizing Small Numbers and the Journey Method (Part 3).......... 40
    Lesson 4: Memorizing Lists of "Familiar Entities" 47
    Lesson 5: Learning and Revisitation Rhythms 60
    Review and Development: Section 1 68

Section 2: Intermediate Memory Development 74

    Lesson 1: Associating "Familiar Entities" 76
    Lesson 2: Associating Two "Unfamiliar Entities"... 83
    Lesson 3: Associating Three or More "Unfamiliar Entities" 97
    Lesson 4: Memorizing Lists of Associated "Familiar Entities"........................... 106
    Lesson 5: Memorizing Lists of (Single or Associated) "Unfamiliar Entities".... 112
    Review and Development: Section 2 120

Section 3: Alternative Memory Development 130

    Lesson 1: The Treasure Map Method 131
    Lesson 2: Meta-Information 141
    Lesson 3: Memorizing Strings of Letters 148
    Review and Development: Section 3 157

Section 4: Advanced Memory Development 169

    Lesson 1: Taking the Journey to the Next Level... 171
    Lesson 2: The Mnemonic Character Library (Part 1) 180
    Lesson 3: The Mnemonic Character Library (Part 2) 203
    Lesson 4: Memorizing People (Names and Faces)... 216
    Review and Development: Section 4 227

Section 5: Bonus Material—Extreme Memory Development 246

Lesson 1: Additional Numerical Mnemonic Skills *248*
Lesson 2: Memorizing Strings of Letters: Advanced Practices *259*
Lesson 3: Indexing Your Life and Remembering Each Day Forever *262*
Lesson 4: Memory Health *284*
Lesson 5: The Profound Effects of Sleep on Memory *288*
Review and Development: Section 5 .... *292*

Conclusion 296

Why Isn't This Taught in School? *297*
Troubleshooting Memory *302*
Beyond This Book *310*
What Does the Future Hold for Memory? *314*
Final Thoughts: Some Words of Caution *316*

Glossary 319

Works Referenced 334

Introduction

He was much shorter than I'd expected.

When you're walking to a small restaurant in Philadelphia to meet someone who had spent years conducting high-risk reconnaissance missions for the US military, you begin to conjure up visions of an action figure—a tall, stern, statuesque machine of a man with a disarming stare. What I found instead was a welcoming man in his late forties, with a receding hairline and more than a slight bulge where his black polo shirt was tucked neatly into his khakis.

He was more *John Lovitz* than *John Cena*, but then again, he'd been retired for quite some time.

Having conducted years of study in the development of this book, I already knew that many of the skills I had uncovered were similar to those used by memory "professionals;" in many cases, the methods I studied were favored by memory competitors, performers, and the like. As I was significantly more interested in the practical side of **Memory Development**, I called in some favors, and—after leveraging the connections of a former coworker—I was able to sit down with someone whose memory had been trained to an elite level by an organization for whom money was no object: the United States government.

I had spoken about **Memory Development** with military personnel before, but never before had the opportunity to speak with someone of this level; I was in the company of a real-life 007.

After an hour of comfortable conversation, a fancy beer (his) and a mediocre coffee (mine), we shook hands and parted ways. It was made clear that I could not use his name or image in this book, but I was free to share some of the methods we discussed. Unfortunately, those methods were virtually identical to the ones with which I had become quite familiar through the countless resources I spent years exploring. As it turns out, the human memory is a very specific type of machine, and the secrets of those who have mastered it—regardless of purpose or vocation—exploit the strengths of this machine in strikingly similar ways.

I walked away, disappointed that several months' worth of phone calls had resulted in a meeting from which I gained little fresh insight. Sure, it was nice to know that I had developed as elite a memory as a highly trained and field-tested government operative, but beyond some geeky bragging rights, what had I gained?

I was convinced there was much more to be discovered, and I vowed in that moment to take **Memory Development** to the next level.

Memory: The Core of All Learning

The ancient Greek tragedian Aeschylus once penned, "Memory is the mother of all wisdom." This is difficult to argue; memory, put simply, is responsible for everything we know. Without a memory, we would have no knowledge, and if we had an absolutely perfect memory, we would have retained all the knowledge we've ever come across. Though the latter is unattainable, the closer we can get to having a perfect memory, the better off we would theoretically be.

How easy would school have been if we could instantly memorize everything we read? In fact, how much easier would life be overall if we could instantly store everything we saw or heard? We wouldn't have to review information; studying would be pointless. We'd never need to write anything down. We could spend more mental energy on the value and consequence of information, rather than on the task of retaining the information itself.

Of course, instant memorization of everything we encounter is not an attainable goal, but by drastically improving our short- and long-term memories (which, as we'll see, is *very much* attainable), we'll be able to tackle increasingly complex mental challenges with a greater degree of ease. Memory is the foundation for learning and skill acquisition; it is the canvas upon which we write out the problems we solve and the journal through which we record our experiences. In short, by developing a well-trained memory, we'll be making our lives much easier.

In fact, I would argue that training your memory is the single most important thing you can do to make your life easier, to improve your productivity, and to improve your relationships.

It's also a lot of fun, as a trained memory presents you with a constant flow of unique cognitive challenges. Take, for example, the world-famous Rubik's Cube. This puzzle has astounded and delighted generations with its frustrating simplicity. Years ago, a gentleman named Denny Dedmore developed a method for solving it. The solution requires the memorization of seven distinct steps, and each step requires several algorithms (a series of twists and turns). The algorithms (eighteen in total) are each up to twenty-two moves in length, and need to be applied to very specific color patterns on the Cube.

Essentially, Dedmore's method allows the solver to exchange a difficult cognitive challenge for a significantly less daunting memorization challenge.

Using the memorization methods discussed in this book, an absolute amateur can spend a single afternoon learning to solve a Rubik's Cube using the Dedmore method, and eventually become comfortable enough to solve the puzzle within a few minutes.

This is just one small, fun example of how a daunting task can become drastically less intimidating with a well-trained memory.

Do yourself a favor: Have patience, learn to enjoy the process, and spend the time allotted for each aspect of this book. In fact, if you enjoy this learning process more than you imagined you would, please feel free to spend even more time than suggested on the individual lessons before moving on. Your sacrifice now will serve you for the rest of your life.

Developing your memory is not about practicing memorization drills the way you were taught in school; it's about learning practical, natural ways to remember, and then reinforcing these methods until they become habitual.

A (Very) Brief History of Memory

Prior to the birth of printing, human memory was valued as a vital narrative tool, as ideas and core cultural knowledge were passed along primarily through the spoken word. As tools developed and evolved that aided mankind's ability to inexpensively record information, memory became less necessary, less sought after, and less often employed. In the grand scheme of human evolution, this transformation occurred relatively recently, and the fundamental structures of our brains have not devolved so as to significantly inhibit our memories. Profound abilities lie dormant within us, waiting to be called into action.

Centuries ago, the methods used to harness the powers of memory were taught to the very young; as a result, it was relatively commonplace for the educated to exhibit abilities that would be considered exceptional by today's standards. According to Derren Brown's book, *Tricks of the Mind*, the lineage of ancient mnemonic systems was all but destroyed in the 1500's by the Puritan reformation, which challenged the (often absurd or obscene) imaginative tools leveraged to remember large amounts of information.

In the more recent past, neuroscientists have studied the actual mechanisms through which short- and long-term memories are stored and retrieved. At the same time, memory enthusiasts (often called "mnemonists" or—until the 1990's—"memory men") have employed specific techniques that augment or supplement our "natural" memories. Aside from these niche pockets of interest, **Memory Development** has largely fallen out of mainstream consciousness and the art of memory has been all but lost.

Despite all of modern humanity's educational advancements, memory is one area wherein we've slowly but measurably regressed. As a result, at this point, most are simply oblivious to the sheer capabilities of human memory.

If you're interested in the history of human mnemonic techniques beyond the short synopsis provided above, I suggest you read *The Art of Memory* by Frances Yates, as it addresses this topic in incredible detail.

Many of the methods most commonly employed by the mainstream public for the purported development of memory are almost entirely useless, and are largely based upon the massive, widespread assumption that **Memory Development** is best achieved through repetition. Our brains simply don't work this way and are constantly giving us clues about it: every time a song gets stuck in our heads; every time we associate two superficially related objects or ideas (such as a spouse's shirt and the restaurant to which it was first worn). Despite such hints, most of us spent our academic lives trying to memorize historical dates, president's names, geometric formulas, and cloud types through use of brute force and repetition.

Oh, to have those years back!

The art of memory has actually enjoyed a bit of press in recent years. At almost the exact time that I finished writing this book, I was delighted to see that a young writer named Joshua Foer published a bestselling (and very enjoyable) account of his journey into the world of competitive memory championships, entitled *Moonwalking with Einstein*. Thanks to such exposure in popular culture, people may one day come to understand the true value of **Memory Development**.

However, let's just worry about *you* for now.

Although his interest was primarily focused on competitive (as opposed to practical) applications, Foer exhibits a deep respect for both the history and art of **Memory Development**. He laments modern society's failure to prioritize memory:

It is not hard to feel as though a tremendous devolution has taken place between that Golden Age [of memory] and our own comparatively leaden one. People used to labor to furnish their minds. They invested in the acquisition of memories the same way we invest in the acquisition of things. But today...the vast majority of us don't trust our memories. We find shortcuts to avoid relying on them. We complain about them endlessly, and see even their smallest lapses as evidence that they're starting to fail us entirely. How did memory, once so essential, end up so marginalized? Why did these techniques disappear? How, I wondered, did our culture end up forgetting how to remember? (p.134)

Embrace Your Imagination

Take a look at this photograph for three seconds, and then look away. Don't cheat; limit yourself to exactly three seconds.

Now look at the following number for the same duration: 149521882819.

The photograph is of a predatory animal; instinctively, this is something that we perceive as a threat to our survival. Over millennia, our minds have evolved such that we can quickly process and retain that information. However, we have not yet evolved to handle the number in the same way. It's mundane, devoid of context, and seemingly unimportant to our immediate primal interests.

In reality, these two things share a comparable level of complexity, but contain two different types of information: one that our minds are equipped to quickly process and retain, and another that is a bit more foreign. Without going back and looking again, think for a moment about how much information you were able to collect in that quick moment you spent looking at the photograph. What type of animal was featured? Was it young or mature? Alone or with others? On the left or right side of the photograph? Was the photo taken during the day or night? Was the creature standing or lying down? Was it on concrete or grass? What was in the background? Were the trees in the background alive or dead?

Can you truly say the photo contained less information than the twelve-digit number?

With this exercise, we unearth clues about the nature of well-formed memories. How do people with incredible "natural" memories retain information? Do they use some complex innate algorithm? Are they simply smarter?

No.

Effective memorization doesn't involve extreme repetition, predisposition, high IQ, or some complex "filing method," but rather engaging your most intimate and natural faculty: your imagination.

One of my best friends can tell me, after a moment of thought, the precise date on which an event occurred in the distant past, going back almost thirty years. This skill is not cultivated; it's a natural ability. His recollection always begins with a particular, strange detail, such as a conversation or a garment that someone was wearing. From there, he builds upon the small memory visually, until the scene unravels before him, eventually providing clues to the date.

Note that this extraordinary skill doesn't come from a lifeless lock-box of stored information; rather, the process is personal, multi-sensory, and—in many cases—emotional.

We can certainly learn what comes naturally to my friend. Later in this book, we'll learn how to perform a variant of this skill ourselves. The sole advantage those with strong natural memories have over normal folks is the fact that they didn't have to first unlearn bad memorization habits. We will.

If you're like most, your short-term memory is so bad that you can't remember an unfamiliar ten-digit phone number for more than about ten seconds. However, there most likely exist several phone numbers you *do* know (such as those of close friends or family). How do you remember them? It's probably not the numbers themselves that you remember. It may be their "shape"—the path your fingers take across the phone's keypad. It may be the poetic rhythm the numbers produce when spoken aloud.

This is another important clue about the nature of human memory.

Humans are an imaginative breed, and even the least creative of us use our imaginations on a moment-by-moment basis. Many would argue that the very depth and complexity of our imaginative capacity inherently separates our consciousness from that of other relatively intelligent creatures, such as primates and cetaceans. This capacity and our ability to visualize are the some of the strongest mental tools we have, providing the means for many of our brain's most complex cognitive functions.

We naturally want to use our imagination to store and recall information, but doing so is in direct opposition to what many of us were taught.

There's a reason why we don't remember everything we do or learn. When we sleep—specifically during REM cycles—our brains sift through the information that we encountered during the previous day. It disregards information that it perceives as useless for survival and stores that which it perceives as useful. In evolutionary terms, it doesn't make sense to retain every minute detail of our lives, as most are relatively insignificant.

However, highly imaginative or interesting information can slip through this housekeeping process. For example, two years from now, you wouldn't likely remember a dress worn by an average woman sitting next to you on the subway today. However, if the same woman were wearing a bright pink tuxedo, you'd likely remember it with an impressive level of clarity. Interesting moments and ideas in our lives tend to stand out in our memories. So, if you're attempting to memorize mundane, "unimportant" information, it makes sense to attach it to something vivid and unusual, therefore lessening the chances of your mind throwing it out with the night's garbage. This is precisely what you'll be learning to do.

Though memories are strongest when multisensory, we'll be focusing more heavily upon imagery than we will sounds, smells, taste, or touch. In some ways, this opposes a common belief about "learning styles"; it was widely accepted for quite some time that each individual has a tendency to learn most successfully through one of the four VARK methods (Visual, Auditory, Reading, Kinesthetic). However, recent evidence actually suggests otherwise; *Psychological Science in the Public Interest*, a leading academic journal, printed a paper in 2008 entitled "Learning Styles: Concepts and Evidence," which suggests that the differences between individuals' learning styles are most likely considerably less varied than previously thought. It seems that most of us share a predilection for visual learning.

It should be noted, however, that though the methods by which we'll be recording memories are predominantly visual, they are not exclusively so. In fact, while vision is the sense most tightly linked to short-term memory, there exists evidence that our sense of smell is vividly bound to long-term memory.

So why focus on the visual?

We have a bit more freedom with vision than our other senses; it's more difficult to conjure up a brand new smell in your imagination than it is to come up with a new image. However, visual scenes can be greatly accentuated with other sensory information. For example, "vividly" imagining a crocodile doesn't simply mean visualizing a still image of it; rather, imagine its smell, the sounds it makes, the feeling of its breath, its movements, and the taste of the swamp water as you struggle to escape its jaws.

The more free and vibrant you allow your imagination to be, the better you'll become at quickly conjuring up strong images and accentuating them with your other senses. This skill will form the foundation of a powerful memory. You'll learn all about this strange and exciting new world shortly.

To put it simply: to train one's memory is really to train one's imagination.

Neuroplasticity and the Brain Capacity Myth

When faced with the idea of improving one's memory, a few common questions arise. One is particularly interesting because it speaks directly to a common misconception about how the brain works, and thus should be addressed:

"If I begin to memorize a vast amount of information," people often ask, "won't my brain get full?"

Even when asked in a more scientific way, there's little validity to this notion. The human brain is a physical entity that takes up a finite amount of space, and memories are stored through the alteration of matter and energy within the brain; therefore the brain must technically have a set upper threshold for memory capacity (some scientists and scholars propose that this storage capacity sits around 2.5 petabytes, or 9,000 large computer hard drives). This theoretical threshold is nothing that any human has ever (or likely *will* ever) come close to reaching.

In short, your brain simply can't get "full" from acquiring too much information.

In fact, most evidence points to the opposite conclusion: the more memory is used to store information, the larger our memory capacity becomes. As we discussed, the use of imagination is key to memorization, and with the development of our imagination, we're essentially creating "new space" in our brains by exercising our ability to forge interesting (and often absurd) connections and associations. We humans tend to equate our brains' memory system to storage concepts we understand, such as file cabinets or hard drives, but that's not how it works. In reality, it's much less structured and much more associative and complex. If you'd like, you can read an interesting study on these misconceptions called, "What People Believe about How Memory Works: A Representative Survey of the U.S. Population."

To quote Nassim Nicholas Taleb's bestselling book, *The Black Swan*, "with so many brain cells—one hundred billion (and counting)—the attic is quite large, so the difficulties probably do not arise from storage-capacity limitations, but may just be indexing problems." (p. 68)

Our brains are constantly adapting, and not just through the subtle connective changes that take place between individual neural pathways during thinking and memory storage. There is a concept known as **Neuroplasticity**, or "brain plasticity," which explains how the brain can physically adapt to accommodate changes in the stimulation it receives. As a simple example, in one experiment performed by MIT's Mriganka Sur, ferrets had their ear-to-brain and eye-to-brain connections switched. After some time, it was found that their brains adapted in order to allow them to both see and hear again.

There are much more extreme examples of this phenomenon, even in humans. Take, for example, the curious case of Brandi Binder, who helped us to discover that the brain is capable of forging a vast number of new connections within allotted real estate. At 13, Brandi endured a traumatic surgery called a hemispherectomy, which literally left her with half of her brain intact. She awoke from surgery, and, as expected, was barely able to walk, talk, or move most of her body. She lost all capacity to understand abstract, creative concepts such as art, analogies, and humor; essentially, she was robbed of skills that were controlled by the removed hemisphere.

However, Brandi resolved to recover beyond the expectations of her family and doctors by placing upon herself a relentless series of challenges. In doing so, she has re-developed many of these lost skills to an extent that once seemed impossible. As one would imagine, this surprised many in the scientific community. Now in her twenties, Brandi is an accomplished artist, swimmer, high school graduate, and active member of society. Extensive study of her case showed that Brandi's remaining brain forged a massive number of new physical connections, effectively turning half a brain into a makeshift, passable full brain.

The "plasticity" of the brain—the same barely-understood series of biological functions that allowed Brandi to overcome her handicap—is precisely the phenomenon that allows us to keep endlessly cramming our skulls with information.

Paradoxically, the more you memorize through imaginative, creative, vivid means, the more you're going to leverage brain plasticity and actually induce an increase in your storage capacity. So, no, your brain isn't going to get full and end up ditching old information to make room for the new, and yes, you can feel free to memorize William Carlos Williams' classic poem, *The Red Wheelbarrow* without having to make space by forgetting *I'm My Own Grandpa*.

Everyone's Invited

Incredible feats of memory aren't reserved for the lucky or talented among us. Realistically, you don't even need to be that "smart" to develop an absolutely amazing memory. There are thousands of mnemonists alive today, and many are involved with competitive memory associations such as the World Memory Championships and World Memory Sports Council. What are the odds that every one of these individuals was born with a mental gift and also happened to have an interest in memory sports? Sure, a predisposition toward an exceptional memory could arguably encourage continued interest, but that surely doesn't apply to every successful mnemonist. To hear some of the great modern memory experts tell it, very few people are born with exceptional memories; most world-class memories are the result of hard work and training.

What Sets Never Forget Again Apart

Many of the memory concepts you'll soon learn about, such as use of one's imagination and the employment of **Journeys**, have been explored for millennia; they've been documented many times and by many people. However, *Never Forget Again* encompasses an entirely new approach to **Memory Development** and explores many unique methods. These include:

- A new and innovative way to structure information, including classifications such as: Familiar vs. Unfamiliar Entities, lists, Associated vs. Non-Associated Entities, and combinations of these types. No other Memory Development program makes distinctions between these different types of information, and doing so provides a distinct advantage, as the brain handles different types of information in different ways. Each type of information comes with a defined rule set; when faced with a memorization challenge, this allows you to instantly determine which method is most appropriate.

- A Memory Development program that focuses on day-to-day, applicable skills, instead of training you as though you were entering competitive memory events. You'll learn the best ways in which to remember many types of practical information, not just 400-digit integers.

- A suite of entirely new and innovative ways to approach information you only need to store for short periods of time (such as The Treasure Map Method).

- An array of unique additions that may be applied to proven classical mnemonic methods, including Contextual Journeys, Transitions between Journey Steps, and treating Temporary and Permanent Information differently.

- The distinction between Linear and Asynchronous Mnemonic Scenes.

- Beginner-to-expert coverage: Although Never Forget Again's Memory Development education begins at the very beginning and assumes no prior experience, it concludes with advanced, expert-level lessons, which many other programs leave out. Most other programs assume that the reader is equipped to continue developing independently once the basics are understood. On the contrary, structured assistance in even the most advanced stages of Memory Development ensures clarity and the reinforcement of strong habits. Would you teach a child addition, subtraction, multiplication and division, and then assume that they'll be able to teach themselves calculus?

- Meta-Information, the idea of storing peripheral information about other, more important information.

- Tested additions to classical Mnemonic Characters and Actions methods (for numerical memorization), including Mirrored Numbers, Negative Numbers, Decimal Numbers, and Repeating Numbers.

- The concept of the Mega-Journey, or an array of adjacent, ordered Journeys.

- The EFL (Exaggerate, First Name-Location, Last Name-Clue) Method for associating people's names with their faces.

- A focus on the imagination and the importance of using absurd, ridiculous imagery to reinforce memories.

Extensive **Mnemonic Vocabularies** for oft-neglected information types, such as the individual letters of the alphabet.

How to include an optional **Precision Check** within numerical information, so as to ensure your recollection is accurate.

The concept of **Daily Indexes**: the ability to combine and utilize **Daily Strings** and **Trigger Memories** in order to remember each day of your life in incredible detail.

It's likely that most of the above features make very little sense to you right now. That's okay; you'll understand them all soon enough.

Let's begin.

Section 1: Basic Memory Development

As we just discussed, memory is the foundation of everything we learn, and we are about to delve into the foundation of **Memory Development**.

That's right, this is the *foundation's foundation*.

In this section, you'll learn how to memorize numbers, associate certain types of words and ideas, remember lengthy lists, and schedule memorization to optimize retention. These skills are incredibly useful on their own but also lay the groundwork for more advanced lessons.

Lesson 1: Memorizing Small Numbers and the Journey Method (Part 1)

> *"THE SOUL NEVER THINKS WITHOUT A PICTURE."*
> —ARISTOTLE, PHILOSOPHER

Of all the objects, places, concepts, and people in the known universe, you're going to begin **Memory Development** with small numbers. Not because they're easy (they're not; they're boring and notoriously difficult to retain), but because the methods used to memorize them will prepare you for many other types of memorization.

Numbers are mundane pieces of data, and, as mentioned in the introduction, the trick to memorizing information like this is to associate it with visual, imaginative scenes and scenarios. You'll begin by learning to store a single-digit number in a specific "space" in your memory, and work up to storing three, four, and even five digits within the same amount of space.

There are two concepts key to memorizing small numbers, which will carry over into many other memorization techniques in this book: the

Mnemonic Vocabulary and the **Journey Method**. Together, they form a tight bond that allows for incredible feats of memory to take place.

The Mnemonic Vocabulary

A **Mnemonic Vocabulary** is a series of words, ideas, or objects used to memorize a specific type of information. For example, if you were to use the color red to remember January, blue to remember February, yellow to remember March, and so on, these colors together form a **Mnemonic Vocabulary** that represents the months of the year. This is a concept we'll revisit over and over.

According to everyone from the ancient Greeks to modern competitive mnemonists, the key to memorizing small numbers is to create **Mnemonic Clues** that represent each number. These **Clues** will serve as our personal **Mnemonic Vocabulary** for single-digit numbers.

Let's create a basic set of **Single-Digit Mnemonic Clues** for all ten single-digit numbers (0 through 9).

Take the number 1, for example. Two examples of possible visual **Clues** for the number 1 are "gun" (which *sounds* like "one") and "pencil" (which is long and thin, so it *looks* like the written character "1"). Examples for 9 could be "wine" (which *sounds* like "nine") and "lollypop" (which sort of *looks* like a "9").

How about 8?

What objects or images look similar to the number 8? One doughnut sitting atop another? A snowman? John Lennon-esque sunglasses? A bra hanging on a laundry line? What about a few objects or images that *sound* like "eight?" A dumbbell (weight)? A gate? Get as creative as you like. How about a kangaroo ("g'day, *mate*")? Choose a single image to use as your **Single-Digit Mnemonic Clue** for the number 8.

The most important thing is that the **Clue** you choose makes sense to *you* and will be easy for you to instantly recall/translate. Other people's suggestions—though they may give you ideas—ultimately don't matter.

You don't necessarily have to choose a **Clue** that looks or sounds like the number; your first instinct is often the best choice: it represents a deeply-rooted gateway into your subconscious, and is therefore likely to be the easiest association to recall quickly. So hey, if you think the number seven looks like a green baseball bat wearing a cowboy hat, so be it. Don't shy away from absurdity, inappropriateness, or downright perversion, as long as it makes *immediate sense to you*.

Do this for every digit from 0 to 9. Grab a pen and fill the table below with your **Single-Digit Mnemonic Clue** images. Choose a single **Clue** for each digit. If you get stuck, read on.

Number	Your Single-Digit Mnemonic Clue
0	
1	
2	
3	
4	

#		
5		
6		
7		
8		
9		

As I said, you should really come up with your own **Single-Digit Mnemonic Clues**. However, if you're stuck, you'll find a few suggestions below. When you're first starting out, it can be difficult to think with creative freedom, but I promise you it will come with time.

#	Looks Like	Sounds Like
0	Baseball, soccer ball, bowling ball, golf ball, basketball, eyeball, apple, clock, Frisbee, bowl, egg, peach	Hero, gyro, Nero
1	Pen, pencil, marker, feather, baseball bat	Nun, gun, sun, bun, clown (fun), sneaker (run)
2	Goose, sickle	Shoe, lawyer (sue), gnu
3	A heavyset person's profile, heart, breasts, buttocks	*Spree* (the candy), flea, knee, bee, tree
4	Knife, triangle, pizza slice	Boar, gore, bore, lore, door, whore, someone's back turned to you (ignore), celebrating soccer player (score)

5	Wheelchair, brimmed hat, snake	Chive, dive, jive, hive, Frankenstein's monster ("it's alive!"), car (drive)
6	Teapot, a stick figure doing a handstand, apple with a big stem	Hicks, sticks, candles (wicks), bricks, chicks, a thirsty dog (licks)
7	Arrow, ledge, elbow, uni-brow, hook, candy cane	Viking hat (Sven), rising bread (leaven), cloud (heaven)
8	One doughnut sitting atop another, snowman, bra, John Lennon-esque sunglasses	Weight, gate, angry face (hate), bait
9	Chain mace, Pac-Man	Twine, vine, mine, wine, sign, line

There is truth in the quote that begins this lesson; we think in pictures and remember in an elaborate and free-flowing amalgamation of emotions and visuals. To harness this is to tap into the mind's natural memory mechanisms.

Your **Clues** should be flexible and dynamic; as you'll soon see, they will be put to use in a wide range of contexts. For example, if you're using "duck" as a clue, the imaginative scenes you'll need to create might require a tiny, pocket-sized duck; a city-sized duck; a red duck; or an anthropomorphic, humanoid duck in a suit and tie. Your imagination is boundless and answers to no one but you. Eggs can be blue and hatch baby cars. Trumpets can shoot lasers. Sharks can print receipts. The moon can fart confetti (and has for me many a time). Let yourself go and get weird.

Once you've established your **Single-Digit Mnemonic Clues** for the digits 0 through 9, take some time and commit them to memory, as you'll need them shortly. Don't move on until you can recite the ten digits and their respective **Single-Digit Mnemonic Clues** with relative ease.

> *Tip: This stuff isn't easy, and the lessons you're about learn may take a while to get down. That said, if you're concerned that your progress is considerably slower than you think it should be, feel free to look ahead at* **Troubleshooting Memory**.

The Journey Method

Next, we'll turn to the **Journey Method** of memorization. According to many scholars, the ancient Greeks first developed this system thousands of years ago, but its roots could possibly be even older. The **Journey Method** is still used by almost every noteworthy modern mnemonist.

The core idea is simple: first, select an ordered pathway along a familiar course (for example, walking through the rooms of a friend's home or through a familiar park). Then, with this pathway in mind, imagine placing **Mnemonic Clues** (for example, the **Single-Digit Mnemonic Clues** you just memorized for the numbers 0 through 9) at each location encountered along the path. These individual locations are simply called "**Steps**," and the whole pathway is called a "**Journey**."

Recent scientific research has revealed that a part of the brain called the hippocampus houses specialized cells that are used specifically to keep us oriented in space. These cells (called "grid," "place" and "border cells") work with the memory to provide accurate spatial records of the places we've been, including their respective layouts, features and scales. The **Journey Method** leverages this function.

Building Your First Journey

Let's begin with a basic exercise to get comfortable with the core concepts of the **Journey Method**. We're going to build a **Journey** based on wherever you're sitting right now. This **Journey** is going to consist of three **Steps**.

The first is where you're sitting right now; it's the table in front of you, your lap, or your chair. Adapt it based on your specific situation.

The second **Step** is the floor nearby, halfway between your current location and the nearest door or entryway. Look at this spot for a moment, and truly take it in; try to notice minute details you might otherwise overlook.

The third **Step** is the nearest door or entryway; take a moment to study this **Step** as well.

That's three **Steps**: your current location, the floor halfway between you and the nearest door, and the nearest door.

Let's say you want to memorize the number 673. First, imagine a **Clue** for 6 (what was your **Single-Digit Mnemonic Clue** for 6?) in your current location (the first **Step**). Then, imagine a **Clue** for 7 on the floor (your second **Step**), and a **Clue** for 3 at the nearest door (your third and final **Step**).

Shut your eyes and picture the **Clues** in their respective locations. Don't simply think about the objects sitting there; rather, work them into the scene in imaginative ways. Push the boundaries of your creativity.

Review the three **Clues** and their respective **Steps** several times. Once you feel comfortable with the **Journey** you've built, walk through the three **Steps** and "retrieve" the **Clues,** translating them back into digits as you go.

This exercise introduces the basic concepts behind the **Journey Method**: things we need to remember (or **Clues** about these things) are placed at each of the individual **Steps** of an imagined **Journey**.

Building a Longer Journey

Take some time and build your own **Journey** of ten **Steps**. For simplicity's sake, start with a familiar place, such as your home.

Make sure to follow logical, natural paths. Don't "teleport" from an upstairs bedroom directly to your basement. If you can't get from point A to point B naturally in real life, the path won't seem natural to you when you're working through it in your imagination.

A good rule of thumb is to walk through the home as though you're giving someone a tour. Think of how a real estate agent would guide a prospective buyer.

Say each **Step** aloud. "**Step** one is my front door. **Step** two is my living room..." and so on, until you reach the tenth **Step**. Say them again and again out loud—a bit faster each time—while imagining not only each **Step**, but also the trip or transition from one **Step** to the next.

Take a number that would ordinarily be difficult to memorize quickly—2,184,094—and memorize it using the **Journey** you just developed. Unlike the first exercise, the starting point of this **Journey**—though familiar—won't necessarily be directly in front of you; you'll have to rely entirely on your memory of the layout.

Imagine the following in great detail: you're alone at the first **Step** of your **Journey**. Take your time and get lost in the scene. What's the temperature? What are you wearing? Is it day or night? In your fantasy, imagine that you shift slightly, and your foot touches something. You look down to find a shoe (shoe sounds like "two"). Imagine your reaction; why is there a shoe on the ground? How would you react in the real world? What does the shoe look like? What does it feel like? Is it a men's or women's shoe? Formal footwear or sneaker?

A shoe may not be your chosen **Single-Digit Mnemonic Clue** for the number two; I'm using **Single-Digit Mnemonic Clues** from the examples only as a guide to help get you used to the process. You should substitute your own **Clues** as needed.

Next, you arrive at the second **Step**, and see that there is a gun lying on the floor ("gun" sounds like "one"). Again, make the image vivid and realistic. Picture the gun; pick it up, feel it, and notice subtle details about it. Is it cold? Is it heavy? Remember that you can be as creative as you want. Instead of a gun, perhaps 1 could be a tiny clown ("fun")? What would a tiny clown look like? Feel like? What would it do?

Now, wander toward your third **Step**. Where are you? Picture as many details as you can. Wherever you find yourself, imagine a woman's bra hanging on the wall, as though it was a piece of art (a hanging bra looks like the number "eight"). What color is it? Is it frilly or plain?

You get the idea: in order to memorize this seemingly complex number, use **Steps** along a familiar path (**Journey**), leaving for yourself at each one a sole **Single-Digit Mnemonic Clue**. Continue memorizing the number 2,184,094 using your ordered **Steps**. As you're using a ten-**Step Journey** to memorize seven **Steps**, you'll end up with three left over.

Take a deep breath, relax, shut your eyes, and imagine yourself walking through your **Journey** from the very beginning. Along the path, retrace your strange experiences, recollecting and deciphering into numbers the **Single-Digit Mnemonic Clues** you uncover. The imaginary events that play out within a **Journey's Step** are referred to as a **Scene**. This method creates such strong impressions that you can usually remember the **Clues** for a long time (especially if you create quirky, distinct scenarios at each **Step**).

> *Tip*: *Once you become comfortable with a particular **Journey**, you may find yourself imagining the transitions between the **Steps** occurring quickly, as though in "fast forward." This is perfectly natural.*

Before moving on, go through your **Journey** once again and retrieve the stored numbers; this time, try to go a bit faster.

Next, we'll continue learning about the **Journey Method** in a bit more detail.

Quick Review

1. Numbers are a good example of mundane information, which your brain tends to discard. In order to retain numbers, you must associate each digit with an imaginative **Clue**, which your brain can usually retain much more easily.

2. A **Mnemonic Vocabulary** is a personalized set of **Mnemonic Clues** that represent specific pieces of mundane information.

3. Creating **Single-Digit Mnemonic Clues** (standardized images or objects that represent each number from 0 through 9) allows you to easily imagine and recall individual digits. Some of the most popular **Single-Digit Mnemonic Clues** are those that either physically resemble ("2" and "a cobra") or sound like ("three" and "tree") the digit.

4. A **Journey** is an imagined path through a familiar setting in which you store information. You can do so by integrating **Mnemonic Clues** (such as **Single-Digit Mnemonic Clues**) within the individual **Steps** that comprise the **Journey**. You can then mentally retrace the **Steps** of the **Journey**, observing the **Mnemonic Clues** and translating them back into information (such as numbers).

Lesson 2: Memorizing Small Numbers and the Journey Method (Part 2)

> *"A MAN'S REAL POSSESSION IS HIS MEMORY. IN NOTHING ELSE IS HE RICH, IN NOTHING ELSE IS HE POOR."*
> —ALEXANDER SMITH, POET

You just learned the basics of **Mnemonic Vocabulary** development and built a great **Mnemonic Vocabulary** for the numbers 0 through 9. You learned about the **Journey Method** and how to use it in conjunction with **Single-Digit Mnemonic Clues** in order to remember small numbers. Now we're going to expand on that idea so you learn how to build quality, memorable **Journeys**.

Beyond Your First Journey

One reason the **Journey Method** is so useful is its expandability; by combining several **Journeys** (for example: your home, then your gym, then your job, then a friend's home), you can memorize incredibly lengthy numbers; with time and effort, you can memorize up to hundreds or even thousands of digits.

"Thousands," you ask?

Absolutely. Of course, in order to do so (and become reasonably fast at this), you'll need to:

- Become so comfortable with your **Single-Digit Mnemonic Clues** that deciphering them to and from their corresponding digits becomes instantaneous.
- Build a mental database that consists of many familiar **Journeys** that you can access quickly.

We'll do both in this book.

For now, however, build a second ten-**Step Journey**. This time, picture your best friend's home or your childhood home. You're going to build this the same way you did before; go through the home's layout and define ten **Steps**, making sure the order corresponds to the path you would naturally take through the rooms; remember, don't jump around arbitrarily from room to room. As before, say the steps out loud; "**Step one is the front door...Step two is...**", and imagine the **Transition** from each **Step** to the next.

Once you have your new ten-**Step Journey** memorized, you're going to want to use an interesting **Transition** to link it to your first **Journey** (the one inside your own home). Perhaps you get from your home to your new **Journey** by flying like a superhero. Perhaps you take a hot pink taxi.

You have the memories of many familiar places stored in your mind. By connecting them through some logical (though perhaps absurd or unusual) means, you can link two ten-**Step Journeys** to create a single twenty-step **Mega-Journey** (an array of two or more individual **Journeys**). You can go from the home of a coworker to a familiar mall (via bicycle), then to the gym (via limo), and then to a familiar vacation spot (via hot air balloon).

Linking individual **Journeys** together in this manner will eventually result in a giant, continuous realm in which you can store information at will.

For now, however, you have constructed a **Mega-Journey** comprised of two ten-step **Journeys**: your home and this new place. Before you move on, recite your first twenty **Steps** aloud. Then do it again, but faster.

Choosing Quality Journeys

Let's take a moment to examine what makes a high-quality **Journey**.

To begin, **Journeys** should always reflect a familiar place, either real or fictional. "Real" places are actual physical locations you know well, such as your home or a local park. A "fictional" place could be the setting of a beloved film or television show; however, *don't simply "make up" a totally fictional place with no frame of reference.*

On this point, I strongly disagree with many modern and early Greek mnemonists, who have suggested using your imagination to provide an endless supply of completely self-constructed **Journeys**. This method has obvious appeal; however, our overall concept of a setting is constructed through both our recollection of the physical space and the memories of our experiences in that place. A completely made-up **Journey** lacks these vital components, potentially impeding our ability to recall the **Steps** quickly or in sufficient detail. For this reason, completely made-up **Journeys** should be avoided.

So while it would be a bad idea to memorize information using a magical wonderland created entirely in your mind, there is no problem with using the set of the TV show *Full House* (if you feel you're familiar enough with the house to navigate through it) or even the levels of a favorite video game.

There's a second, equally important reason to avoid completely imaginary **Journeys**: it's unnecessary. Although it may be difficult to recite them offhand, we're all intimately familiar with hundreds upon hundreds of unique locations. The human mind is good at storing information about the places we've been, and when you begin to list them, you'll be amazed at how much you've retained.

Journey Standardization

When it comes to indoor **Journeys**, rooms have multiple corners and often contain beds, tables, and other noteworthy fixtures or characteristics that could serve as **Steps**, and it can seem wasteful to extract only one **Step** from each room; however, at this point, it's more important to keep things simple than it is to stretch your **Journeys** and extract every possible **Step** from them.

Furthermore, it's important to ensure each **Journey** contains a set number of **Steps**. Most people like to use ten or twenty. In doing so, when transitioning between **Journeys** (such as from a diner to your old middle school), you always know you're at an increment of ten or twenty **Steps**. This also makes it more difficult to miss **Steps** (or second-guess whether or not you missed **Steps**) or to lose a sense of exactly where you are in a **Journey** at a given time.

Extending Your Mega-Journey

Your **Mega-Journey** will eventually serve as a priceless companion that travels with you at all times, like a mental sheet of paper. Let's make it larger.

You're now going to build a third ten-**Step Journey**. Perhaps your sibling's home? The local convenience store? Your place of business? Record store? Pet shop? Subway station? Whatever the **Journey**, decide upon and recite your ten chosen **Steps** aloud. If you're having trouble, shut your eyes, regulate your breathing, and try to relax. In the beginning, this can be quite difficult; rarely-accessed parts of your imagination are at work, and, for many of us, concentration itself can be difficult.

Once finished, imagine a **Transition** from your second **Journey** to this new one. Out loud, recite your thirty-**Step Mega-Journey** twice, back-to-back. First, go slowly, and imagine each **Step** in as much detail as possible. What do you smell? What do you hear? Feel the floor beneath your feet. Feel the texture of the walls and hear the wind whistling through the windows. The second time, go a bit faster.

Congratulations, you now have thirty **Steps** in your **Mega-Journey**. Thirty **Steps** means that you've created storage for thirty distinct pieces of information. Since you now have a **Mnemonic Vocabulary** for each single-digit number, this means you can now memorize a number up to thirty digits in length.

Each **Journey** you add to your personal **Mega-Journey** is like adding a memory chip to a computer, increasing the capacity of the device (in this case, your brain) to store mundane information.

Spend some time reviewing both your personal **Mnemonic Vocabulary** for each number from 0 to 9 and your **Mega-Journey** (the three ten-step **Journeys** you created).

Once you're comfortable with these, memorize the three numbers below. Start each number at the beginning of one of your individual ten-step **Journeys** (for now, don't worry about the fact that you're not using every **Step**).

1. 2,390 (use your first 10-step **Journey**)
2. 34,982 (use your second 10-step **Journey**)
3. 129,001,923 (use your third 10-step **Journey**)

Take your time; this isn't easy in the beginning. Go slowly and use your imagination. As time progresses, you'll become faster, your **Mnemonic Vocabulary** will grow beyond simple numbers, and your **Journeys** will multiply. When I first started, I had trouble with a single ten-**Step Journey**. A few years later, my **Mega-Journey** consists of hundreds upon hundreds of distinct **Journeys**.

Once you've memorized the three above numbers, occupy yourself with something else for a few minutes, and then come back and recite them. Beginning with the first ten-**Step Journey**, mentally travel through each **Step**, retrieving the **Mnemonic Clues** for each digit in the first number. Decipher the **Clues** into their corresponding digits. Do the same for the second and third numbers. Take your time, and if you find yourself getting stuck, relax your mind and allow your imagination to flow; envision the **Step** in as much detail as you can.

How did you do?

With time, you'll learn to love your **Journeys**. Use them often, and you'll learn to recall and populate them quickly and automatically.

Next, you're going to memorize four more numbers. You'll be using the same three **Journeys**, so you're simply going to overwrite the **Clues** for the last numbers with these new ones. Before you begin, take a short break. Stand up, stretch, think of something else, and clear your mind.

Now take a look at the numbers, but don't begin yet.

1. 6,372
2. 100,293,194
3. 761
4. 475,382

You may notice that—at this point—there are four numbers, and yet you only have three ten-**Step Journeys**. Fear not; you'll be using the same three **Journeys** as before; however, this time, instead of starting each number at the beginning of a different **Journey**, you'll stack the four numbers back-to-back.

For example, since the first number (6,372) is four digits long, this will only require four **Steps**; thus, you can begin memorizing the second number at the fifth **Step** of the first **Journey**.

In order to know where one number ends and the next begins, you should leave for yourself some indicator at the end of each number. Such an indicator will come after the "2" in the first number (6,37<u>2</u>), but before the "1" in the next number (<u>1</u>00,293,194). You can represent this any way you like; you could work a stop sign into the **Scene** located at the last **Step** of a given number. If the number "2" at the end of 6,37<u>2</u> were represented by a goose, for example, you could imagine the goose attempting to take flight, but unable to go far because it's tethered to the stop sign.

Such a Mnemonic Clue is called a Finality Indicator.

This is a bit of an advanced concept, but it's important to learn how to use a single **Journey** to store multiple pieces of information. Life doesn't always hand you information that fits snugly into ten-**Step Journeys**, and this helps you to avoid wasting unused **Steps**. Furthermore, this practice will equip you to deal with numbers that exceed ten digits and therefore span multiple **Journeys**.

Using **Finality Indicators**, take a few minutes and memorize the four numbers as discussed.

Once finished, shut your eyes, take a deep breath, and work through your **Journeys**. Decipher the individual digits and recite the numbers. Take your time.

After you've gone through your **Journeys** and recited each of the four numbers, take note: if you ignore the "stop signs," you just memorized a twenty-two-digit number:

6,372,100,293,194,761,475,382

Memorizing such a long number would have been a daunting task mere days ago. If you managed to perform this feat after two lessons, do you see now that memorizing incredibly long numbers (up to hundreds of digits) will be possible after a bit of hard work and practice?

The art of integrating imagined information (such as **Single-Digit Mnemonic Clues**) into the constructs of the real world can be challenging at first, but the mind is actually quite adept at it. We have all experienced daydreams. We have all thought we saw something that wasn't actually there. There are even negative examples of this; all over the world, people suffer from hallucinations due to drugs, mental illness, sleep deprivation, and the like. Long-time habitual video game players can even begin to suffer from a condition known as "Game Transfer Phenomenon," which causes them to see video game-like attributes scattered throughout real world settings. Our imaginations are powerful; we just need to learn to let them work freely and to our advantage.

At this point, you need to practice. Your life won't change simply by reading this book; you must put in some effort. Don't move on until you feel very comfortable with your **Single-Digit Mnemonic Clues**, your three-part **Mega-Journey**, and the ideas and terminology outlined in this lesson.

One of the great things about numbers is that they are all around us, meaning you can practice anytime. You can memorize the numerical portions of license plates or the number of the bus or train car you're on. You can memorize the time when you leave the house and the time when you return. You can memorize the numbers on bar codes. You can memorize friends' birthdays and anniversary dates.

The world is full of numbers just waiting to be memorized. Get to it.

Quick Review

1. When building **Journeys**, it's wise to restrict them to a standard length, such as ten or twenty **Steps**.

2. The more vivid and imaginative you make **Scenes** (the imagined interactions between **Mnemonic Clues** and a **Journey's** individual **Steps**), the easier it will be for your brain to retain the information over a long period of time. Absurdity, humor, and realistic details all help to strengthen the types of artificial memories discussed in this lesson.

3. A **Finality Indicator** is a **Clue** placed within a **Journey** that alerts you that you've reached the end of a certain piece of information.

4. A **Transition** is an imagined occurrence that takes place in order to bridge adjacent **Journeys** or **Journey Steps**.

5. A **Mega-Journey** is an ordered array of adjacent **Journeys**.

Lesson 3: Memorizing Small Numbers and the Journey Method (Part 3)

> "ALL OF US HAVE PHOTOGRAPHIC MEMORIES, BUT SPEND A LIFETIME LEARNING HOW TO BLOCK OFF THE THINGS THAT ARE REALLY IN THERE."
>
> —GRANGER, *FAHRENHEIT 451* (RAY BRADBURY)

We are almost finished learning about small number memorization and the **Journey Method**. There are just a few more details to cover.

Contextual Journeys

By now you may be thinking, "This system is fine for memorizing a few numbers, but once I have many things memorized, how will I recall which **Journey** goes with which information?" The answer lies in *context*; you must use a **Journey** that relates to the context of the number.

If done properly, you can easily connect information (numerical or otherwise) to specific people, places, or things by using **Journeys** based on locations that pertain to them. These types of **Journeys** are called

Contextual Journeys, and your choice of **Contextual Journey** relies on whether the information is **Permanent** or **Temporary**.

Permanent Information

When it comes to memorizing a small piece of static (generally unchanging) numerical information related to a particular person (such as a phone number, address, or social security number), you can use a **Journey** based on that individual's home, office, or other (also generally unchanging) place that comes to mind immediately when thinking of them.

For example, when I need to remember a number associated with my friend Dave, my mind immediately transports me to his house. I have his address, phone number, birthday, old addresses and more all stored as separate **Journeys** within his home.

Information that doesn't change (or at least doesn't often change)—like someone's birthday or phone number—is called **Permanent Information**.

I will forever remember the number of steps in the basement staircase of my first home, the numerical combination to my gym locker, dozens of ID and account numbers, and so on, simply because I've attached these numbers (via narrative **Scenes**) to the locations which most remind me of them (the bottom of my basement steps, the gym locker room, etc.). By storing these constructed memories inside contextually significant **Journeys**, I ensure easy access to the information they represent.

Temporary Information

Sometimes it's necessary to store **Temporary Information** related to a particular place or individual. A few examples of numerical **Temporary Information** are an individual's hotel room number, their flight arrival time and gate, the keypad entry code to a rented vacation home, or the section, row, and seat numbers of tickets to a baseball game. **Temporary Information** is "throwaway," in that it is to be used for a short time and then discarded.

In such cases, it's best to avoid **Journeys** that have a permanent attachment to relevant individuals (such as their homes). In the example of someone's flight arrival time and gate, you could use a **Journey** based in a familiar airport (ideally the one where the individual is arriving). As this information does not need to be associated with the individual for an extended period of time, you can store it in a less permanent (but still appropriate) context. Let's look at an example.

Imagine you're at work and need to dial into an important conference call. Your company has a dedicated line for such calls (which you use all the time), and so you already have the phone number memorized. However, each participant was given a unique access code that must be entered in order to join this particular call. Just as you're getting ready to dial, something goes wrong with the company's email server, and all of your calendar events disappear, including the event that provided the call details. You have no way to pull up your access code.

Sounds unlikely? It happened to me on Monday, June 28, 2010 at approximately 1:58 PM. So, yes, this sort of thing can indeed happen. Luckily, employing the very skill you just developed, I had memorized the access code on sight when I first received the calendar event. When I saw it, I pictured a short **Journey** from my office to the office of the woman who had called the meeting, and populated it with my access code. Associating the numerical information with this woman's office provided a stronger connection than attempting to store the access code inside an arbitrary **Journey**.

In that instance, I used a **Contextual Journey** to store **Temporary Information**. Please note: this same woman's office number and phone extension were already stored in my memory in a **Journey** based in her office. These numbers would be considered **Permanent Information**.

Contextual Journeys are incredibly useful for memorizing **Temporary Information** such as gift card balances, dates and deadlines. Sometimes **Temporary Information** can stick around for a long time: many years ago, a friend was partway through a book—*Eating the Dinosaur* by Chuck Klosterman—and suggested I read it. As he was about to go on a trip, I borrowed the book during his absence. He handed it to me outside his townhouse, and I saw that he had placed a bookmark at page sixty-seven. I didn't want to lose his spot, so I immediately created a **Scene** relating to the number sixty-seven that took place on the stoop of the townhouse. When I returned the book weeks later, my mind naturally whisked me back to that **Contextual Journey**, and I was able to place his bookmark back on page sixty-seven. Note that this required no hard work, no brute force memorization, and no repetition. Just my imagination.

Years later, he may not even recall that he loaned me the book. Meanwhile, I still remember the exact page number he had bookmarked when he loaned it to me.

The "Decimal Clue"

When dealing with the conversion of numerical information to or from **Mnemonic Clues**, you often need to keep track of a decimal. You should establish a personally significant **Mnemonic Clue** that represents a decimal point—we'll call this a **Decimal Clue**—to inject into **Journeys** as necessary.

This concept should sound familiar, as it shares attributes with your **Finality Indicator**. Unlike a **Finality Indicator**, however, a **Decimal Clue** should take up an entire **Step** of your **Journey**. You can choose anything that works for you (perhaps an arrow, a construction cone, or a tiny skyscraper, since they can remind you of a "point").

For example, if you were to memorize the number 314, you'd simply recall your **Single-Digit Mnemonic Clues** for 3, then 1, then 4, placed within three individual consecutive **Steps** of a chosen **Journey**. However, if you were to memorize the number 3.14 (the first digits of pi), you would use four **Steps**: 3, **Decimal Clue**, 1, and 4.

Spend a few moments carefully selecting your **Decimal Clue**, as you'll be using it for the rest of your life. Then, quickly memorize the following numbers before continuing:

1. 8.64
2. 71.70
3. 0.991

Why Learn This?

"Wait a minute," you may be thinking, "Phone numbers? Arrival gates? Hotel room numbers? Do you know what year it is? I have a smart phone, a tablet, a laptop computer, a pad of sticky notes…"

Here in the modern age, people tend to use tools like smart phones and computers to store small bits of information; most folks are not used to relying on memory for that type of thing. We have at our disposal convenient recording media the likes of which the ancient Greeks could never have imagined when training their memories.

We depend upon these tools because we were taught to. Without needing to rely upon our memories, they've become undisciplined and therefore untrustworthy. The constant scramble to record, locate, and retrieve information from external sources may not seem stressful and time-consuming, but once you break free of the shackles, you'll realize how freeing it can be.

As you develop your memory, you'll find yourself using paper or gadgets to store information less and less often; at first in order to practice, but eventually because recording things in your mind will truly be easier than writing them down. It may be hard to imagine now, but trust me, the day will come, and it's truly liberating.

Methods for memorizing numerical information don't end here. Later in this book, you'll learn how to easily fill a single **Journey Step** with two, three, four, and even five digits. Earlier, you memorized a twenty-two-digit number using twenty-two **Steps**; by the end of this book, you'll be able to memorize the same twenty-two digits in only six.

So far, we've only discussed numbers; however, the **Journey Method** is useful for storing many other types of information. In the next lesson, you'll branch out beyond numbers.

Quick Review

1. When memorizing information (numerical or otherwise), it's best to use a **Contextual Journey** somehow associated with the information you're attempting to remember.

2. Select a location for a **Contextual Journey** based on the permanence of the information. For example, when dealing with **Permanent Information** (information that doesn't change, or changes very infrequently) related to an individual, choose a setting such as the individual's home or place of business for your **Contextual Journey**. When dealing with **Temporary Information** (such as the individual's flight number, hotel room, or raffle ticket number), choose a **Contextual Journey** that relates to the specific information (such as an airport for the flight, a hotel lobby for the room number, and a raffle ticket booth for the ticket number).

3. A **Decimal Clue** is a **Mnemonic Clue** that represents a decimal, allowing you to place a decimal inline within a number when storing it using the **Journey Method**.

Lesson 4: Memorizing Lists of "Familiar Entities"

> *"IMAGINATION IS MORE IMPORTANT THAN KNOWLEDGE."*
> —ALBERT EINSTEIN, PHYSICIST

Though Einstein was referring to creativity's role in innovation, this quotation is also relevant to **Memory Development**; as you learned, imagination is the most natural mechanism by which to accrue and retain information.

By now, you should have a good sense of how small numbers are best memorized. As simple as they may seem, the methods you just learned are pared-down versions of the ones used by the world's most seasoned mnemonists; for the most part, the pros simply have a good deal more experience than you do. We are going to step away from numbers for a bit and learn how to memorize small lists of **Familiar Entities**.

What is a "Familiar Entity?"

A **Familiar Entity** refers to a noun (person, place, or thing) that you have some sort of pre-existing idea about. Computers, coffee mugs, cousins, lamps, and next-door neighbors are all **Familiar Entities**, as they are nouns for which you have a frame of reference.

Proper nouns can also be **Familiar Entities**, as long as you're familiar enough with them that you can picture them in your mind. For example, the names of your children, hometown, or high school math teacher can be **Familiar Entities**. However, "Shawn Linus Black" or "Harrowingston Manor, Texas" are **Unfamiliar Entities**, because you have no knowledge about or connection to them. You can't picture or cite any distinguishing attributes about these **Unfamiliar Entities** and thus can't imagine them in a vivid, real-life context (the most powerful tool in your mnemonic arsenal).

Familiar and **Unfamiliar Entities** require different memorization methods. First, we'll discuss the method for memorizing lists of **Familiar Entities** before delving into **Unfamiliar Entities** later on.

How to Memorize Lists of Familiar Entities

The method for memorizing lists of **Familiar Entities** is similar to the number memorizing method in two ways:

- Both require creative, personally significant thinking; and
- Both make use of the **Journey Method**.

However, memorizing **Familiar Entities** is different from memorizing numbers in that no **Mnemonic Vocabulary** is needed.

Let's explore this concept with an exercise. Imagine that you have to memorize this shopping list:

1. Cat litter
2. Two red mugs
3. A USB thumb drive
4. A case of bottled water
5. A harmonica
6. A photocopy of the deed to your house

How would you do it without a written list, such as a paper note or smart phone reminder?

Luckily, these are all **Familiar Entities**; you've likely encountered each item before, in some capacity. You have a frame of reference and can picture each in your mind. As with numbers, you'll use a **Journey** to store this information. Since there are six things you need to purchase at the store, you need to decide upon a **Journey** with at least six **Steps** and imagine placing one of the items within each of the **Steps**.

Let's Begin the Journey

You'd most likely want to use a **Contextual Journey** for this **Temporary Information**, but for the sake of the example, let's go on a **Journey** through your workplace. If you aren't employed, or if you're a contractor who's constantly in different locations you'll have to choose a different **Journey** (perhaps an old job).

To start your **Journey**, you might imagine being unable to enter the building because a cat is sitting in a litter box in front of the door, blocking it (a reminder for the cat litter). Imagine the cat staring up at you, smugly defying your attempt in that way only a cat can. What color is the cat? Big or small? Fluffy or short-haired? Do you smell anything? What does the litter box look like? Then, imagine you pull the door hard enough to move the cat and litter box (much to the cat's irritation), and continue on to the next **Step** in this **Journey**. Where is the next **Step**? How would you work two red mugs into the **Scene**?

Before continuing with this example, let's talk about building **Transitions** between **Steps**.

Building Step Transitions

You already learned the importance of building **Transitions** between **Journeys** (for instance, imagining a trip from your home to your local mall by horse or blimp). The same concept applies to the smaller **Transitions** between the individual **Steps** of a single **Journey**.

You can reinforce memorized information by forging creative **Transitions** between each **Step**, with each **Transition** involving the **Entities** from two adjacent **Scenes**. Good **Transitions** are useful in the event that you "blank" on a particular **Step**, because the **Transition** to the **Step** from the previous **Step** could help to jog your memory.

Let's Complete the Journey

Let's apply this principle to our current example. The first **Step** involved the office door and cat litter, so, as a **Transition**, you might imagine yourself chasing the cat from this **Step** to the second, where you find the second list item (two red mugs), stacked perilously on the floor. Like before, use absurdity and humor to reinforce the memory: perhaps the mugs are filled with rainbow-colored liquid. Imagine that the cat runs by and knocks one of the mugs over. The mug shatters, causing a puddle of rainbow-liquid to expand across the floor as a **Transition** to the third

Step in the **Journey**, where a glowing USB thumb drive (item three) forms and rises from the puddle.

Next, imagine that someone comes along and picks the dripping drive out of the puddle. With the thumb drive in his hand, he dances over (**Transition**) to the fourth **Step**, where he puts it in an empty plastic water bottle and shakes it (a reminder for item four, the case of bottled water).

Let's keep going.

A poodle in a top hat (added for uniqueness) grabs the water bottle in her mouth and takes it (**Transition**) to the fifth **Step**, where she sits up on a stool, places the water bottle next to her on a table, and begins playing the blues on a harmonica (the fifth item). Behind her, a band rises from the ground on a platform and accompanies the melody. Upon closer inspection, the band has no drummer; a drum set sits in the background, unoccupied. The stage grows wheels, and the poodle and band are wheeled over (**Transition**) to the sixth and final **Step** of the **Journey**. Here, they meet the drummer, who is sitting on a photocopier instead of a drum stool, photocopying his exposed behind (a reminder to photocopy the deed to your house, the sixth list item).

Immerse yourself in the **Scenes** and absorb all the details you can. The lights are dim and a spotlight shines on the poodle-led band. Imagine the smell of smoke and whiskey as the band of weathered old bluesmen turns your workplace into a makeshift Memphis nightclub. What song are they playing? What do they look like? How many of them are there? Is the poodle wearing clothes aside from the top hat? Describe the copier—is it white? Gray? Tan? Is it an expensive, large commercial copier, or a less extravagant, "small business" copier? Imagine the noise and light coming from the copier.

Although you can use the **Scenes** and **Transitions** described in the example given, you're encouraged to develop your own, as this will help you to cultivate your imaginative powers.

Right now, the more buttoned-up of you may be staring slack-jawed at this page or screen, moderately appalled that *Never Forget Again* would suggest such absurd and playful images. Harmonica-playing poodles? Drummers making butt-copies? Is this a joke?

Far from it. This is how the brain works, and you can either accept and work with it, or deny it and struggle. I challenge you to memorize the above list in the same amount of time (or less) using brute force repetition, and without using a similar creative device. More importantly, I challenge you to recall the list verbatim four days later.

This example demonstrates the core ideas behind the memorization of **Familiar Entities** and many other types of information: imagine placing the objects you're trying to remember within the **Steps** of a (ideally **Contextual**) **Journey**, using vivid **Scenes** that invoke multiple senses.

The details are what make the difference, and, in the above example, the smell of the litter box, the vividness of the rainbow-liquid, or the smokiness of the nightclub can mean the difference between a mediocre, forgettable imaginative **Scene** and a fantastic, memorable one that lingers in your mind for a long time. Right now, details come at a price—time—but this cost will decrease after some practice.

Take a deep breath, close your eyes, and relax. Walk through your **Journey** and extract the six-item list you stored. Go at your own pace and embrace the details.

How'd you do? If you ran into any problems, focus on the **Steps** that caused confusion. Consider that you may have rushed, created inadequately memorable **Scenes**, or failed to add enough detail.

Once you feel comfortable with the **Journey** and can extract the items somewhat quickly, you can move on.

> *Tip*: Since **Journeys** are based strictly upon familiar linear settings you can easily imagine traversing, you can also retrieve the stored items in reverse order. You simply need to imagine yourself walking backward through your **Journey**, starting at the end (the final **Step**; in the above case, the sixth). In fact, with strong **Transitions** and rich **Scenes**, you can begin at any **Step** in a **Journey** and move forward or backward from there with relative ease.

Let's Memorize Some Lists

Work out seven **Steps** within an indoor **Journey** of your choosing, starting at the front door or entrance, and moving naturally throughout the building or setting. Imagine the familiar sights, smells, sounds, and—perhaps most importantly—emotions associated with this place. Say your seven **Steps** aloud, and imagine placing each object from the list below into the **Steps** you've chosen.

1. A black cowboy hat

2. A computer monitor
3. A can of tuna
4. A Rubik's Cube
5. A green piggy bank
6. A jack-o'-lantern
7. A high school math textbook

Note that some of these items are a bit more specific than those in our last example. The cowboy hat and piggy banks are particular colors, and the math textbook is high school level.

Once you've placed the items in their respective **Steps**, walk through the **Journey** and retrieve them. Do this several times, and once you feel comfortable with the list, try traveling through the **Journey** backward and collecting the items in reverse order.

This type of memorization is useful for a variety of practical applications. Some examples:

- Speeches or presentations: each **Step** could contain a **Mnemonic Clue** representing a paragraph or speaking point; good **Transitions** allow you to pick back up if you lose your place.
- Grocery lists
- Separate default "checklists" for work, school, weekend trips, etc., to make sure you aren't forgetting something you'll need
- Things to check/do when closing up the house for the night
- Gift ideas for friends and family
- (For servers) A list of the night's specials
- (For students) A roster of classes
- (For musicians) A "set list" of songs to be played at a concert
- (For salespeople) A list of product offerings

Surely you can come up with additional applications specific to your lifestyle. With time, memorizing a lengthy grocery list or class roster will be no more demanding than a simple two-item list.

More important than the practical examples given above, cultivation of this skill through structured practice will drastically improve your ability to confidently record and recall information of all types when needed; once we move beyond **Familiar Entities**, you'll need to leverage the imaginative skills you've cultivated for other (often more complex) memorization tasks.

Let's work through the "class roster" scenario from the above list as another example. Imagine you're a student with a five-day schedule. You could choose a different **Journey** for each day of the week and recall each one based on some personal **Contextual** connection between each **Journey's** setting and that particular day. It may seem like a stretch at first, but if you let your emotions work freely, you may very well have deeply-rooted associations between days and places; perhaps you spent Sundays at your grandmother's as a child, or had Tae Kwon Do practice every Thursday after school?

Once your **Journeys** are chosen for the individual days, you can begin to fill each **Journey's Steps** with **Clues**. Imagine you need to attend history, philosophy, physics and German classes on Monday; therefore, Monday's **Journey** would consist of four **Steps**. The first **Step** will require a **Clue** about history. The **Scene** you construct could feature a flamboyantly attired fifteenth-century explorer, who—in a French accent—frantically implores you to help him decipher the contents of a tattered map (a reminder that you have history class). You eventually wrestle the map off him, roll it up, and use it to knock his bicorn (little pointy hat) off. Imagine feeling the impact of the map on the hat. Watch the hat slide across the floor. Smell the acrid stench of the man, who's evidently spent months at sea. Both you and the explorer watch in bewilderment as the hat, now on the ground, sprouts a tiny sail and floats toward the second **Step** in your **Journey**. This is your **Transition**.

At the second **Step**, perhaps there is a sculpture of a man sitting with his chin resting upon his fist and his elbow propped on his knee, like Rodin's famous sculpture, *The Thinker*. The man is staring at the sailing hat, as though contemplating it. This reminds you that philosophy class is next. As though suddenly frustrated by an existential realization, the man picks up the hat, angrily balls it in his fist, and throws it (your **Transition**) toward the third **Step**.

Upon landing at the third **Step**, the balled-up hat unfolds into a flat, checkered two-dimensional plane. You hear the deep, looping hum of a recorded sine wave. A woman in a lab coat approaches the strange plane and studies it closely (a reminder for physics class).

The woman gestures for you to follow her, and walks with you toward the fourth and final **Step**. As you walk, she begins to take the lab coat off (the final **Transition**). After shedding the layer, you see she was concealing traditional Bavarian attire. At the fourth and final **Step**, accordion music plays and she breaks into a traditional German dance (a reminder for German class).

This array of **Scenes** contains all the attributes of a well-formed **Journey**. It's **Contextual** (Monday's list is set within a **Journey** associated with Monday). It contains strong **Transitions**, which help to clue you in about the next **Step** should you "blank" on it. You're incorporating as many of your senses as you can (the explorer's stench, the accordion music, the sine wave, etc.). It's full of detailed, unique imagery and **Clues** that are immediately relatable to the **Familiar Entities** (in this case, the classes) being listed.

Use this as a model for your own **Journeys**, and keep in mind that ignoring any of these key concepts compromises the potential strength of the memory or speed of recall.

In a coming section, you'll learn how to attach additional relevant information (such as class times, room locations, etc.) to these **Clues**. For now, however, spend some time practicing these basics. Before moving on, memorize the following three lists of randomly chosen **Familiar Entities**. Take your time and focus on details.

1. A whistle, a folder, a lifeguard, a rabbit, and a plaid shirt
2. A violin, a coat hanger, a steering wheel, the family member with whom you most recently spoke, and a barrel
3. A VHS copy of *Platoon*, a Sharpie marker, a fancy watch, your next door neighbor, an original 8-Bit Nintendo system, a smoke detector, and a plastic plate

Handling Abstract Familiar Entities

The word "noun" was defined at the beginning of this lesson as a "person, place, or thing." However, an idea can also be a noun; thus, a familiar idea can be considered a **Familiar Entity**. For example, if you for some reason have to memorize a list of emotions (perhaps for a game played with children), this technique can still work. In this case, rather than imagining the placement of physical items in the **Journey**'s individual **Steps**, instead imagine the placement of **Clues** relating to the ideas (since emotions are intangible). We touched upon this when explorers, philosophers, and Bavarian dancers represented different classes in the previous example.

In other words, "happiness" can be represented by something usually associated with happiness, such as a clown, a sunflower with a smiling face, or a dog wagging its tail. You could also choose something personally associative, such as a friend or family member who generally makes you happy (although less direct associations are more likely to introduce confusion). Sadness could be represented by a gravestone, a frowning mask, or even a dropped pizza lying face-down on the ground (hey, if that doesn't make you sad, you're probably a serial killer). You can choose symbols for other dispositions or actions; for instance, a stereotypical movie villain could represent cruelty and a seesaw could represent indecisiveness.

Feel free to create associations as absurd as you like, as long as they immediately trigger the memory of the intended idea.

Create a **Journey** that contains **Clues** about the following list of abstract **Familiar Entities**:

1. Procrastination
2. Repetition
3. Power
4. Failure
5. Flavor
6. Luck

If that was difficult, don't be discouraged; abstract **Familiar Entities** can be difficult for even experienced mnemonists to memorize quickly. Challenging memorization tasks like these will further develop your ability to think creatively and strengthen your memorization skills across the board.

Quick Review

1. **Familiar Entities** are nouns (persons, places, things, or ideas) for which you have some frame of reference; you've had past contact with these **Entities** and can thus immediately imagine either the **Entities** or **Clues** about them.

2. To memorize lists of **Familiar Entities**, you must employ the **Journey Method** (using a **Contextual Journey**, if possible), develop **Mnemonic Scenes** that involve each of the **Entities** (or, if abstract, **Clues** about said **Entities**) and work these **Scenes** into the **Journey's** individual **Steps**.

Lesson 5: Learning and Revisitation Rhythms

> "THERE ARE SOME THINGS YOU LEARN BEST IN CALM, AND SOME IN STORM."
>
> —WILLA CATHER, AUTHOR

People subscribe to a wide range of beliefs about the nature of knowledge, ranging from the pure empiricist belief that all knowledge is derived from the senses to the pure rationalist belief that true knowledge is the intrinsic product of reason. Regardless of your thoughts on the subject, most would agree you were born with no knowledge at all (aside from instinct); that is to say, everything you now know had to be learned for the first time at some point. You've spent years cultivating knowledge and forging the associations that make you who you are today. How did you do it? How did you learn? How did you retain this information?

Over the last few centuries, science has come to better understand these learning processes. It turns out that the brain does not function as a single unit, but rather as a network of interrelated parts that serve vastly different functions. The areas responsible for learning are numerous and complex; for example, it's been determined that a small area called the *Basal Ganglia* is specifically dedicated to the retention of repetitive tasks (such as tying your shoes). This is almost entirely removed from the part that handles the recollection of trivia (such as the year man first landed on the moon), and this in turn is separate from the part that remembers visual information (such as what plaid looks like). Relatively recent discoveries even show that faces are learned and remembered differently from other visual information.

Due in part to the complexity of the brain's physical structure and internal clock, the success with which we learn and remember can vary due to situational and timing factors. We're going to take a quick break away from learning technique and explore how to leverage this fact to your advantage. Here, we're going to discuss two concepts that are incredibly important for the long-term retention of new information.

Learning Rhythms: Study Smarter, Not Harder

Memorization can be challenging, especially when learning large amounts of totally unfamiliar information, as students are often expected to do when studying. Whether using the old, difficult, "brute force" method or the more sophisticated imagination-based methods taught in this book, you don't want to overload your mind in a single session, as doing so risks damaging the integrity of the very information you're hoping to retain. But how can you know when you've studied enough in a single session?

Attention spans are highly individual. People learn differently, and likewise have different levels of tolerance for knowledge acquisition; each individual needs to determine and respect his or her own attention span threshold and learn to take breaks when information begins to blur together. While some may benefit from taking a study break every twenty minutes, that frequency may feel more like an undue interruption for someone with a higher threshold.

In the same way, for someone who is perhaps only able to focus and retain new information in ten-minute intervals, trying to memorize information or learn a new skill for twenty straight minutes can be taxing and counterproductive. For this reason, it's best to determine your own **Learning Rhythms** by listening to and obeying your instincts; when you're burned out and having trouble learning anything more in a particular session, you know it. Don't fight it—stop trying.

Study time should be set strictly into repeating cycles; for example, someone with a particularly short attention span may need ten minutes of distraction-free study followed by five minutes of leisure or distraction. For others, it may well be forty minutes of study with a ten-minute break. The clues your brain provides can serve as a foundation on which to build a structured study plan.

To determine your initial baseline **Learning Rhythm**, sit down (while rested, not overly caffeinated, and in good health) and study something that you consider a bit dull or mentally taxing. How long can you go before becoming antsy, cross-eyed, or distracted? Set this as your default "on" time interval (round up to the nearest five-minute mark), and make your "off" time half as long. For example, if you find yourself distracted and bored after seventeen minutes, your "on" and "off" times should be twenty minutes and ten minutes, respectively. If you're unable to determine your ideal **Learning Rhythm**, start out with twenty minutes "on" and ten minutes "off."

When studying ("on" time) or taking breaks ("off" time), use the following guidelines:

"On" Time:

- Remove all potential distractions: phones, email, other people, music, and access to distracting websites. There are free services like RescueTime (rescuetime.com) that allow you to turn off access to the latter. If you're on a computer but not using the Internet, turning off your Internet connection has essentially the same effect.

- Use a clock. Stop working immediately when "on" time is over, even if things seem to be going well.

"Off" Time:

- Use a clock for this too. End your break immediately when the allotted time ends. Stop even if something you're doing (like watching a television show) only has a minute or so remaining. Police yourself and know that allowing flexibility in your timeline will only lead to more and more flexibility as time goes on.

- Don't allow yourself to think about your study topic when relaxing. Even if you feel like you're having an idea or breakthrough, ignore it. It may be hard to adjust to breaks, but just because society, peers, parents, and a lifetime of teachers taught you to feel lazy for taking regular breaks from study doesn't mean they were right.

If you find yourself unable to focus for extended periods of time, you're only partially responsible; media and technology have made it feel unnatural to focus on one thing for more than a few minutes at a time. This is something that can be repaired with practice.

Once you settle on a good **Learning Rhythm**, remember it's not set in stone. Your rhythm may change over time as your ability to focus improves. Allow yourself to adjust your "on" and "off" times every week (starting on Monday morning) by five minutes "on" while keeping your "off" time the same.

Revisitation Rhythms

Revisitation Rhythms refer to the manner in which you revisit information after you've initially learned it.

With patience and structured practice of the skills taught in this book, you'll soon find yourself able to record information immediately—whether interesting or mundane—and recall it easily for extended periods of time. As you learned, the most important factor in the "sticking power" of information is the creativity employed in crafting the visuals you use to represent it; the more vivid, stimulating, absurd, and multi-sensory a narrative you create, the better off you'll be.

The second most important factor is **Revisitation**. Structured **Revisitation** of this imaginative information is vital for long-term retention. There are many schools of thought about the best way to do this, but most experts seem to agree on two basic principles: for information to transition from short- to long-term memory, it must be 1.) reviewed *almost immediately*, and 2.) reviewed *several times*.

In *Quantum Memory Power*, famed mnemonist Dominic O'Brien cites nineteenth-century German psychologist Hermann Ebbinghaus, who is responsible for a great deal of what is known about the minds' reaction to study. He coined such widely-used terms as "spacing effect" and "forgetting curve"; "spacing effect" refers to the fact that humans learn listed information more effectively when studied slowly over a long period of time, and "forgetting curve" refers to a formula ($R = E - [t/s]$) illustrating how our memories fade with time, and how the fade rate is essentially a function of the "strength" of the memory itself.

Ebbinghaus proved that revisiting new information five times at specific intervals maximizes retention. Based on Ebbinghaus' research, O'Brien goes on to suggest revisiting newly learned information according to the following schedule:

1. Immediately after learning
2. 24 hours later
3. 1 week later
4. 1 month later
5. 6 months later

In light of recent discoveries in neuroscience, this interpretation of Ebbinghaus' work seems somewhat incomplete. You should add one more **Revisitation**—arguably the most important one of all: revisit information *immediately before going to sleep* on the day you learn it.

In his talk "Secrets of the Sleeping Brain," Matt Walker (professor of Psychology and Neuroscience at Berkeley) explores in detail the relationship between sleep and memory, and explains how sleep can drastically impact the "stickiness" of newly-learned information. This research will come up again when we discuss *The Profound Effects of Sleep on Memory* later in this book. However, the takeaway is simple: recent science has proven that lack of sleep severely degrades one's ability to create and store new memories, and studying information (or learning brand new information) right before sleeping significantly increases the likelihood of retention.

Sorry, college students, but pulling an all-nighter to cram for a test doesn't work; you're much better off cramming until bedtime and then getting some high-quality sleep.

That said, the ideal (more complete) **Revisitation** sequence is as follows:

1. Immediately after learning
2. Immediately before going to sleep
3. 24 hours later
4. 1 week later
5. 1 month later
6. 6 months later

Obviously, you can't always manage to revisit everything you learn exactly six months after learning it, but for really important information, don't be put off by the idea of setting a few cell phone calendar reminders to review. **Memory Development** takes some effort, and occasionally—in cases like this—it involves practices that may now seem to be odd or invasive. You can't expect to simply read this book and walk away with a drastically improved memory; you must make a few lifestyle changes and embrace some new customs to achieve your goals.

Keep **Learning Rhythms** in mind as you work your way through *Never Forget Again*, and use these concepts to maximize the efficiency of your learning. Leverage what you've just learned about **Revisitation Rhythms** in order to maximize the "stickiness" of the things you truly want to remember.

Next, it's time to review and practice everything you learned in *Section 1*. Once you're ready to move on, you're going to take concepts you've already come to understand (such as the **Journey Method, Mnemonic Vocabularies,** etc.), and extend them to memorize new types of information.

Quick Review

1. **Learning Rhythms** are the patterns of study you should use when initially developing skills or learning new information.

2. When learning something new, never attempt to force study when you're tired, restless, or unfocused. Take breaks at predetermined times; after determining the ideal intervals of time for study and breaks, enforce these timelines strictly, obeying them down to the second.

3. **Revisitation Rhythms** are schedules for revisiting information after initially learning it. Newly learned skills or information should be revisited six times—at specific intervals—in order to maximize long-term retention.

Review and Development: Section 1

In *Section 1*, you learned methods for memorizing numbers and lists of **Familiar Entities**, and in doing so became familiar with some of the most important and widely used tools in **Memory Development**. We'll develop and expand upon these core concepts through the rest of the book, as they are fundamental to the memorization of almost all types of information. Let's quickly review what you've learned so far.

Review

1. **Creativity is Key**: Numbers are a good example of mundane information, which your brain tends to discard. In order to retain numbers, you must associate each digit with an imaginative **Clue**, which your brain can usually retain much more easily.

2. **Mnemonic Vocabulary**: A **Mnemonic Vocabulary** is a personalized set of **Mnemonic Clues** that represent specific pieces of mundane information.

3. **Single-Digit Mnemonic Clues**: Creating **Single-Digit Mnemonic Clues** (standardized images or objects that represent each number from 0 through 9) allows you to easily imagine and recall individual digits. Some of the most popular **Single-Digit Mnemonic Clues** are those that either physically resemble ("2" and "a cobra") or sound like ("three" and "tree") the digit.

4. **Memorizing Numbers**: When memorizing numbers, use **Single-Digit Mnemonic Clues** to represent each digit. Place

each **Clue** inside an individual **Step** within a **Journey** of your choice.

5. **The Journey Method**: A **Journey** is an imagined path through a familiar setting in which you store information. You can do so by integrating **Mnemonic Clues** (such as **Single-Digit Mnemonic Clues**) within the individual **Steps** that comprise the **Journey**. You can then mentally retrace the **Steps** of the **Journey**, observing the **Mnemonic Clues** and translating them back into information (such as numbers).

6. **Mega-Journey**: A **Mega-Journey** is an ordered array of adjacent **Journeys**.

7. **Contextual Journeys**: When memorizing information (numerical or otherwise), use a **Contextual Journey** whenever possible—one that is somehow associated with the information you're attempting to remember.

8. **Journey Standardization**: When building **Journeys**, restrict them to a standard length, such as ten or twenty **Steps**.

9. **Finality Indicator**: A **Finality Indicator** is a **Clue** placed within a **Journey** that alerts you that you've reached the end of a certain piece of information.

10. **Decimal Clue**: A **Decimal Clue** is a **Mnemonic Clue** that represents a decimal, allowing you to place a decimal inline within a number when storing it using the **Journey Method**.

11. **Transition**: A **Transition** is an imagined occurrence that takes place in order to bridge adjacent **Journeys** or **Journey Steps**.

12. **Permanent vs. Temporary Information**: Select a location for a **Contextual Journey** based on the permanence of the information. For example, when dealing with **Permanent**

Information (information that doesn't change, or changes very infrequently) related to an individual, choose a setting such as the individual's home or place of business for your **Contextual Journey**. When dealing with **Temporary Information** (such as the individual's flight number, hotel room, or raffle ticket number), choose a **Contextual Journey** that relates to the specific information (such as an airport for the flight, a hotel lobby for the room number, or a raffle ticket booth for the ticket number).

13. **Get Weird**: The more vivid and imaginative you make **Scenes** (the imagined interactions between **Mnemonic Clues** and a **Journey's** individual **Steps**), the easier it will be to retain the information over a long period of time. Absurdity, humor, and realistic details all help to strengthen the types of artificial memories discussed in this section.

14. **Familiar Entities**: **Familiar Entities** are nouns (persons, places, things, or ideas) for which you have some frame of reference; you've had past contact with these **Entities** and can thus immediately imagine either the **Entities** or **Clues** about them.

15. **Memorizing Lists of Familiar Entities**: To memorize lists of **Familiar Entities**, you must employ the **Journey Method** (using a **Contextual Journey**, if possible), develop **Mnemonic Scenes** that involve each of the **Entities** (or, if abstract, **Clues** about said **Entities**) and work these **Scenes** into the **Journey's** individual **Steps**. *Example of a list of Familiar Entities: Bow tie; shotgun; parrot; duct tape; cell phone.*

16. **Learning Rhythms**: **Learning Rhythms** are the patterns of study you should use when initially developing skills or learning new information. When learning something new, never attempt to

force study when you're tired, restless, or unfocused. Take breaks at pre-determined times; after determining the ideal intervals of time for study and breaks, enforce these timelines strictly, obeying them down to the second.

17. **Revisitation Rhythms**: **Revisitation Rhythms** are schedules for revisiting information after initially learning it. Newly learned skills or information should be revisited six times—at specific intervals—in order to maximize long-term retention.

Development

You should spend a minimum of seven days learning to use these skills. The schedule outlined below represents the minimum suggested amounts of time; however, you should feel free to spend additional time on any particular subject.

Days 1 - 2

Once per day, quickly review all three parts of *Memorizing Small Numbers and the Journey Method*. Get comfortable with the concepts by memorizing numbers out in the wild; try to memorize every three- to ten-digit number you come across throughout the day (within reason). This could include the numerical portions of license plates, zip codes, phone numbers, bus numbers, UPC codes, etc. Continue to get used to your **Mnemonic Vocabulary** for the digits 0 through 9, and become more comfortable with the **Journeys** you've developed so far. Build strong **Transitions** between **Journey Steps** as quickly as possible.

Day 3

Review *Memorizing Lists of "Familiar Entities"* today. Begin to memorize as many lists of **Familiar Entities** as you can. You can find lists on the Internet relevant to topics you're interested in, but try to use real-world examples whenever possible. Resist the urge to write down small lists throughout your day; instead, use only your mind.

As you interact with people, try to catalog them using a **Journey**, creating a long list that you can add to and review throughout the day. Essentially, make a hobby out of memorizing **Familiar Entities**; the more you enjoy the process, the easier it will be.

Continue to memorize numbers, as well; while focusing on one set of skills, don't abandon the development of earlier ones, as they feed upon each other in many ways. Remember, your brain can't "fill up."

Days 4 - 6

If your situation allows, spend at least an hour each day walking around and honing your skills using the things around you. If possible, do so in an unfamiliar place.

Day 7

Either create or have someone generate for you a list of eight random six-digit numbers. Attempt to memorize them in under five minutes, and recite them after a ten-minute break. If you can't do it in this amount of time, start over with a fresh list. Only move on once you can perform this feat in the allotted timeframe.

Have someone generate for you a list of thirty random **Familiar Entities**; this list can include friends, family members, neighbors, locations, institutions, teachers, organizations, landmarks, objects, or any other nouns you're familiar with. Attempt to memorize the list in under eight minutes. If you can't do it in this amount of time, start over with a fresh list. Again, only move on once you can perform this feat in the allotted timeframe.

Before Moving On…

If at any time you feel that your progress is being compromised because you haven't established enough **Journeys**, sit down and map out a few new ones. If it helps, write them out in detail. Some popular **Journeys** include friends' homes, recreational spots, family members' homes, malls, stores, gyms, schools, parks, vacation spots, past workplaces, etc.

In implementing the **Journey Method**, you constantly revisit the memory of a setting, and thus enjoy the additional benefit of keeping these places fresh in your mind, regardless of how infrequently you find yourself able to visit them physically. I often imagine walks through museums and exotic locations I visited years ago.

Every place you visit throughout your life has the potential to be another **Journey**, essentially adding another chip to your internal memory capacity.

Section 2: Intermediate Memory Development

Think back to a conversation from your distant past. If you were to imagine a genie in place of the other person, how could you tell which version of the event actually occurred?

In this case, there are at least three indicators:

1. Genies are fictional.
2. You would remember this exercise and thus purposely implanting the genie in the memory.
3. You have not experienced the consequences of having a conversation with a genie (such as the need to realign your beliefs about what is and is not real).

Still, these factors aside, if you concentrate hard and add enough detail to the false memory, doesn't it almost seem as though it happened? Can't you picture it just as vividly as the memory of an actual past event? Aside from context and consequence, what differentiates an imagined memory from a real one?

Such is the power of the imagination; or, arguably, such is the weakness of memory.

Physiologically, memories aren't static mental images to be accessed at your whim; revisiting a memory is more like reading a script that you retrieve and reenact. It's colored by context and your mood at the time of retrieval. Pablo Picasso once said, "Everything you can imagine is real," and in many ways, a vividly imagined visual **Scene** can seem as real as a memory of a past event.

If you're reading this, it means that you know how to memorize numbers and lists of **Familiar Entities** effectively. It's time to move on, expand upon these methods, and apply them to new types of information. You have only scratched the surface of the nearly limitless capabilities of your memory.

In this section, you'll learn to link **Entities** into **Associated** (connected) **Entities**. This entails taking two or more words, phrases, or ideas, putting them together, and remembering the association between them. You'll learn first how to connect **Familiar Entities**, followed by **Unfamiliar Entities**. Although the last section only touched briefly on **Unfamiliar Entities**, these are people, places, things, or ideas for which you have no frame of reference. An example of **Associated Unfamiliar Entities** could be an unfamiliar family's last name and the street on which they live ("the Weldons"/"Canterberry Court"). After you're comfortable pairing up two or more **Entities** as **Associated Entities**, you'll learn how to memorize lists of such **Associated Entities**.

As you expand your use of creativity-fueled mnemonic methods, storing information in these ways will seem less like work and more like the natural way to do things. Let's get started.

Lesson 1: Associating "Familiar Entities"

> *"NO ONE IS POOR, EXCEPT HE WHO LACKS KNOWLEDGE."*
> —*RABBI KRUSTOFSKI, THE SIMPSONS (SEASON 3, EPISODE 6)*

In *Section 1*, you learned how to memorize lists of **Familiar Entities**, but not how to connect two of them together. For example, you may need to remember a familiar food and its primary ingredient (hummus : chick peas), or a particular item and its location (phone charger : top drawer), or a musical instrument's location in an orchestra (violins : front). These unlikely examples aside, we often encounter a practical need to connect two familiar words or concepts for later retrieval. Additionally, developing this skill flexes your imaginative muscles in general, and strengthens your ability to associate and remember all types of information.

Take two random words: "rooster" and "hot air balloon." These are two **Familiar Entities**; even if you've never seen a rooster or hot air balloon in person, you should at least be able to imagine both. To connect these (thus forming a pair of **Associated Familiar Entities**), a **Journey** is unnecessary, as there is no list involved; you just need to *create an imaginative connection* between the two.

Start simply: envision a hot air balloon with a giant rooster design on it. Get a bit more creative: now picture a human-sized rooster piloting a hot air balloon. In fact, for the sake of humor and ease of recall, give the rooster a chef's hat and a bow tie. Can you hear the rooster? Can you smell the balloon's burning fuel? What do you see down below? Are you over a prairie, city or forest? How is the rooster reacting? Is it day or night? Sunny or overcast?

Alternatively, imagine yourself as the sole human in the basket of a hot air balloon with dozens of roosters. Shut your eyes and actually imagine it; you're knee-deep in a basket of panicking roosters, scratching against your legs. Imagine the fluttering wings, loose feathers in the air, and earthy smell of livestock. Lose yourself in the noise and commotion. Imagine your reaction to this situation. Are you frightened? Amused?

When it comes to associating a rooster with a hot air balloon, the options are numerous and limited only by the boundaries of your imagination. If approached creatively, this association has the potential to stick with you for a long time. Think of other ways to connect these two ideas. Don't be afraid to venture into the bizarre or inappropriate. First come up with a few on your own, and then when you're done (or if you get stuck), take a look at some examples below:

- A human-sized rooster is walking down the street, holding a string that's tied to a tiny hot air balloon. The balloon follows behind him high up in the sky, like a kite.
- You're standing in a hot air balloon and floating over an ocean of hot lava, while flying roosters attack like Kamikaze pilots, trying to poke holes in the balloon. With each puncture hole, the balloon creeps farther downward, inching ever closer to your molten demise.

- You're standing in a hot air balloon that is fueled not by propane, but by roosters tossed into the burner by a small catapult-like mechanism. Each rooster combusts when propelled into the flame, resulting in a loud, feathery "poof" (sorry, PETA).

- You're standing in a basket that's attached not to a hot air balloon, but to a giant rooster. The basket jerks and swings as the huge bird flaps its wings. Every time it slows or starts to sink, you pull the trigger on the burner, which ignites a flame under the rooster. This sends the giant beast into a panic and it flies with renewed vigor.

The possibilities are endless. With time and practice, quickly conjuring completely silly, absurd scenarios like the ones described above will get easier. The real trick is learning to let your imagination loosen up and play freely.

Another example: a friend has asked you to check his mail and water his plants a few times while he and his wife are away on vacation. He tells you the door key is "hidden underneath a stone turtle in the backyard." Though this is fairly simple to remember on its own because it is easily visualized, you can reinforce the "key : turtle" association exponentially by constructing a clever and elaborate narrative **Mnemonic Scene**.

First, think of your friend. Picture the back of his home or apartment and imagine walking up to the back door, when suddenly you feel a quick, sharp nip on your left calf. You look down to find an angry turtle with an old-fashioned brass key taped to its shell chasing after you and biting at your legs. You try to get the key away from the turtle as it snaps at you viciously. How big is the turtle? Does it make any noise? Is it slow or fast? Does anything else happen? Picture your surroundings. What does the key look like? Is it attached with duct tape? Electrical tape? Scotch tape?

Is it day or night? How close are you to the back door when the attack occurs?

Now, when you visit your friend's yard, you'll certainly remember where the key is. For quite some time, you should be able to retain a life-like recollection of the brutal turtle battle, solidifying in your mind the association between "turtle" and "key" (two **Familiar Entities**) in the **Context** of your friend's backyard.

It's time for an exercise. You'll use the exact same method to associate and memorize the following pairs of seemingly-unrelated items.

Write down only the first half of each pair on a piece of paper. Once you've copied them down, start studying the full list. Keep in mind that you're memorizing the individual **Associated Familiar Entities** (pairs); you don't have to memorize the list as a whole, so the **Journey Method** won't be needed. The goal here is to associate each pair of items such that when you encounter one of the words, you're able to reply immediately with its respective mate.

- Robe — Graffiti
- Magazine — Rat
- Viking hat — Picture frame
- Lacrosse stick — Hulk Hogan
- New York City — Couch
- Car trunk — Koala
- Television — Pony
- Vincent Van Gogh — Forklift
- Birthday card — President
- Stove — Root beer float
- Mickey Mouse — Doorknob

- Bamboo — Clown nose

Read through the list several times and create powerful associations for each pair. Like with numerical mnemonics, strive to create logical relationships between the **Entities**, but remember that "logical" doesn't necessarily mean "sensible" or "realistic." To understand the distinction, consider the following example: "a clown pulls off his shiny red nose and throws it into the air, where it gets snatched by a swooping pink eagle." This is *logical*: real-world physics and cause-and-effect apply, but it's not necessarily *sensible* or *realistic*. It is the absurdity itself that helps to reinforce the memorable nature of the narrative **Mnemonic Scene**. Try to use bizarre, sexual, violent, surprising, or humorous situations to create **Scenes**, as these stick most tenaciously in the psyche. So, "logical" is good—"sensible" and "realistic" are overrated.

Once you think you have the **Associated Familiar Entities** above committed to memory, go through the list one last time, take a two- to five-minute break, and then come back to the paper you used to record the first word of each pair. Fill in the missing halves without referencing the list.

How did you do? Don't get discouraged if you have trouble with this the first few times; most of us spent our entire lives trying to connect **Entities** through non-methodical brute force, so it can take time to allow yourself to engage your imagination this way. If any of the pairs gave you a particularly hard time, go back and build upon your original **Scene**. Add strange elements and additional sensory stimuli.

Below are some more **Associated Familiar Entities** to practice with. As before, copy down only the first half of each pair on a sheet of paper, study the whole list, then revisit your paper and fill in the blanks.

- The Pope — Watermelon
- Mike Tyson — Radiator
- Record player — Wig
- Honda — Jungle
- Cinnamon — Pinocchio
- Cell phone — Brick wall
- Wood — Sky
- Mermaid — Taco
- Bookshelf — Business card
- Baseball bat — The Rolling Stones
- T-Shirt — Your mother
- Laser — Oprah Winfrey

You'll spend some more time on this at the end of the section. For now, though, don't move on until you have the hang of it.

When you're ready, move on. Next, you'll learn how to memorize **Associated Unfamiliar Entities**.

Quick Review

1. Familiar Entities are nouns (persons, places, things, or ideas) for which you have a frame of reference. You have encountered these Entities in the past and can immediately imagine them or imagine Clues about them.

2. The best way to associate two Familiar Entities is to construct creative, fun, memorable Mnemonic Scenes that involve both Entities. If the association pertains to a particular place or

individual, construct an associative Scene in a context that reminds you of that place or individual.

Lesson 2: Associating Two "Unfamiliar Entities"

> *"IT'S BETTER TO BE ABSOLUTELY RIDICULOUS THAN ABSOLUTELY BORING."*
>
> —MARILYN MONROE, ACTRESS

By now, you understand the differences between **Familiar** and **Unfamiliar Entities**, and should be comfortable associating and memorizing lists of **Familiar Entities**. Now, you'll learn the best way to connect pairs of **Unfamiliar Entities** (as you've probably guessed, these pairs are called **Associated Unfamiliar Entities**).

To recap, **Unfamiliar Entities** are persons, places, things, or ideas (though most often proper nouns) for which you have no frame of reference. "Shamus Lorenzo McCullen" and "Bucaramanga, Columbia" are good examples of **Unfamiliar Entities**; due to your lack of familiarity with these two **Entities**, you can't picture them, have no emotional connection to them, and can't easily visualize **Clues** that could help you remember them (unless you just so happen to be familiar with Bucaramanga or know someone by that name).

Less often, common (non-proper, non-name) nouns can also be **Unfamiliar Entities**. For example, if you don't know what "monotremes" or "singleton patterns" are, they are **Unfamiliar Entities** to you, even though they are technically common nouns.

Consider an example that requires the need to associate two **Unfamiliar Entities**: imagine you're scheduled to meet with a board of eight speakers. Each of them is the owner of a mid-sized company. Prior to the meeting, you were supposed to have researched them and learned their names as well as which company each of them owns. However, the event completely slipped your mind. To make matters worse, five of them are from foreign countries, and their names are a little tougher to remember than "Dick Jones" or "Jane Smith." It looks like you're in trouble.

So, you hop on a computer, quickly look them up, and jot down the bare minimum before heading out the door: a simple list consisting of the eight individuals and their respective companies. Surabh Patel owns PyroTechnica Online, Gladys Baum owns Lotus Industrial, and so on. You use every traffic light on the way to the event to furiously study the scribbled name/company pairs.

Using classical, brute-force repetition, this would be a real pain, and you'd most likely show up to the event under-prepared despite your frantic efforts. However, you know better than to memorize this way; instead, you're going to relax and let your imagination take over. The associations you create will stick with you much longer than would be possible using brute-force memorization.

However, let's begin with a simpler example: world countries and their respective capitals (incidentally, this will also prove to be a more useful example if you ever end up on *Jeopardy*). World capitals are perfect for learning to associate **Unfamiliar Entities**; they are abundant and often difficult for westerners to pronounce. While you may be familiar with some, many of the world's countries are probably completely unfamiliar to you. Growing up, I used to call these countries "Olympics countries," because I never heard anything about them until their representatives came running out during the opening ceremony of the Olympic games ("and representing Tuvalu...").

Before associating world countries with their capitals, let's discuss the best approach. You don't need any new skills, but rather a different way to implement ones you've already learned.

To associate pairs of **Unfamiliar Entities**, you'll use imaginative **Mnemonic Scenes**, but no **Journeys**, as **Journeys** are only necessary for lists and numbers. In fact, you'll essentially approach this the same way you did when associating pairs of **Familiar Entities**; this time, instead of creating **Mnemonic Scenes** involving the two associated **Entities** themselves, you'll instead create **Mnemonic Scenes** involving *Clues* about the two **Entities**.

Broken down, this skill comprises four simple steps:

1. Take the first **Entity** and extract some sort of imaginative **Clue**(s) from the word itself that will allow you to recall the word.
2. Do the same for the second **Entity**.
3. Create an imaginative **Mnemonic Scene** that involves the two **Clues**, thus connecting them.
4. When recollecting the **Mnemonic Scene** at a later time, "play detective" and decipher the **Clues** you left for yourself.

Example: the capital of Albania is Tirana (sometimes spelled Tirane). Some people—mostly Albanians—know a good deal about this country, and probably already have some simple, emotionally relevant associations between "Albania" and the name of its capital (thus making it a **Familiar Entity**). Personally, I'm not one of these people, so for me this is an **Unfamiliar Entity**. When I hear the word "Albania," I immediately think of film actress Jessica Alba, because "Albania" starts with "Alba."

Unless you happen to have emotionally relevant connections to Albania or Tirana, do exactly the same: *go with the first, most natural thing that pops into your brain*, no matter how ridiculous it may seem.

Like the "Albania/Alba" connection, when I hear "Tirana," I think of a Tyrannosaurus Rex. Given these two **Clues**, I create a narrative **Mnemonic Scene** in my mind in which a Tyrannosaurus Rex is chasing Jessica Alba. As you can see, I extracted a **Clue** from each of the words (steps one and two), and then paired them together in a **Mnemonic Scene** (step three).

However, would you call "a Tyrannosaurus Rex chasing Jessica Alba" colorful? Memorable?

Extracting **Clues** from two unfamiliar words is the easy part. The challenge lies in creating detailed imaginative **Mnemonic Scenes** that involve the two **Clues**. It can be difficult at first to build connections that prove memorable enough to fulfill their purpose (step four) long-term; however, as you grow more accustomed to this technique, you'll begin to embrace your imagination and work more absurdity and detail into narrative **Mnemonic Scenes**.

For the "Albania — Tirana" example, I have constructed the following **Scene**: it's a hot summer afternoon in a small city, and the prehistoric predator is flipping cars and racing through the streets, only a few paces behind the sweating, panicking actress. The **Scene** is pure bedlam, and pedestrian bystanders race to find shelter. I hear car alarms and the thundering of the monster's feet against the caving blacktop. Alba, wearing a white t-shirt and jeans, abruptly turns right and runs down a narrow brick alley. The beast turns after her and slams its skull into the alley's opening, unable to squeeze through the space. Despite the presence of countless other fleeing humans, the Tyrannosaurus seems single-mindedly bent on pursuing the star.

Bricks are falling with every furious thrust of the monster's face against the two buildings that bookend the alley, and Alba, a few meters into the alley, finds her escape blocked by a tall, rusty chain-link fence. She is facing the beast with her back pressed into the fence. Panting and fighting back tears, she and the fence are just deep enough into the alley that the Tyrannosaurus can't reach her; however, its nose is coming closer with each snap of its mighty jaws.

I succumb to a stifling sense of claustrophobia at the merciless intersection of entrapment and dense, humid summer air. I can see and smell dust from the loosened bricks and mortar, and can feel the subtle heat of the monster's breath. I can see Alba's quivering jaw and hear police sirens growing closer in the distance. She grips the fence with a white-knuckled, desperate intensity. She turns her head away from the nightmare, squeezes her eyes shut, and quietly repeats, "This isn't happening. This isn't happening. This isn't happening."

Now if someone says "Albania," what will I think of? I often use the above example when speaking on this subject, and have had people tell me many years later that they can still effortlessly recall the capital of Albania.

I apologize to my Albanian readers for my lack of knowledge about their homeland. I also apologize to Jessica Alba for casting her in such an uncomfortable **Scene**; Jessica, if you're reading this, please get in touch with me; I'll gladly apologize over dinner.

Note that the city where the **Scene** takes place is not a **Journey** and is therefore not broken into individual **Steps**. It is rather a single fictional setting that serves as the vehicle for a narrative about this particular pair of **Associated Unfamiliar Entities**. As an exercise, spend some time performing this type of creative association for all the world's countries whose names begin with "A" or "B"; please keep in mind that the world is an ever-evolving place, and so the list may have changed slightly since this was written. Some of these will be difficult to remember and associate at first, but reach deep to find connections, take your time, and embrace your first impressions, as they often create the strongest links. Create imaginative, funny, sexual, violent, perverse, weird, and frightening associations.

Though she was referring to her public persona (as opposed to mnemonic devices), take Marilyn Monroe's quote from the beginning of the lesson to heart; it's better to be ridiculous than boring. The mental pictures you paint are yours and yours alone, so don't settle for something weak, and don't worry about justifying your choices. Channel strong, emotional, weird images and you'll recall the **Scene** much more easily.

- Afghanistan — Kabul
- Albania — Tirana
- Algeria — Algiers
- Andorra — Andorra la Vella
- Angola — Luanda

- Antigua and Barbuda — Saint John's
- Argentina — Buenos Aires
- Armenia — Yerevan
- Australia — Canberra
- Austria — Vienna
- Azerbaijan — Baku
- The Bahamas — Nassau
- Bahrain — Manama
- Bangladesh — Dhaka
- Barbados — Bridgetown
- Belarus — Minsk
- Belgium — Brussels
- Belize — Belmopan
- Benin — Porto Novo
- Bhutan — Thimphu
- Bolivia — Sucre
- Bosnia and Herzegovina — Sarajevo
- Botswana — Gaborone
- Brazil — Brasilia
- Brunei — Bandar Seri Begawan
- Bulgaria — Sofia
- Burkina Faso — Ouagadougou
- Burundi — Bujumbura

Like I did in the "Albania" example, use as much sensory detail as possible. Though your associations should be personal and natural, this can be difficult for the inexperienced. If you get stuck and need inspiration, you'll find below some of my more interesting personal narrative **Mnemonics Scenes** relating to this list; the examples should illustrate the ideal level of detail to include when constructing such **Scenes**.

Armenia — Yerevan: A burly, bearded man with huge, unrealistically muscular arms walks up to me on a city street (Armenia = "arms"). The town is paved with cobblestone and has a certain degree of ambiguous old-world European charm. It's dusk, and I hear music and people in the distance. This strange man accuses me of being a van, as though that were something a person could be.

"Hey," he yells as he approaches, "You're a van!"

Confused, I look around, confirm he's talking to me, and reply timidly, "No, I'm a person." At this, the burly stranger repeats his accusation, and I find myself becoming indignant at the bizarre claim.

"Yeah? Maybe *you're* the one who's a van," I yell back, and come closer to him, preparing for the strangest fight of my life. He smiles broadly, and again tells me that I'm a van.

Despite my initial indignation, I find myself laughing at the absurdity of the scenario; as I realize that I'm involved in some sort of odd game, I return the allegation. Back and forth we go, laughing harder each time. "You're a van" = "Yerevan."

Australia — Canberra: I apologize to my elementary school geography teacher for the following confession: even though I've visited Australia, I thought its capital was Sydney until I decided to memorize these world capitals.

Taking this into consideration, in my scenario I step off a small plane in Sydney, looking at a big blue sign that says, "Welcome to Sydney!" It is a hot morning and the air ripples above the tarmac and airport terminal before me. I'm dressed as the archetypal tourist: weighed down with pamphlets, multiple cameras dangling by neck straps, and an excess of luggage. A mustachioed Australian man approaches me; he is gaunt, seems to be in his early fifties, and has leathery skin from living for years in the unforgiving Australian sun.

I raise my index finger into the air and command in an exaggerated and comical manner, "Good sir, show me around your illustrious capital."

Chewing on something, he shakes his head and says, "This ain't it, mate. Sorry."

I look at him, bewildered, and, after a moment, he says, "Oi. You want a berry?" I look down to see a crude aluminum can full of raspberries (Canberra = "can of berries") in his left hand. The subtle fruity smell of the berries reaches my nose as the last of the passengers exit the **Scene**, leaving me alone with my strange companion.

I stammer, "This—this isn't the capital?" Still eating berries, he shakes his head and calmly gazes off into the distance, as though distracted or disinterested in my problem. I find myself gazing off as well. I sigh and eat a berry.

> *Tip*: Note that in the above example I don't rely on **Clues** about the word "Australia," because the country is familiar enough to me that I have some points of reference (such as my companion's accent, my incorrect perception of the capital, the climate, and so on). In contrast, countries like Armenia or Benin, which are completely foreign to me (except for some vague geographical sense of where they exist on the globe), require sound **Clues**, as I'm forced to rely entirely on the names of the countries themselves.

Benin — Porto Novo: Although it's pronounced more like "ben-*neen*," Benin reminds me a bit of Mennen, the company who makes *Speed Stick* deodorant. In the 1980's, their television commercials ended with a manly chorus singing, "By Mennen!" Hence, for me, deodorant is a **Clue** for Benin.

When it comes to the capital, Porto Novo, I need **Clues** as well. My friend Lionel grew up in Puerto Rico (Porto), and when I hear Novo, I think of the television series *Nova*, and therefore outer space. So, in my scenario, my Puerto Rican friend Lionel is wearing a space suit and floating out in the cosmos while carefully applying deodorant to the armpits of his suit. He is tethered to a nearby ship with a long, snaking cable.

Putting it all together, when I hear the name "Benin," I think of "Mennen," which makes me think of deodorant, which triggers the image of Lionel applying deodorant as he is floating through space. From there, I decipher Puerto Rico and Nova, and this in turn triggers recall of Benin's capital, Porto Novo.

The Bahamas — Nassau: Before we were married, my wife went on a trip to the Bahamas with two friends and returned with many photographs, including one of a particular restaurant where they had eaten. The restaurant was on a dock, and every so often, the restaurant staff would throw discarded food into the water, prompting a feeding frenzy among the sizable resident sharks (much to the delight of the patrons).

When I hear "Bahamas," I first imagine the restaurant and beach as I remember them from the photograph; this serves as both a setting and a **Clue**. Because of this association, I don't need to create a separate **Clue** for the word "Bahamas." Without the benefit of my personal familiarity with a photograph of the Bahamas, I'd probably have created a word **Clue** from Ebenezer Scrooge's catch phrase, "Bah Humbug!" as this is among my first natural associations with the word "Bahamas."

The scene from the photograph comes alive in my mind. I'm standing on the dock at dusk, surrounded on three sides by calm water, taking in the view. I sigh sadly and begin to walk away, as though coming to terms with the end of my vacation on the beautiful island.

On my way back to the hotel, a tall local man walks up to me holding a fruity drink (with a tiny umbrella) and looking relaxed. Behind him, tourists are enjoying themselves at a small beachfront resort. The stranger asks, "J'oo leavin', mon?" and I nod sadly. He holds up a finger, wags it side to side, and says, "Nah-ahhh. Not so fast. You can stay t'ree more days!" Just then, as though on cue, the people in the background break into dance as music begins blasting from an unseen source. My vacation miraculously extended, I dance my way over to the party and join in.

"Not so" sounds like "Nassau" in the man's thick island accent, thus triggering the necessary association in my mind.

Belarus — Minsk: When I hear "Belarus," I think of a walrus. For me, the words sound somehow related; this is a prime example of going with your gut instinct, even if the association wouldn't necessarily make much sense to anyone else.

I imagine sitting on a train next to a wealthy walrus, who is wearing a monocle and tuxedo. I smell a mixture of expensive cologne and fish. It's daytime, but a bit overcast. The walrus ignores me and reads a newspaper. A bit put off by the strangeness of seeing a walrus dressed like the Monopoly guy and riding a train, I pretend to read so as not to appear rude, but study him out of the corner of my eye. After a moment, his wife (also a walrus) joins us, wearing a flamboyant mink coat ("mink" reminds me of "Minsk").

Bolivia — Sucre: "Bolivia" immediately brings to mind the word "bowl," and "Sucre" sounds like "sucrose," a type of sugar. So, for me, the Bolivia/Sucre connection instantly translates into a "bowl of sugar," which I imagine being glued to South America on a globe. The globe sits on a bronze stand in an expensive-looking private study or library, and the setting smells a bit like a church (old wood, incense, and musty books).

I notice the bowl and find it strange that its contents don't spill out, since Bolivia is south of the equator, and thus the bowl is almost upside down. Curious, I poke the substance with my finger; it flakes off as though it had once been wet and sticks together now that it's dry. I break a tiny piece off and taste it, confirming that it's sugar. This is enough to trigger my memory.

Note how I used multiple senses to paint each **Mnemonic Scene** in detail. As mentioned, the more senses invoked, the easier the **Scene** will be to retain long-term.

Continue memorizing the list of "A" and "B" countries and their capitals. If you get stuck, consider it a chance to challenge yourself to be absurd and inventive. Push the boundaries. Even the most difficult **Unfamiliar Entities** in this list sound like *something* if you stretch your mind enough. "Ouagadougou" = "I wag a dog, do you?" "Bandar Seri Begawan" = "A band of cherries begging for a wand?" "Bujumbura" = "Boo! Jumbo bra?"

Once finished, you should be able to hear the name of any country from the list and immediately recite its respective capital. Conversely, you should be able to hear the name of any capital and immediately recite its country. Don't move on until you're confident with each pair.

Spend as much time on this exercise as necessary before moving on. In the coming sections, you'll make heavy use of the free-flowing imaginative processes you're cultivating here.

Quick Review

1. **Unfamiliar Entities** are nouns (persons, places, things or ideas) for which you have no frame of reference. You've never encountered these **Entities** in the past, and thus cannot immediately imagine them.
2. The best way to associate two **Unfamiliar Entities** is to construct creative, fun, narrative **Mnemonic Scenes** that involve **Mnemonic Clues** about both **Entities** (usually in the form of references to the words themselves). If the association pertains

to a particular place or individual, construct the **Scene** in a setting that will remind you of that place or individual.

Lesson 3: Associating Three or More "Unfamiliar Entities"

> *"IF YOU ARE NOT WILLING TO RISK THE UNUSUAL, YOU WILL HAVE TO SETTLE FOR THE ORDINARY."*
>
> —*Jim Rohn, Motivational Speaker*

When connecting or associating **Unfamiliar Entities**, you'll most often have to associate two such **Entities**, as you just learned to do. Sometimes, though, you might need to connect three or more. Examples include:

- An unfamiliar person (first, middle, and last names)
- An unfamiliar location (city, state/jurisdiction, and country)
- An unfamiliar record (musician, album title, and record label)
- An unfamiliar vehicle (the manufacturer, model, and dealership)

You'll still need to create **Mnemonic Clues** for each **Entity** and associate them with one another through a shared imaginative **Mnemonic Scene**. However, dealing with three or more **Unfamiliar Entities** introduces an additional consideration: in many cases, it will also be necessary to keep track of each **Clue's** role.

A good illustration of this is the "first, middle, and last name" example. If you're dealing with only two names, and are able to extract from your **Clues** the names "Dennis" and "Bowers," cultural cues allow you to deduce which name comes first ("Dennis" is a common first name, and "Bowers" a common last name, but not the other way around).

As many westerners have middle names that could also be used as a first name, adding the middle name into the mix can cause confusion. If you extracted from your **Clues** the names "Howard," "Dennis," and "Bowers," it would be difficult to tell if you were trying to recall "Howard Dennis Bowers" or "Dennis Howard Bowers." For this reason, it's important to provide information about the <u>role</u> (in this case, first, middle, or last name) of each **Clue**.

You can remember Entity roles via Linear Scenes.

Linear and Asynchronous Scenes

There are two special types of **Mnemonic Scenes**. Each has its own purpose.

Linear Scenes

In a **Linear Scene**, the narrative action takes place in a set order, as the result of imagined cause and effect relationships. An example of this would be a mouse (a **Clue**) knocking over a bookshelf (a **Clue**), causing a book to fall into a fish tank (a **Clue**). In this case, you'd need to first imagine the mouse in order to think of the bookshelf, and so on; aside from the first, each **Clue** relies on the prior **Clue** to drive the narrative forward. When you need to memorize a **Entities** that need to be recalled in a specific order (example: first, middle, and last name), use a **Linear Scene** to do so.

Let's work through an easy **Linear Scene** together. Imagine that you're tasked with remembering the term Sodium Lauryl Sulfate (a chemical found in many detergents and shampoos). First, choose a location for your **Scene**; perhaps your shower would be appropriate, as that's most likely where you shampoo your hair. Note that this isn't really a "**Journey**," as you'll only use a single location.

First, create a **Clue** for "Sodium." Perhaps a salt shaker? A can of soda pop ("soda" sounds like "Sodium")? Picture that **Clue** positioned way up high, perhaps balanced perilously atop your showerhead. It falls off the showerhead and strikes the "Lauryl" **Clue**. Do you know someone with that name? How about Lauren? Lawrence? Hugh Laurie (the actor)? Laurel (the type of flower)? A lawyer? Finally, imagine the "Lauryl" **Clue** doing something strange when it is struck by the "Sodium" **Clue**—exploding, melting, vibrating, changing color or shape—and thus generating your final **Clue** for "Sulfate." Perhaps a book of matches ("Sulfer")? Something that will remind you of "soul fate?"

And just like that, you've managed to fit three **Clues** into a single **Mnemonic Scene** in a way that retains their order.

> *Tip: Linear Scenes aren't necessarily reserved for three or more Entities; sometimes you have to connect two Unfamiliar Entities that are so foreign to you it would be impossible to intuitively deduce their order. For instance, if you memorized the name "Boaght Tchar" (an actual name I've come across), and then recalled the two words later, would you be able to tell which came first? Even though it's only comprised of two Entities, you could use a Linear Scene to retain the proper order in your memory; in the Scene, the Clue for "Boaght" would perform some action that causes/spawns the Clue for "Tchar."*

Asynchronous Scenes

An **Asynchronous Scene** is one in which multiple actions are happening simultaneously and can be observed as a whole, in any order. An example would be two blue robots (**Clue**) dancing in front of a burning building (**Clue**) while airplanes (**Clue**) soar in circles overhead. The **Scene** can be viewed as a whole, with no **Clue** relying on another in a cause-and-effect manner; as far as we can tell, the robots didn't cause the fire, the fire didn't create the robots, neither the robots nor the fire caused the airplanes to appear, etc. These are great for **Entities** that can be recalled in any order.

If you had to remember the first names of a coworker's three children, an **Asynchronous Scene** would work well. You could imagine your coworker's home or workspace, pick a single location within it, and store the three name **Clues** in a single **Mnemonic Scene**, as order doesn't matter (unless, for instance, you need to store them in ascending age order).

Linear vs. Asynchronous Scene Comparison

While **Linear Scenes** make the most sense for ordered information and **Asynchronous Scenes** are best suited for unordered information, you could use a **Linear Scene** to remember the names of your coworker's three children, even if the order doesn't matter.

Linear Scenes, rich with cause-and-effect relationships, can be easier to recall and therefore a more powerful mnemonic tool. The drawback: if a single **Clue** is forgotten, you might lose the context relied upon to remember the rest of the **Clues**. **Asynchronous Scenes** can be slightly more difficult to recall wholly since they lack cause-and-effect connections to lead you from one **Clue** to the next; however, this gives you more creative freedom. Since you don't have to worry about creating cause-and-effect relationships, you can usually develop **Mnemonic Scenes** much more quickly by simply stacking **Clues** into a given **Scene** as needed.

As a rule of thumb, it's safer to stick with **Linear Scenes** whenever possible, though they require a bit more effort to compose.

Let's do an exercise. Take a look at the **Scenes** below and assess whether each is **Linear** or **Asynchronous**.

1. Two dogs play in a puddle while—in the distant sky—the sun's color fluctuates rapidly from yellow to purple.
2. A boy knocks an exotic bird off a mailbox with a slingshot. When the bird hits the ground, it explodes into an orange mist, which floats away while emitting a high-pitched squeal.
3. A baseball player hits a ball, which is caught by the Grim Reaper (who is sitting in the stadium crowd like any other spectator).

The Reaper reaches back behind his seat, grabs a seatbelt, and snaps it over his chest. The row of seats in which he's sitting begins to pull away like a roller coaster.

4. A man sitting in a large wooden chair spins in circles while balancing on a raft in an ocean of bright green water.

Answers:

1. Asynchronous
2. Linear
3. Linear
4. Asynchronous

If you got any of these wrong, go back and think about them again. All **Asynchronous Scenes**—though they may involve action of some kind—contain no distinct cause-and-effect relationships, while **Linear Scenes** rely on cause-and-effect to continue the action.

Meta-Information

Meta-Information will be covered more formally later on, but for now, just know that **Meta-Information** is basically "information about information." In the first/middle/last name example, you needed to determine how to convey information about each word's role so you could remember the correct order. Though you used a **Linear Scene** in that example, you could also use an **Asynchronous Scene** paired with **Meta-Information**.

To do this, create an **Asynchronous Scene** and attach information to each of the individual **Clues** that would tip you off about where they belong in a given order. For instance, you could imagine the **Clues** finishing a race (coming in first, second, and third place). You could exaggerate the size of the **Clues**, with the first name appearing abnormally large, the last name abnormally small, and the middle name at roughly normal size. A simpler way would be to imagine a **Scene** where the **Clues** appear in ascending age order from left to right (the order in which they'd be read).

The options are limited only by your imagination, and as long as you're able to convey this information to your future self in some distinct and reliable way, there are no strict rules determining how to do this.

The "three sizes" or "left-to-right" methods could also work for the city/state/country example, as cities are smaller, states are larger, and countries are the largest of the three. But how would you tackle the musician/album title/record label example? Size or order won't reliably capture the role of each **Clue**, so you need to apply more contextual **Meta-Information** to each **Clue**.

Consider the following set of information: *Delectrothrone* (the band)/*Sombrero-Optional Party* (the album title)/*Make-Up Records* (the record label). You need to create a **Mnemonic Scene** depicting **Clues** about all three **Entities**. You could decorate the *Delectrothrone* **Clue** with an instrument (to remind you this is the band name), the *Sombrero-Optional Party* **Clue** with a record sleeve or CD case (to remind you this is the album), and the *Make-Up Records* **Clue** with a cheap, tacky suit (to remind you of a record label, using the stereotype of a sleazy record executive).

Including **Meta-Information** can be a bit difficult when you're first starting out, but it will become more natural with practice. If you can work sensory details into your **Mnemonic Scenes**, you can certainly add **Meta-Information** as well.

Work through the following example on your own: you need to remember the king of a small country and his two sons. The king is named Caliban, his elder son is named Julius, and his younger son is named Rafael. Use an **Asynchronous Scene** to store the individual names, and add **Meta-Information** to record their respective roles (king, elder son, younger son).

The Difference Between Multiple Associated Entities and Lists

It's important to understand the differences between **Associated Entities** and lists, as these two types of information are best memorized using very different methods. The distinction lies more in size or scale than context.

Here's an example to illustrate what I mean.

Imagine that you must memorize 2009's top oil-exporting nations, which were Saudi Arabia, Russia, and the United Arab Emirates (in order from first to third). This is an example of **Associated Entities** (whether they're **Familiar** or **Unfamiliar** depends on your personal familiarity with the three nations). You could remember this with a single **Mnemonic Scene** by taking a place that reminds you of oil—perhaps a gas station—and constructing an ordered **Linear Scene** there involving three **Clues**.

For three nations, this is a piece of cake; however, if you had to memorize the top *twenty* nations, you would definitely have a list on your hands, and should approach it as such (using a **Journey**).

This example illustrates how the sheer volume of information determines the method best used to memorize it. With some practice using **Mnemonic Techniques**, it's fairly easy to record three **Clues** (with accompanying **Meta-Information**) in a single **Mnemonic Scene**. Beyond that, most people run the risk of losing things.

To be safe, a good rule of thumb is "four or more items requires a list," though this number is not set in stone. In fact, a better rule is, "if it doesn't feel natural, don't push it." Lists are much easier to memorize when treated as lists, so don't stress yourself out trying to shove a ton of information into a single **Mnemonic Scene**.

Quick Review

1. The best way to recall ordered **Associated Unfamiliar Entities** is to imagine a **Linear Scene** in which the individual **Clues** interact through cause-and-effect relationships. This will facilitate **Entity** recall in a specific, scripted sequence.

2. You can use an **Asynchronous Scene** to memorize unordered **Associated Unfamiliar Entities**. If necessary, the role of each **Entity** can be coded into the **Scene** by the use of **Meta-Information**, or information attached to each **Clue**.

3. If you need to memorize too many **Entities** to fit comfortably within a **Scene**, the **Entities** may be better suited for memorization as a list.

Lesson 4: Memorizing Lists of Associated "Familiar Entities"

> *"I WORKED HARD AT MEMORIZING LISTS OF FACTS AND FIGURES."*
>
> —CHARLES VAN DOREN, THE CONTESTANT INVOLVED WITH THE FAMED QUIZ SHOW SCANDAL OF 1959

Van Doren wasn't born with innate encyclopedic knowledge; neither was brainy game show host Ben Stein, nor even the more recent *Jeopardy* champion Ken Jennings; they all memorized and retained the trivia that brought them fame. It wasn't magic, and you should by now have a good sense of the types of methods that can help you retain such knowledge yourself. In this lesson, you'll continue learning how to memorize specific types of information.

You already learned how to associate two **Familiar Entities**; however, you may sometimes need to memorize lists of **Associated Familiar Entities**.

To illustrate this, let's expand upon some examples from earlier. Instead of having to memorize a single food and its primary ingredient (hummus : chick peas), imagine you have to memorize a list of foods and their respective primary ingredients. Instead of a single musical instrument's location in an orchestra (violins : front), what if you needed to do so for an entire orchestra and recite the list back without being fed the first **Entity** of each pair?

Here are some practical uses for memorizing lists of **Associated Familiar Entities**:

- Memorizing the parts of a lengthy speech or presentation and their core concepts or arguments, then recalling them in order without forgetting or skipping any of them. Introduction : "puppy" anecdote; Recent studies overview : disprove the old model…

- Remembering a list of familiar people who are coming to an event (their names) and a contextual attribute for each, such as their dish for a pot luck dinner. Donnie : soup; Sasha : dip…

- During a touring vacation or work trip, remembering which city you'll be in on each day. Monday : Albuquerque; Tuesday : Santa Fe…

Remembering directions in a familiar area. Left on Thompson Avenue; Left on St. John Place; Right on Water Street…

The practical applications are numerous, and this method can even be used for such purposes as remembering sports team schedules, academic papers and their authors, and the amounts of money owed to you by specific individuals (for all the bookies reading this).

To memorize this type of information, you'll need to combine the **Journey Method** (which you used for simple **Familiar Entity** lists) with the type of creative association skills you just employed during the **Associating Unfamiliar Entities** lesson.

Let's break it down into three steps:

1. Choose a **Journey**.
2. For each pair of **Familiar Entities**, construct an imaginative **Mnemonic Scene** that involves both **Entities**.
3. Place each of the **Scenes** within a **Step** of the **Journey**.

To make sense of the process, we'll begin by reviewing the **Associated Familiar Entities** we used previously. First, prepare an array of **Journeys** that add up to a minimum of thirty **Steps**. *[If you can't do this by now, reread the lessons on the Journey Method.]*

1. Robe — Graffiti
2. Magazine — Rat
3. Viking hat — Picture frame
4. Lacrosse stick — Hulk Hogan
5. New York City — Couch
6. Car trunk — Koala
7. Television — Pony
8. Vincent Van Gogh — Forklift
9. Birthday card — President
10. Stove — Root beer float
11. Mickey Mouse — Doorknob
12. Bamboo — Clown nose
13. The Pope — Watermelon
14. Mike Tyson — Radiator
15. Record player — Wig
16. Honda — Jungle
17. Cinnamon — Pinocchio
18. Cell Phone — Brick wall
19. Wood — Sky

20. Mermaid — Taco
21. Book shelf — Business card
22. Baseball bat — The Rolling Stones
23. T-Shirt — Your mother
24. Laser — Oprah Winfrey

When you first learned how to associate **Familiar Entities** using these pairs, you trained yourself to recall each of the words when presented with its mate. As you studied this list somewhat recently, there's a good chance you can still recall many of the associations, especially if you used strong visual **Mnemonic Scenes** as instructed. However, this doesn't mean you'll know the entire list by heart or in order, since you memorized only the individual associations, and not the list as a whole.

To memorize the entire list, simply place the **Clue** pairs you already know along the **Steps** of a **Journey**. Instead of "Robe : Graffiti" being an isolated pair of **Associated Familiar Entities**, they're now going to be a pair of **Associated Familiar Entities** stored in the first **Step** of a **Journey**. Use logical **Transitions** from one **Step** to the next; as usual, the **Scenes** and **Transitions** should be personally intuitive.

To give you an idea of how this should work, consider the following narrative, in which I illustrate one possible way to store the first three **Steps** of the list (in a **Journey** that begins in your old high school's library):

The late Hugh Hefner, wearing his trademark <u>robe</u>, stands on <u>the front steps of your old high school library</u> (**Step** one). A bunch of little animated thugs run around him, spray-painting <u>graffiti</u> on him. Can you smell the paint? Hefner—seemingly unaffected—simply tokes at his pipe and looks off into the distance, obviously deep in thought about the many women of his past. The thugs are laughing and making a racket, which upsets a nearby <u>human-sized rat</u>, who sits in <u>the library's foyer</u> (**Step** two). Is the rat dressed in human clothing? What is he wearing? "Hey! Will you kids knock it off? I'm trying to read here," the rat yells, as he shakes a copy of *Rodents* <u>magazine</u> (the rat equivalent of *People*). The rat continues to read for a moment, then tears a page out of the magazine, walks to <u>the library's front desk</u> (**Step** three), and quickly creates an impressive origami <u>Viking hat</u>. He puts it on and holds up an empty <u>picture frame</u> so he's centered within it. He poses, and the woman behind the counter takes a photograph of him with an old-fashioned camera. Does the rat smile? How does he pose? What does the librarian look like?

Because the list is made up of arbitrarily chosen **Entities**, there was no opportunity to choose a **Journey** based upon context. When facing real-world applications, you'll most likely be able to associate a given list with a suitable **Contextual Journey** with some emotional significance; you should use such a **Journey** whenever possible.

Spend a few minutes studying the entire list in order. Once you think you have it properly memorized, recite it aloud a few times, moving faster with each round. On your last recital, speed up or "fast forward" the **Journey** and attempt to recall the pairs as quickly as possible. Pretend you're practicing for a timed memory competition, and attempt to exceed a comfortable pace.

Once confident, check your memory against the list. How did you do? Don't be discouraged if you didn't get everything exactly right, but scrutinize each missed association. Why didn't the image stick? Did you overestimate your familiarity with the particular **Step** of the **Journey**? Were the **Mnemonic Clues** used not powerful or creative enough? Did you incorporate insufficient sensory detail? Did weak **Transitions** between **Steps** cause you to lose your place? Determine the most likely reason for each failure, adjust your **Scenes** accordingly, and try again.

Memorize and recite back the following short list of **Associated Familiar Entities** in order. You should be able to memorize this type of list in under sixty seconds. Don't move on until you can.

1. Purple — Sunflower seed
2. Steel Drum — Machine gun
3. Chalk Board — Rapper
4. Demon — Throne
5. Aluminum foil — Handcuffs

As you continue to develop the skills taught in this section, your powers of imagination and association will grow; these benefits will reach beyond the realm of conscious memory and mnemonics. These skills will manifest themselves in decision-making, problem solving, and creative thinking. You'll begin to make more free-flowing, zany connections and expand your mind.

Quick Review

1. To memorize lists of **Associated Familiar Entities**, use the **Journey Method** and creative association. First, forge strong creative associations between each pair of **Familiar Entities**, painting vivid narrative **Mnemonic Scenes** in which they interact. Then, mentally place each **Mnemonic Scene** within an individual **Step** of a **Journey**.

Lesson 5: Memorizing Lists of (Single or Associated) "Unfamiliar Entities"

> *"LISTS ARE ANTI-DEMOCRATIC, DISCRIMINATORY, ELITIST…AND SOMETIMES THE PRINT IS TOO SMALL."*
>
> —DAVID IVES, PLAYWRIGHT

Right now, you have to think consciously about which method you should use to memorize a particular type of information; with time, the correct method will come naturally.

Now that you've learned a few methods, you may have noticed some patterns; there are a few steadfast rules that can be used alone or in any combination, depending on the type of information:

1. When associating two or more **Entities**, connect them using creative imagery (e.g., "mug : electrician" = "an <u>electrician</u> installing a glowing <u>mug</u> in your wall").

2. When memorizing three or more **Entities** or pairs of **Associated Entities**, you're usually dealing with a list. Use a **Journey** (e.g., "dog, flowers…" = "a furry <u>dog</u> at **Step** one is wearing a fedora, which he takes off and throws [**Transition**] to **Step** two. <u>Flowers</u> grow out of it after it lands…").

3. When memorizing an **Unfamiliar Entity**, break it down into a **Clue** or series of **Clues** that will tip you off about its nature or pronounciation (e.g., "Melanie Burton" = "Melon Brrr Ton" = "a <u>melon</u>, while <u>shivering</u> with cold, is crushed by a giant one-<u>ton</u> weight").

Keeping all this in mind, let's examine a challenge you may one day face: the imposing task of memorizing lists of **Unfamiliar Entities**.

Lists of Individual Unfamiliar Entities

In some cases, these lists may consist of individual **Unfamiliar Entities** (invoking rules two and three). An example of a list of individual **Unfamiliar Entities** would be an alphabetical inventory of the counties of New Jersey (Atlantic, Bergen, Burlington…). To memorize the list, you would need to generate creative **Clues** for each **Entity** ("Atlantic" = "Atlas," "Bergen" = "Burger," "Burlington" = "Burly Tony…") and place each **Mnemonic Clue** within the ordered **Steps** of a **Journey**. After completion, you should be able to recite the counties in order, without missing any.

Take a crack at memorizing this list now. If you're from New Jersey, feel free to substitute this list with the counties of a different state (but don't use Delaware, which only has three counties). Don't move on until you can perform this task and feel comfortable with the method.

1. Atlantic
2. Bergen
3. Burlington
4. Camden

5. Cape May
6. Cumberland
7. Essex
8. Gloucester
9. Hudson
10. Hunterdon
11. Mercer
12. Middlesex
13. Monmouth
14. Morris
15. Ocean
16. Passaic
17. Salem
18. Somerset
19. Sussex
20. Union
21. Warren

Lists of Associated Unfamiliar Entities

In other cases, you may need to memorize a list containing pairs of **Associated Unfamiliar Entities** (requiring all three of the memorization rules listed). An example of such a list could be an alphabetical roster of the thirty-two children in your daughter's first grade class (first and last names). You would need to transform each first and last name into **Clues**. Then, using creative association to connect the **Clues**, you would create **Scenes** to place within the ordered **Steps** of a **Journey**.

Let's use this example to practice this skill. First, decide on a setting. This example is the perfect time to use a **Contextual Journey**; you can use your daughter's actual classroom (if you happen to have a daughter, she's in school, and you're familiar with her classroom), or just a memorable classroom from your own time in school. Though this example requires thirty-two **Steps** and will thus call for the **Journey** to continue beyond a single classroom, you can start there. Use creative, logical **Transitions** to travel to the next segment of your **Mega-Journey** once the classroom's capacity has been reached.

Imagine the first fictional classmate on the list is named Michelle Casey, and construct a **Mnemonic Scene** containing **Clues** to tip you off about her first and last names. Perhaps imagine Michelle Obama dressed as a train conductor (a reference to famed conductor Casey Jones). Picture her standing at the first **Step** of your **Journey**. What is she doing? How is she interacting with the setting?

As you know, a great way to reinforce a mnemonic narrative vehicle is by creating logical (but not always sensible) **Transitions** between each **Step**. Using **Transitions**, a **Journey's** individual **Steps** become part of a larger story, rather than isolated thoughts; this reinforces the stickiness of the memory. For instance, Michelle Obama can take off her conductor's hat, reach inside and pull out a rabbit, which scampers to the **Journey's** second **Step**. Or perhaps she blows a train whistle, which elicits a reaction from the **Clues** at the second **Step**.

We won't go through the entire class together, but let's think of a clue for Paul Zahodski, the final student on the list. You might envision drag diva RuPaul asleep at your final **Step**, using a pair of skis as a pillow. Cartoonish "Z's" flow from the slumbering star's mouth. Some object from the penultimate **Step** rolls into the **Scene** (the **Transition**), brushes her leg, and startles her awake. When recollecting this **Journey**, you might decipher the **Clues** by saying to yourself, "RuPaul? Asleep? Skis? Paul...sleep...nap...catching Z's...Z...skis? Paul Z-skis? Paul Zahodski!"

Let's tackle an example that's difficult but practical. Remember the countries and capitals you memorized earlier? You should still be able to connect any "A" or "B" country to its respective capital (or vice versa). However, if you were asked to recite the entire list in order, could you? Of course not; you didn't approach the exercise as a list and didn't use a **Journey**, so you would have no way of ensuring you didn't miss any countries along the way. Luckily, half the work is done for you, as you've already built creative **Mnemonic Scenes** for each of the **Associated Pairs**; you only need to fit each **Scene** into the ordered **Steps** of a **Journey**.

Prepare an array of **Journeys** and begin memorizing the entire list. What **Contextual Journey** makes you think of world countries and capitals? For instance, you could begin with your elementary school's geography classroom or the set of *Jeopardy*. Here's the list again:

1. Afghanistan — Kabul
2. Albania — Tirane
3. Algeria — Algiers
4. Andorra — Andorra la Vella
5. Angola — Luanda
6. Antigua and Barbuda — Saint John's
7. Argentina — Buenos Aires
8. Armenia — Yerevan
9. Australia — Canberra
10. Austria — Vienna
11. Azerbaijan — Baku
12. The Bahamas — Nassau

13. Bahrain — Manama
14. Bangladesh — Dhaka
15. Barbados — Bridgetown
16. Belarus — Minsk
17. Belgium — Brussels
18. Belize — Belmopan
19. Benin — Porto Novo
20. Bhutan — Thimphu
21. Bolivia — Sucre
22. Bosnia and Herzegovina — Sarajevo
23. Botswana — Gaborone
24. Brazil — Brasilia
25. Brunei — Bandar Seri Begawan
26. Bulgaria — Sofia
27. Burkina Faso — Ouagadougou
28. Burundi — Bujumbura

It may at first be a bit difficult to take your pre-existing narrative **Mnemonic Scenes** and fit them into the **Steps** of a **Journey**, but this is a great exercise for your creativity.

Take your time, and don't stop until you have this list reasonably memorized. As you did when learning to memorize lists of **Familiar Entities**, recite the list of **Associated Entities** over and over, going faster each time, until you're pushing the boundaries of your comfort.

Let's next work on a list of **Associated Unfamiliar Entities** that you haven't previously memorized, so you can see what it's like to go through all the required steps. These are the Lord Mayors of London from 2001 to 2010:

1. Michael Oliver
2. Gavyn Arthur
3. Robert Finch
4. Michael Savory
5. David Brewer
6. John Stuttard
7. David Lewis
8. Ian Luder
9. Nick Anstee
10. Michael Bear

For each, forge a creative, associative **Mnemonic Scene** involving **Clues** about both the first and last names. Then, use a ten-**Step Journey** and store these **Mnemonic Scenes** within its **Steps**.

Move on once you feel comfortable reciting the list. How did you do? Did you struggle with anything? What type of **Clues** did you use? Did Oliver remind you of olives or olive oil? Did Finch remind you of a bird?

During *Review and Development* for *Section 2*, we'll examine some real-world applications of this method.

Quick Review

1. To memorize lists of individual **Unfamiliar Entities**, create imaginative **Clues** that represent each **Entity**. Use the **Journey Method** (with a **Contextual Journey**, if possible), develop **Mnemonic Scenes** that involve each **Clue**, and work these **Scenes** into each of the **Journey's** individual **Steps**.

2. Lists of **Associated Unfamiliar Entities** are memorized much like lists of individual **Unfamiliar Entities**, but the **Mnemonic Scenes** you develop will involve multiple **Clues**. Be sure to forge creative associations between **Unfamiliar Entities** by painting vivid, narrative **Mnemonic Scenes** in which the **Entities' Clues** interact.

Review and Development: Section 2

At this point, you've learned how best to memorize several different types of common information. It's a lot to take in at once, so let's review how to best approach each type.

Review

1. **Associating Familiar Entities**: The best way to associate two **Familiar Entities** is to construct creative, fun, memorable **Mnemonic Scenes** that involve both **Entities**. If the association pertains to a particular place or individual, construct an associative **Scene** in a context that reminds you of that place or individual. *Example of a pair of Associated Familiar Entities: George Washington — Record Player.*

2. **Memorizing Lists of Associated Familiar Entities**: To memorize lists of **Associated Familiar Entities**, use the **Journey Method** and creative association. First, forge strong creative associations between each pair of **Familiar Entities**, painting vivid narrative **Mnemonic Scenes** in which they interact. Then, mentally place each **Mnemonic Scene** within an individual **Step** of a **Journey**. *Example of a list of Associated Familiar Entities: (1) Scarecrow — Security system; (2) Cinnamon — Mouse pad; (3) Tornado — Book; (4) Laser pointer — German Shepherd.*

3. **Unfamiliar Entities**: **Unfamiliar Entities** are nouns (persons, places, things, or ideas) for which you have no frame of reference. You've never encountered these **Entities** in the past, and thus cannot immediately imagine them. *Three examples of*

Unfamiliar Entities: (1) *Bradley J. Whitehead*; (2) *Hvammstangi, Iceland*; (3) *Distal phalanx*.

4. **Associating Unfamiliar Entities:** To associate two or more **Unfamiliar Entities**, construct creative, fun, memorable **Mnemonic Scenes** that include **Mnemonic Clues** about the **Entities** (usually references to the words themselves). If the association pertains to a particular place or individual, construct the **Scene** in a context that will remind you of that place or individual. The best way to recall ordered **Associated Unfamiliar Entities** is to imagine a **Linear Scene**, in which the individual **Clues** interact through cause-and-effect relationships that facilitate **Entity** recall in a specific, scripted sequence. You can use an **Asynchronous Scene** to memorize unordered **Associated Unfamiliar Entities**. If necessary, the role of each **Entity** can be coded into the **Scene** by the use of **Meta-Information**, or information attached to each **Clue**. *Two examples of Associated Unfamiliar Entities:* (1) *Hamburgville — Laurie*; (2) *Francesca — Corpus Callosum*.

5. **Associated Entities vs. Lists:** If you need to memorize too many **Entities** to fit comfortably within a single **Scene**, the **Entities** may be better suited for memorization as a list.

6. **Memorizing Lists of Unfamiliar Entities**: To memorize lists of individual **Unfamiliar Entities**, create imaginative **Clues** that represent each **Entity**. Use the **Journey Method** (with a **Contextual Journey**, if possible), develop **Mnemonic Scenes** that involve each **Clue**, and work these **Scenes** into each of the **Journey's** individual **Steps**. *An example of a list of Unfamiliar Entities: Fruitland; Middlesex; Adamsville; Tawnton.*

7. **Memorizing Lists of Associated Unfamiliar Entities**: Lists of **Associated Unfamiliar Entities** are memorized much like lists

of individual **Unfamiliar Entities**, but the **Mnemonic Scenes** you develop will involve multiple **Clues**. Be sure to forge creative associations between **Unfamiliar Entities** by painting vivid, narrative **Mnemonic Scenes** in which the **Entities' Clues** interact. *Two examples of lists of **Associated Unfamiliar Entities**:* (1) *Shawn Masterbergen, Desmond Jones, Angie Bishop;* (2) *Franklintown — Bradford, Bridgeport — Essex, Coopersburg — Lawnton.*

Take a moment to ensure that you understand the different types of information and the correct methods used to memorize each. Come up with two examples of each type on your own.

- Associated Familiar Entities
- Associated Unfamiliar Entities
- Lists of Familiar Entities
- Lists of Unfamiliar Entities
- Lists of Associated Familiar Entities
- Lists of Associated Unfamiliar Entities

Development

Spend some time practicing each of the memorization methods learned in *Section 2*. Be sure to take your time on each; don't skip ahead, as continued practice helps ingrain the core principles into your mind, allowing them to become your natural recourse for memorization. Keep this goal in mind; you want to be able to evoke these methods promptly when presented with memorization tasks.

Day 1

Review *Section 2* in its entirety. Make sure you're comfortable with everything covered in the section. By the end of the first day, you should be able to:

- Identify different types of information (Associated Familiar Entities, Associated Unfamiliar Entities, lists of Familiar Entities, lists of Unfamiliar Entities, lists of Associated Familiar Entities, lists of Associated Unfamiliar Entities).

- Determine the appropriate method for memorizing each type of information (e.g., lists of Associated Unfamiliar Entities: "Create **Clues** representing each of the Entities, then associate the Entities' **Clues** within the context of narrative Mnemonic Scenes, then work the Scenes into the individual Steps of a Journey"). You don't need to reproduce these definitions verbatim as long as you understand the fundamental concepts.

Practice memorizing a short list of **Entities**. Below is a list of the twenty-seven highest-grossing films of all time (at the time of this writing—you will probably want to look up the latest rankings). If you've seen or heard of the films, you may consider these **Familiar Entities**; you could imagine the films' main characters acting out plot points in the individual **Journey Steps**. If you're unfamiliar with some of the films, you can treat them as **Unfamiliar Entities**, meaning you'll need to create **Clues** relating to each title. You can mix and match **Familiar** and **Unfamiliar Entities** as needed.

1. Avatar
2. Titanic
3. Star Wars: The Force Awakens

4. Jurassic World
5. The Avengers
6. Furious 7
7. Avengers: Age of Ultron
8. Harry Potter and the Deathly Hallows – Part 2
9. Star Wars: The Last Jedi
10. Frozen
11. Beauty and the Beast
12. The Fate of the Furious
13. Iron Man 3
14. Minions
15. Captain America: Civil War
16. Transformers: Dark of the Moon
17. The Lord of the Rings: The Return of the King
18. Black Panther
19. Skyfall
20. Transformers: Age of Extinction
21. The Dark Knight Rises
22. Toy Story 3
23. Pirates of the Caribbean: Dead Man's Chest
24. Rogue One: A Star Wars Story
25. Pirates of the Caribbean: On Stranger Tides
26. Despicable Me 3
27. Jurassic Park

Don't move on until you have the list comfortably memorized using the appropriate methods.

Day 2

Today, you'll work on associating **Entities**. Take the following list of **Familiar Entities** and associate them. Don't worry about memorizing them as a list. Instead, focus on their associations with one another.

For example, if someone were to say "cannon," you should be able to reply immediately with "speaker" (and vice versa).

- Cannon — Speaker
- DVD — Tire
- Church — Fire alarm
- Novel — Japan
- Cello — Scarecrow
- Egg — Suit
- Toy — Prize
- Stained glass window — Computer
- Toilet — Wheelbarrow
- Wooden log — Thesis paper
- One-way mirror — Lightning

Next, take the following list of **Unfamiliar Entities**—first and last names—and memorize them. As before, don't worry about memorizing them as a list, but rather focus on the individual associations.

So, for example, if someone were to say "Lexington," you should be able to immediately reply with "Bonnie" (and vice versa).

- Bonnie Lexington
- Chris Stein
- Charles Whitt

- Dave Donovan
- Michelle Chesterfield
- Kim Wong
- Mike Lassater
- Jeff Albany
- Joanna Fredrick
- Les White
- Nancy Blumenthal
- Ben Jalon

Day 3

Today, you'll practice memorizing more lists, beginning with a list of **Associated Familiar Entities**. Do this one on your own: develop a list of twenty vegetables and a list of twenty things you regularly carry with you (such as the contents of a purse, backpack, or wallet). If you don't carry that many things on you, you can also include the contents of your car's trunk or glove box. Write the list of vegetables next to the list of items such that each vegetable is associated with a corresponding item (example: Avocado — Hairbrush). Prepare a **Journey** and add to each **Step** a **Mnemonic Scene** that involves both the vegetable and the item. If you can't name twenty vegetables, use fruit as well.

Don't move on until you've memorized this list and can comfortably recall it in order. Next, memorize this small-but-challenging list of **Unfamiliar Entities**: the largest cities in Tunisia (ordered by population). Again, don't move on until you can recite it back in order.

1. Tunis
2. Sfax

3. Kairouan
4. Sousse
5. Ettadhamen
6. Gabès
7. Bizerte
8. Aryanah
9. Gafsa
10. El Mourouj

Next is a list of **Associated Unfamiliar Entities**. This time, you'll be memorizing a list of DC Comics' most popular Middle-Eastern superheroes and their respective powers.

1. Aminedi — Invisibility
2. Arabian Knight — Magic weapons
3. Black Raazer — Spells, sorcery
4. Dust — Turns to sand
5. Living Monolith — Absorbs energy from cosmic rays
6. Sabra — Mutant strength and agility
7. Sirocco — Alters weather
8. Veil — Secretes a gaseous cloud
9. Faiza Hussain — Controls living creatures

Days 4 - 5

For the last two days, you'll work to memorize two more lists of **Associated Unfamiliar Entities**: an alphabetical list of your state's members of congress, and a list of the United States' Bronze Medal Winners from the 1952 Olympic Games.

This is admittedly a boring homework assignment, but that's the point; you'll need to find creativity in mundane information when using these methods for practical applications. Use a **Journey** (**Contextual**, if possible) to remember order; use creative **Clues** to remember both the first and last names; and use **Mnemonic Scenes** to link the first and last names together.

Your state's members of congress are easy to locate online (HOUSE.GOV/REPRESENTATIVES). This doesn't only work for congress—if you live outside the United States, choose your local representatives (titles vary greatly by country).

The United State's Bronze Medal Winners from the 1952 Olympic Games were:

1. James Gathers
2. Ollie Matson
3. Arthur Barnard
4. James Fuchs
5. James Dillion
6. Floyd Simmons
7. Bob Clotworthy
8. Zoe Olsen-Jensen
9. Juno Irwin
10. Charles Hough, Jr.
11. Walter Staley
12. John Wofford
13. Arthur McCashin
14. John Russell
15. William Steinkraus
16. Matthew Leanderson

17. Carl Lovested
18. Albert Rossi
19. Alvin Ulbrickson
20. Richard Wahlstrom
21. Arthur Jackson
22. Jack Taylor
23. Evelyn Kawamoto
24. Joan Alderson
25. Evelyn Kawamoto
26. Jacqueline LaVine
27. Marilee Stepan
28. Josiah Henson

Feel free to spend a few extra days working on these challenging lists.

On top of these prescribed lists, begin using your new creative memory in your everyday activities. Use these skills to memorize any practical information that you find interesting.

Challenge yourself, and you'll be rewarded with great powers (a gong resounds softly in the distance). Like bodybuilders lifting weights far heavier than they'd ever need to in daily life, memorizing difficult or boring pieces of information as quickly as possible is the best way to prepare yourself so you'll be equipped to handle real-world situations requiring rapid memorization.

In the next section, *Alternative Memory Development*, you'll learn a few methods for memorizing other types of common information.

Section 3: Alternative Memory Development

In *Section 2, Intermediate Memory Development*, you learned how best to memorize and retain different types of information for long periods using a defined set of rules and methods. *Section 3* will expand upon some of these concepts.

You'll learn the **Treasure Map Method**, a way to leverage your newly turbocharged imagination to store temporary information in your physical surroundings for retrieval in the near future.

Then, we'll explore the concept of **Meta-Information** (touched upon briefly in the last section), where you'll learn to attach information to other information to increase the storage capacity of each **Journey Step**.

Finally, we'll conclude the section with a simpler subject: developing another **Mnemonic Vocabulary** (like you did for 0 through 9), this time for the letters of the alphabet (A through Z).

This section will act as a conceptual bridge between intermediate and advanced mnemonic skills. The skills covered in *Section 3* are not only intrinsically useful; they also serve to increase the capacity and effectiveness of your memory by challenging your imaginative capability.

Lesson 1: The Treasure Map Method

> *"As humans we look at things and think about what we've looked at. We treasure it in a kind of private art gallery."*
>
> —Thom Gunn, Poet

After becoming comfortable with the concepts covered in *Section 2*, you have an array of new memorization tools at your disposal and will likely begin automatically using your imaginative skills in other ways. The **Treasure Map Method** leverages this natural progression.

Like a squirrel tucking away acorns, you can store imagined short-term information or **Mnemonic Clues** *within your current real-world surroundings*. This is similar to the way you learned to store longer-term information or **Mnemonic Clues** within the **Steps** of imagined **Journeys**.

The basic process goes like this: take an **Entity** you need to remember—or, with your newfound associative powers, derive a **Clue** from the **Entity**—and mentally set the **Entity** (or **Clue**) within your real-world surroundings, where you imagine it interacting with real objects. For example, if you need to remember to call someone named Frank in a few minutes, you could imagine a hot dog next to the phone. Creating a strong imaginative **Mnemonic Scene** prompts you to "see" the hot dog when you next look at the phone, and thus remember to make the call.

You could place imagined **Entities/Clues** on a tissue box, next to a pair of headphones, in your neighbors' yards, or in the toilet bowl. They can stand in your way when attempting to board a bus. They can hang from the garage wall. Weaving imaginary **Entities** or **Mnemonic Clues** into the fabric of reality gives you the ability to embed short-term reminders all around you. Whenever your gaze passes over those places, you'll imagine the **Entities** or **Mnemonic Clues** and be reminded of the information. The name for this practice, which we'll now discuss in more depth, is the **Treasure Map Method**.

When placing the **Entities** or **Clues** into your physical environment, they must have connections to real-world objects and surfaces to create strong bonds with the setting. As your field of view changes constantly, weak **Clues** are likely to get lost in the shifting of scenery. Therefore, the **Entities** or **Clues** must interact with the actual environment in realistic (but creative) ways.

The **Treasure Map Method** is best used for short-term information (needed for less than one day). Used correctly, a **Treasure Map** provides a convenient alternative to a short **Journey**.

Reflective Treasure Mapping

A **Reflective Treasure Map** involves mentally placing imagined **Entities** or **Clues** into your current setting, then later forcing your consciousness to return to that location for retrieval.

Say you have two tasks to perform: first, you need to pick up your friend from the airport at 7:00 PM, and then you need to stop at the store to pick up a saw, some trash bags, and a bottle of bleach. You obviously have...something important to take care of.

To use the **Reflective Treasure Map** method to remember these tasks, store **Clues** in the scene you're currently observing. In this example, imagine you're leaving your home through the front door. You pause, take a deep breath, and absorb the scene before you. From this vantage point, you can see your neighbor's house across the street, some small trees, and a few parked cars. Take the items you need to remember (friend, saw, trash bags, bleach), and create fictitious scenarios for each that involve objects in your field of vision; ideally, you would imagine one in the top right part of the scene, one in the bottom right, one in the top left, and one in the bottom left. These four quadrants act as the equivalent of the **Steps** you're familiar with.

Like all the methods you've learned so far, this only works if you use imaginative, colorful, vivid, and realistic connections. To illustrate the concept, I'll present one possible **Treasure Map**; though you'll of course have to use your own imagination and construct your own **Scenes**, this should give you a sense of how a successful **Reflective Treasure Map** can be built:

In the top right area of my view from the front stoop, my friend who needs a ride from the airport is hanging from a tree by one hand, in a tutu, yelling for help in a comically high-pitched voice. The tutu and high-pitched voice are completely unrelated to the task at hand, but they create a memorable, humorous **Scene**; humor always helps to reinforce a **Mnemonic Scene**, and you probably wouldn't confuse these additions with important information, especially when storing the **Scene** for only a short period. From the ground, Australian Aborigines assault him with boomerangs (well, who else would have boomerangs?), hoping to make him fall. A boomerang is my **Single-Digit Mnemonic Clue** for the number 7, reminding me that his flight lands at 7:00 PM.

In the bottom right area of the scene, there sits a (real-world) mailbox. In my imagination, however, it is covered with a trash bag. A troll rides a lazy old bloodhound up to the mailbox and peeks under the trash bag. He begins to giggle as if he saw something funny, and—with a crack of a tiny whip—commands his canine companion to continue on. It's quite a scene to behold. I'll now remember the trash bags.

Next, I have to work the saw and the bleach into the scene. As the troll rides the dog away from the mailbox, they pass a real-world car, which is parked in the bottom left of my field of vision. In my mind, the troll brings the dog to a halt, pulls out a large saw, and begins to saw at the rear tire of the car. I stare in disbelief as he saws and saws until the tire finally pops and hisses. As it deflates, I imagine the rear of the car sinking and the bloodhound shifting uncomfortably in reaction to the loud, unfamiliar noise. From this, I'll remember the saw.

In the top left area of my field of vision, a bottle of bleach sits upon the roof of my neighbor's house. I imagine the bottle rolling off the ledge and landing in front of the troll. The dog sniffs the bottle cautiously, and then the troll pours the bleach (the final item I must remember) into the car's gas tank before riding away. The car turns a stark white color, as though bleached from within.

Later, I'll say, "Wait, what time do I have to pick up my friend? What supplies do we need to pick up to 'take care of that thing'?"

Thinking back to the moment I was leaving the house (where I constructed the **Treasure Map**), I can mentally collect the items I planted within the setting. The **Clues** are all there, woven into the fabric of reality, and I used vivid, memorable devices to make sure I remembered everything. Some of the **Clues** are reinforced with helpful additions: even if I forget that the troll poured bleach into the gas tank, I'll imagine the car turning white and wonder why; I'll then remember the action that caused this.

This is the core concept behind the **Treasure Map Method**: you leave **Mnemonic Clues** in a real world setting and retrieve them later. Though you can use something like a cell phone to-do list, you'll find with practice that it's so easy to use a **Treasure Map**, you'll prefer it to constant note-taking. As you become more confident in your mnemonic skills, you may discover it can be fun and freeing to use your memory in this way and reduce your reliance on organizational tools.

Look up now at the scene before you; it doesn't matter if you're in a park, in your living room, on a bus, in an office, or in bed. Keep your head still and use your eyes to look up and to the left, up and to the right, down and to the left, and down and to the right. You should find multiple surfaces and objects; every one of these has the potential to hold an imagined object or **Clue**.

Practice by using a **Reflective Treasure Map** to memorize the following unordered list of items. Use your current surroundings and attempt to recite the list from memory. You should also try to recall it again in a few hours to see how well you retained it.

- A Milwaukee Brewers baseball cap
- A VHS copy of *Star Wars*
- A rotary telephone
- An electrical outlet (still in its packaging)

Once you've comfortably memorized and recalled those items using a **Reflective Treasure Map**, move to a new location and practice one more time with the following items:

- A purse
- A thick binder holding hundreds of sheets of paper
- A framed antique Roy Orbison concert poster
- A jar of pickled Chili peppers

Again, attempt to recall these items a few hours later.

Projected Treasure Mapping

There's another way to use the **Treasure Map Method**; however, while potentially more powerful, it requires a very well-trained imagination. Whereas **Reflective Treasure Maps** involve the placement of **Clues** in a *current setting*, **Projected Treasure Maps** involve the placement of **Clues** in a *future setting*.

The **Projected Treasure Map Method** requires you to forecast settings and places you'll encounter in the near future, and to fill these places with **Entities** or **Clues** about information you need to remember. Upon physically arriving at the location where you've mentally placed the **Entities** or **Clues**, the setting should trigger recall.

This is especially useful when you come up with an idea or need to remember a task, but are unable to record a physical reminder. For instance, imagine you're in bed and under the covers on a cold night when you suddenly remember you need to make a vet appointment. You're comfortable enough that you don't want to get up to find a pen and paper, and your smart phone is plugged into the wall across the room (and if you own a voice-controlled smart assistant you can speak with, imagine that you're instead in a foreign hotel room and away from such luxuries). You could create a **Clue** (perhaps the family cat wearing a stethoscope) and imagine it in a physical location you'll encounter in the morning (such as the bathroom sink).

Let's look at another example of a **Projected Treasure Map**. Imagine you're exercising at the gym when your see a potted plant and realize you desperately need to water the plants at your house. You're wearing only a t-shirt and shorts without pockets; there's nowhere to write down a reminder, and you don't have your phone on you.

To make sure you'll remember this when you need to, you can use a **Projected Treasure Map**. Shut your eyes, breathe deeply, and picture what you see when you enter your home. Maybe you usually hang your jacket in the hall closet, so that's what you'll likely see first; or perhaps you have a specific spot for your keys. Regardless of the setting, construct a vivid **Mnemonic Scene** that will remind you to water the plants.

This **Scene** could feature a few plants, huddled together. When you arrive, they clamor for water, shaking empty canteens. To add some memory-boosting humor, imagine them producing incoherent humanoid noises like "Animal" from *The Muppet Show*. How would you actually react? Would you be surprised, afraid, or confused?

Now, when you get home, you'll be greeted with this reminder. Even if the image doesn't jump right out at you, a vague sense of déjà vu should accompany your arrival, causing you to pause and eventually retrieve the **Scene**.

You may worry that merely arriving at your destination won't do enough to trigger the reminder. As your creativity develops, so too will your ability to interweave imagination and reality; with time, these fictitious projections will become nearly as strong as memories of actual events. You'll become the architect of an imaginary realm where you can splice fiction with the real world for your own purposes, conjuring and erasing images at will.

Memorize the following unordered group of objects using a **Projected Treasure Map**. Use a place you'll likely encounter in the next hour or so. Recall should be triggered immediately upon reaching your projected setting. Keep in mind that this is a foreign skill, and you might not get it at first—you may well arrive at the projected location and completely forget the **Treasure Map**. If that happens, try to determine why the **Scene** failed, and try again (using different locations) until you succeed.

- A top hat
- A knit sweater with a Koala embroidered on it
- A gallon of distilled water
- A light bulb

Store each item in a specific quadrant of the setting, as with **Reflective Treasure Maps** (top right, bottom right, top left, bottom left). Build **Mnemonic Scenes** that incorporate multiple senses.

Once you successfully retrieve this **Projected Treasure Map**, create another arbitrary four-item unordered list on your own. Again, use a **Projected Treasure Map** to memorize it. Keep practicing. Only move on once you're able to create **Projected Treasure Maps** that consistently trigger recall immediately upon arriving at the projected location.

The **Treasure Map Method** is a practical skill that—like some others you have learned—becomes second nature after a while. Your rewired brain will begin to regard it as the default way to remember a small series of short-term tasks or items.

You'll occasionally come across situations that require you to memorize short-term information that's too large to fit into a **Treasure Map**. At this point, you have enough experience with memorization tools that you've likely begun to develop and cultivate your own unique style. It's entirely up to you how to handle such situations, but two logical options are:

- Jam more information into the **Treasure Map** by adding more "quadrants" (such as "top center").
- Use a **Treasure Map** to remind you of **Journeys** that contain your information.

Either way, find a solution that feels intuitive to you and stick with it. You won't always be able to predict where you'll end up, especially when traveling or exploring new places; this is why you must develop your ability to create both **Projected** and **Reflective Treasure Maps**.

Quick Review

1. The **Treasure Map Method** involves placing imaginary **Mnemonic Clues** within the context of real-world settings. There are two methods: **Reflective Treasure Mapping** and **Projected Treasure Mapping**.

2. To use a **Reflective Treasure Map**, work vivid imagined information (**Mnemonic Clues**) into real-world settings you're currently observing in real time. Later, transport your awareness back to the scene where you recorded the information, then extract the imaginary **Clues** and decipher their meanings.

3. To use a **Projected Treasure Map**, work imagined information (**Mnemonic Clues**) into real-world settings you're reasonably certain you'll encounter in the near future. Vividly imagining this real/imaginary hybrid scene prompts you to recall the meaning of the **Clues** upon arriving at the setting.

Lesson 2: Meta-Information

> "IT IS A VERY SAD THING THAT NOWADAYS THERE IS SO LITTLE USELESS INFORMATION."
>
> —OSCAR WILDE, AUTHOR

As time passes and new technologies develop, it becomes faster and cheaper to deliver content to the masses. In the past, the expense and limited availability of printing ensured some level of natural content filtration, whereas the Internet makes available an ever-expanding amount of superficial information; as a result, expectations surrounding the absorption and digestion of information have likewise increased. Wilde's quip applies just as much in our time as it did during his short life. With massive amounts of information available at all times, we are left to our own devices to determine what is and isn't worth knowing.

This book can't help you make such decisions; it can, however, help you develop the tools necessary to more effectively retain the material that makes the cut. **Meta-Information** is one such tool.

When committing a recipe to memory, you must of course memorize the ingredients as a list of **Familiar Entities**. But that's not all: you also need to remember the quantities for each ingredient. One way to accomplish this is to attach **Meta-Information** (information *about* information) to each memorized ingredient.

For this example, imagine you're memorizing a recipe for cake, which reminds you of a park where you once ate some cake on a picnic (a **Contextual Journey**). Suppose the first **Step** is a bench in that park. There, you'll store the **Clue** for the first ingredient (sugar). You may be inclined to envision a bag of sugar (a **Familiar Entity**) sitting on the park bench. Though somewhat uncreative, this could be sufficient if you were only memorizing the ingredients (a list of **Familiar Entities**) and not the amounts needed of each. The recipe calls for three cups of sugar, so you need to add a **Clue** to the "sugar" **Clue** that indicates the amount. This kind of sub-**Clue** is an example of **Meta-Information**.

My personal means of attaching the **Meta-Information** would be to picture an enormously obese man with a tiny tree growing from his head (my **Single-Digit Mnemonic Clue** for the number 3). The man is shirtless and wearing a bra made of teacups (if I forget the unit of measurement, I'll picture the bizarre bra and remember "cups"). The heavyset gentleman sits on the bench and stares sadly into the distance while eating sugar directly out of the bag with his bare hands. Clumps of saliva-tainted sugar fall down into his dense, matted chest hair. Slack-jawed children stare at him as they walk by, but he ignores them and continues to eat sugar by the fistful. To add some quirky, memorable details, he's wearing swim goggles and mumbling to himself in a creepy baritone, like the character Buffalo Bill from the film, *The Silence of the Lambs*.

I bet you didn't expect you'd be imagining things like *that* when you started reading this book. Yes, it's creepy and off-putting. But you have to admit, it's memorable.

From here, you move on to the next **Step** (remembering to create a **Transition**), where you'll store a **Clue** about both the next ingredient (water) and its amount (6 fluid ounces). What would your personal **Mnemonic Scene** involve? How would you transition here from the first **Step** (in my case, the sad sugar man)?

For me, this could mean an office-style commercial water cooler (a **Clue** for "water") with an over-sized bandage across the front ("ouch" = "ounce") and pronounced, human-like abdominal muscles ("six pack" = 6).

Try this brief **Meta-Information** exercise. Imagine you need to memorize information about the starting lineup of the 1991 Oakland Athletics (a very talented ball club during that particular period). If you happen to be from Oakland and are a big enough baseball fan to remember this lineup by heart, look up similar information about a team you don't know as well and perform the same exercise. Practice integrating **Meta-Information** into your **Journeys** by including each player's respective position and total number of home runs during the season:

Position	Player	# of Home Runs
Catcher	Terry Steinbach	6
1st Base	Mark McGwire	22
2nd Base	Mike Gallego	12
3rd Base	Ernest Riles	5
Shortstop	Mike Bordick	0

Left Field	Rickey Henderson	18
Center Field	Dave Henderson	25
Right Field	José Canseco	44

Select a **Contextual Journey** that reminds you of baseball. Perhaps a little league field? The house of a friend who's a huge baseball fan? Your local Major League team's stadium? For each **Step** of the **Journey**, create a **Clue** for each player's first and last names using the skills learned in *Memorizing Lists of (Single or Associated) "Unfamiliar Entities."* Then, attach one **Meta-Clue** for his position, and another **Meta-Clue** for his home run count (using **Single-Digit Mnemonic Clues**). Each **Step** of the **Journey** requires storing two pieces of **Meta-Information** on top of the **Core Information** (the player's full name).

This is not easy, but with practice, this type of challenge will become drastically easier.

If you're having trouble getting this right, let's go through one together. First, break the name "Terry Steinbach" into two **Clues**, and then decide how to work them into a **Mnemonic Scene**. For me, the name "Terry" immediately brings to mind "terrycloth." "Steinbach" makes me think of a "stein" (as in a large, German-style beer glass) and "back" (the part of the body). Combining all of these, I picture a man bending over at the waist, wearing a thick terrycloth robe. He has a large stein of beer balanced perilously on his upper back ("stein back"). I smell the beer and see his body quivering slightly as he tries to balance the stein (vivid, imaginative details). The stein begins to fall off, and the man spins around with superhuman speed to snatch it out of thin air (a **Clue** about him being a "catcher"). He sips the beer, gags a few times, and dramatically vomits a small, sleepy newborn duck (my **Single-Digit Mnemonic Clue** for the number six).

When recalling the **Scene** and trying to decipher my own **Clues**, I'd say to myself, "why a robe? Robe. Robe. Is it the color of the robe? What's the robe made of? Cotton? Silk? Terrycloth? ...Terry! With a big glass mug on his back. A mug. A stein? Terry...Stein...Back. Terry Steinbach. Catching the falling stein... catcher! Then he vomits a baby duck. Why? The duck is my **Single-Digit Mnemonic Clue** for the number six, so Steinbach must have hit six home runs. Terry Steinbach, catcher, six home runs."

Continue this exercise on your own. The second player is Mark McGwire. What combination of **Clues** would you use to remember his name, position, and number of home runs? Develop a vivid **Mnemonic Scene** involving all the necessary information.

Take as much time as you need to memorize this list. Don't move on until you're confident you can recite it. It may be difficult (and you may not care about baseball history), but this exercise will reinforce a free-flowing imaginative skill set you'll use more and more as you continue exploring **Memory Development**. The storage of **Meta-Information** is less standardized than many other aspects of **Memory Development** and relies on the adoption of an amorphous, highly personal sense of creativity.

Let's look at another (vastly more difficult) example of **Meta-Information** before moving on. What follows is a list of the ten tallest buildings in the world (at the time of this writing), including their respective location, height, and year construction was completed.

Name	City	Height (ft.)	Year Completed
Burj Khalifa	Dubai	2,717	2010
Taipei 101	Taipei	1,667	2004
Shanghai World Financial Center	Shanghai	1,614	2008
International Commerce Centre	Kowloon	1,588	2010
Petronas Tower 1	Kuala Lumpur	1,483	1998
Petronas Tower 2	Kuala Lumpur	1,483	1998
Nanjing Greenland Financial Center	Nanjing	1,476	2010
Willis Tower	Chicago	1,451	1974
Kingkey Finance Tower	Shenzhen	1,440	2011
Guangzhou West Tower	Guangzhou	1,435	2010

This example contains an abundance of **Meta-Information**; for each **Step** in the **Journey** (hopefully you've chosen a **Contextual Journey** related to skyscrapers), you must store **Clues** about the building name (the **Core Information**), as well as three pieces of complex **Meta-Information**: the city, the height, and the year.

Let your imagination run wild and create detailed **Mnemonic Scenes** containing all the necessary elements. Don't let this exercise intimidate you.

> *Tip*: *While constructing **Mnemonic Scenes**, ensure the words (the building names vs. the cities) and the numbers (the heights vs. the years) can be contextually differentiated. Since many of the words may be unfamiliar, you could easily confuse the two. ("Was 'Petronas' the name of the city or the building?")*

Keep trying until you've managed to memorize the list perfectly. This may take some time and patience, as this is the most complex challenge you've faced so far.

Meta-Information is an important part of many **Memory Development** techniques you'll soon learn, as you can apply it to almost any type of information. Take as long as you need to become confident with this skill. There will be more opportunities to practice at the end of this section.

Quick Review

1. Attaching **Meta-Information** (additional information) to **Mnemonic Clues** is a fantastic way to organize complex, multi-faceted material using the **Journey** or **Treasure Map Methods**. By constructing creative and elaborate **Mnemonic Scenes**, you can fill an individual **Step** with both **Core Information** and **Meta-Information**.

Lesson 3: Memorizing Strings of Letters

> *"'C' IS FOR 'COOKIE'—THAT'S GOOD ENOUGH FOR ME."*
> —Cookie Monster

"GZDGAB"

How would you memorize this? Some people would pronounce it phonetically, resulting in something that sounds like "Goes-duh-gab," but this is an error-prone approach. Others would try "brute-force" memorization: "G...Z...D...G...A...B. Okay... G...Z...D...G...A...B. Okay...G...Z..."; this is difficult, and doesn't scale well when it comes to longer strings of letters.

Imagine you've witnessed a car accident, and the driver is attempting to flee the scene. It's hard enough to memorize license plate numbers using brute force under normal circumstances, and in your state of surprise, it would be even tougher than usual. As the car quickly fades into the distance, you'd most likely be left with only a vague idea of the perpetrator's plate number.

It's difficult to find guidance on how to memorize this type of information.

You often need to memorize lengthy numbers, and you've already learned to do so quite effectively. Throughout your day, you encounter phone numbers, retail product UPC or model numbers, bank account numbers, addresses, office/room numbers, class numbers, receipt numbers, credit card numbers, zip codes, dates, and the like.

Similarly, it's common to have to memorize strings of letters, such as: abbreviations (like state abbreviations or airport codes), website URL's, TV or radio station call signs and stock exchange symbols. Companies (such as IBM, GE, or MGM) are often better known by their shorthand names than their full-length monikers. Memorizing strings of letters is also useful for remembering the spelling of unconventional or foreign names, places, foods, and objects.

Arguably more common than strings of letters or numbers, many pieces of information are "alphanumeric" (a mix of letters and numbers). Examples include license plates, automatically generated passwords, car VIN numbers, product models, account ID's, and train or bus lines.

In case you haven't guessed, you're going to create a **Mnemonic Vocabulary** consisting of pre-defined **Letter Clues** for each individual letter of the alphabet, just like when you created a **Mnemonic Vocabulary** of **Single-Digit Mnemonic Clues** for the numbers zero through nine. You'll incorporate these **Clues** into **Journeys**.

Choosing Your Letter Clues

So, how do you choose **Mnemonic Clues** to represent letters?

Simplicity and Ease of Recall

Use **Clues** that come naturally to you, as they're quickly accessed and retrieved. Channel your inner three-year-old: "A" is for "apple," "B" is for "banana," "C" is for "cat," "D" is for "dog," etc. Be careful: don't use a **Letter Clue** you've used as a **Single-Digit Mnemonic Clue**. For instance, don't use "zebra" for "Z" if that's already your **Clue** for the number two.

Go back in your mind to the hit-and-run accident you just imagined witnessing. You've glimpsed the driver's license plate; if your instincts tell you to remember "ADF" as "apple, dog, fire hydrant," accept it and work quickly to construct a **Mnemonic Scene** around these **Clues**, instead of wasting precious moments trying to recall overly sophisticated or clever pre-defined **Clues**.

Anthropomorphism

While your initial instinct can work, living or anthropomorphic beings make excellent **Clues**, since they can move around and are more easily imagined performing actions and interacting with their environment. You can find an animal to represent almost every letter (anteater, bear, cat, dog, elephant, ferret, giraffe, hamster, iguana, jackal, kangaroo, lion, monkey, narwhal, etc.). Of course, there are a few letters that present a challenge; for example, most people don't know of any animal beginning with the letter "X" (though a "xiphosuran" is a horseshoe crab and a "xiphias" is a swordfish). In such cases, it's usually smarter to make exceptions to the animal rule.

When it comes to exceptions, try to stick to the "living or anthropomorphized creature" rule. For example, "U" could be "umpire,"

"V" could be "vampire," "X" could be "xenomorph" (from the *Alien* film franchise), and "Y" could be a "yogi" (a practitioner of yoga). Sticking to living things will enable you to employ letter memorization shortcuts later on (something you'll learn about in *Memorizing Strings of Letters: Advanced Practices*).

Choose your **Letter Clues** now and write them down.

Letter	Letter Clue
A	
B	
C	
D	
E	
F	
G	
H	
I	
J	
K	
L	

M	
N	
O	
P	
Q	
R	
S	
T	
U	
V	
W	
X	
Y	
Z	

One way to fill this chart with instinctual **Clues** is by closing your eyes, putting your finger on a random letter, and immediately naming the first animal that comes to mind. Harnessing your subconscious in this way ensures you're choosing immediately accessible **Clues**.

Using Your Letter Clue Mnemonic Vocabulary

As with all **Memory Development** methods, it's vitally important to create vivid images. A cat (should a cat represent the letter "C" for you) should never be "just" a cat in your **Mnemonic Scenes**; rather, it should be something like an opera-singing cat in a suit or a juggling cat in a sombrero. Use absurdity, sex, humor, etc. String these **Letter Clues** together using logical connections and **Transitions**. For example, the "opera cat" representing "C" in this example could hit a high note that breaks a glass of water in the hand of a breakdancing ferret ("F") at the next **Step**.

Imagine you signed up for a job training session. When you arrive at the massive training center, you'll have to provide the receptionist with the class code, which is BKE-10069C.

You'd naturally be tempted to write the code on a small piece of paper or record it in your cell phone; however, relying on your mind will prove to be convenient once you're used to this method and—by flexing your creative muscles—will improve your ability to memorize many different types of information. Constantly recording information on an external medium is something that you'll come to regard as tedious.

To memorize the class code, first form a nine-**Step Journey** (you could use the training center itself if you're familiar with it). The first **Step** needs to contain a **Clue** for the letter "B." What's your **Letter Clue**? Bear? Bobcat? Beetle? Beaver, bat, bunny, boobie, or baboon? If you've chosen to ignore the advice to use animals or living things as your **Letter Clues**, is it basketball, bomb, bicycle, bassinet, bayonet, babaganoush, booger, bag, balloon, bassoon, belly, bass, bagel, bean, beef, beer, bikini, blood, brain, bubble, bucket, bugle, or blast?

Regardless, place your "B" **Clue** at the first **Step** of the **Journey**, then move on to the second and third **Steps** (using **Transitions**, of course), which should contain **Letter Clues** for the letters "K" and "E," respectively. After the "E," you have to memorize some numbers, and should use your **Single-Digit Mnemonic Clues** for the numbers zero through nine.

Let's say that your **Letter Clue** for "B" is "bunny" (get creative: a bunny dressed as a waiter). He pulls from his ear an over-sized ball of wax and rolls it from the first **Step** to the second like a bowling ball, where it knocks over a cheerleading pyramid of cigar-smoking koalas (assuming "koala" is your **Clue** for "K"). After the koalas tumble into a pile in complete disarray, one of them rolls to the foot of a chair. In the chair (the third **Step**) sits a coiled electric eel (if "electric eel" is your **Clue** for "E").

The eel is attached to jumper cables, and the jumper cables snake from the chair to the fourth **Step**, where a cartoonish baseball bat with a humanoid face mans a strange control panel, as though he's harvesting electric current from the eel (if "baseball bat" is your **Single-Digit Mnemonic Clue** for the number 1). The baseball bat turns away from the control panel toward the fifth **Step**, following with his eyes a cluster of wires leading to what looks like a guillotine. The guillotine's blade is about to fall on a soccer ball (if "soccer ball" is your **Single-Digit Mnemonic Clue** for the number 0).

The guillotine cuts the ball in two with such force that one half slides aggressively toward the sixth **Step**. Sitting in the center of the half-ball is what seems to be a big meatball. Upon closer inspection, it's a smallish, brown soccer ball (again, if "soccer ball" is your **Single-Digit Mnemonic Clue** for the number 0). An old farmer picks the ball up and walks it to the seventh **Step**, where it cracks open like an egg to reveal a tiny demon (if "demon" is your **Single-Digit Mnemonic Clue** for the number 6). The demon (who has a tiny pink Mohawk and poodle-like tail) runs angrily to the eighth **Step**, snorting and screaming the whole way. At the eighth **Step**, it finds and picks up a lollipop (if "lollipop" is your **Single-Digit Mnemonic Clue** for the number 9), unwraps it clumsily, and begins to eat it. Finally, switching back to letters from numbers, the tiny demon tosses the half-eaten lollipop to the ninth and final **Step** in your **Journey**, where it sticks to the black fur of a surprised cat (if "cat" is your **Letter Clue** for "C").

You could significantly strengthen the mnemonic impact of your **Journey** by adding multi-sensory details—smells, tactile stimuli, etc.—but you should know that by now, so I left such details out of the description for the sake of brevity.

This example should have given you an idea of how to memorize alphanumeric strings, but you should of course create your own narratives.

Before moving on, memorize the following:

1. SDJ
2. COIS
3. PIOSDB
4. CVD9EJ2
5. B8JG7823T
6. 309848TUSD
7. 0938UET23DG00

Quick Review

1. To memorize strings of letters (or the letter portions of alphanumeric strings) create a **Mnemonic Vocabulary** of **Letter Clues**. Associate each individual letter of the alphabet with a specific **Mnemonic Clue** (an easily-imagined noun whose name begins with that letter). Integrate these **Clues** into **Journeys** or **Treasure Maps** as you would any other type of **Clue**.

2. It's important to ensure your **Letter Clues** don't conflict in any way with the **Single-Digit Mnemonic Clues** you selected for the numbers zero through nine.

3. Like all other types of mnemonics, the more vivid and creative the **Scene**, the easier it will be to retain and recall. Whenever possible, use the **Letter Clue** that comes to you most readily. People tend to have success choosing living or anthropomorphized **Entities** such as animals (anteater, bear, cat, dog...) as their **Letter Clues**.

Review and Development: Section 3

Alas, good friend, we've come to the end of *Section 3*. We discussed **The Treasure Map** method, **Meta-Information**, and how to memorize strings of letters or alphanumerics. Be sure to savor the below review and development, because play time is over, soldier; the next section is entitled *Advanced Memory Development*, and in it, we'll tackle some effective-yet-challenging ways to drastically build upon the skills you've learned so far.

Review

1. **The Treasure Map Method**: The Treasure Map Method involves placing imaginary Mnemonic Clues within the context of real-world settings. There are two methods: **Reflective Treasure Mapping** and **Projected Treasure Mapping**.

2. **Reflective Treasure Maps**: To use a **Reflective Treasure Map**, work vivid imagined information (**Mnemonic Clues**) into real-world settings that you're currently observing in real time. Later, transport your awareness back to the scene where you recorded the information, and then extract the imaginary **Clues** and decipher their meanings.

3. **Projected Treasure Maps**: To use a **Projected Treasure Map**, work imagined information (**Mnemonic Clues**) into real-world settings you're reasonably certain you'll encounter in the near future. Vividly imagining this real/imaginary hybrid scene prompts you to recall the meaning of the **Clues** upon arriving at the setting.

4. **Meta-Information**: Attaching **Meta-Information** (additional information) to **Mnemonic Clues** is a fantastic way to organize complex, multi-faceted material using the **Journey** or **Treasure Map Methods**. By constructing creative and elaborate **Mnemonic Scenes**, you can fill an individual **Step** with both **Core Information** and **Meta-Information**.

5. **Memorizing Strings of Letters**: To memorize strings of letters (or the letter portions of alphanumeric strings) create a **Mnemonic Vocabulary** of **Letter Clues**. Associate each individual letter of the alphabet with a specific **Mnemonic Clue** (an easily-imagined noun whose name begins with that letter). Integrate these **Clues** into **Journeys** or **Treasure Maps** as you would any other type of **Clue**. It's important to ensure your **Letter Clues** don't conflict in any way with the **Single-Digit Mnemonic Clues** you selected for the numbers zero through nine. Whenever possible, use the **Letter Clue** that comes to you most readily. People tend to have success choosing living or anthropomorphized **Entities** such as animals (anteater, bear, cat, dog...) as their **Letter Clues**.

Development

You're going to spend some time practicing each of the **Memory Development** methods you learned in *Section 3*. Be sure to spend the allotted time on each exercise; don't skip ahead, as only through the appropriate amounts of practice will you ingrain these principles into the recesses of your mind and allow them to become the natural means by which you memorize the respective types of information.

Day 1

Skim the entire section and make sure you're comfortable with everything discussed. You should be able to explain the above review points to someone with no **Memory Development** experience. Spend a few minutes explaining them aloud, either to yourself or to a patient acquaintance. Spend extra time reviewing any lessons that seem particularly challenging to you.

Day 2

Spend *Day 2* working with the **Treasure Map** method and begin using it as often as possible in your daily life. If you spend some time honing this skill very deliberately, it should work its way into your natural repertoire after some time. Take a "reminder holiday," and refuse to write small lists (five or fewer items) down. Anything small you need to remember or accomplish should be remembered with no to-do-lists, notes, cell phone reminders, or calendar events; instead, use only the **Treasure Map Method**. Don't become frustrated if it doesn't come naturally at first; these adjustments take time, as we've all come to rely heavily on external tools.

In addition, begin to imagine fictitious objects sitting in front of you whenever you have free time. Try it while you're at work, on the bus, walking through a mall, etc. Truly concentrate on the act of placing an imagined object within the setting so vividly that when you think back to the location, you imagine the object there as though it actually existed. This purposeful, mindful projection will help to reinforce the imaginative skills necessary to quickly construct stable **Treasure Maps**. While performing this exercise, focus on making the **Scenes** seem as real as possible. Imagine realistic reflections, shadows, and textures. Start simply, by imagining an old book or shiny green apple, and work your way up to more detailed objects.

You're also going to perform two specific exercises on *Day 2*. First, using a **Projected Treasure Map**, store the following unordered list of objects within a setting you'll find yourself in later today:

- A bag of coffee
- A laptop computer with a broken monitor
- A dozen paper cups with male names written on them in script
- A large, grandiose throne
- A wicker basket full of snakes

Take care to integrate these items into the projected future setting using as much detail as you can muster. Utilize multiple senses. Later, after you actually arrive at this location, note whether or not the **Treasure Map** presented itself naturally. If not, take some time to reflect upon what you could have done differently.

Next, tackle a **Reflective Treasure Map**. This might be a bit more difficult. Store the below unordered list of objects in your current field of vision, wherever you happen to be right now. You're going to retrieve this information later. Before you begin, send yourself a note, create a calendar event, have someone remind you, or otherwise ensure that later tonight you'll be prompted to retrieve information from this **Treasure Map**. When the time comes, project your consciousness back to this place and retrieve the **Clues** as needed. Here's the list:

- A hockey stick (very beaten and worn, with a good deal of dirty tape on it)
- Three pairs of sneakers

- A blue bucket full of chalkboard erasers
- A photograph of John F. Kennedy in a wooden frame (with small seashells glued to it)
- A celebrity gossip magazine in what seems to be an unfamiliar Eastern European language

Days 3 - 5

Though daunting to begin with, **Meta-Information** will become more natural as you learn to harness your imagination in new and exciting ways. You're going to challenge the boundaries of your comfort zone and see how much **Meta-Information** you can store in a single **Step** without losing track of any of it.

You're constantly presented with opportunities to practice using **Meta-Information**. With time, you'll likely discover that very few pieces of information worth memorizing are single-dimensional. As on *Day 2*, you should put aside your tools and third-party reminders and use only your memory and imagination. Do you have a desk job? If so, memorize appointments and meetings (the topics, key participants, and the location/room numbers). Are you a contractor or tradesperson? Memorize the addresses of your jobs, the work that needs to be performed, the name of the homeowner or GC, etc. Are you in customer service? Memorize ticket numbers related to hot issues, the nature of the issues, and the names of the individuals to whom they pertain. Whether you're a physical therapist, police officer or glassblower, you should be able to identify and memorize multi-faceted pieces of information that will actually be useful.

You're going to memorize a very difficult list that includes a wealth of **Meta Information**: every Major League Baseball World Series from 1970 to 2012, including the year, the name of the winning team and coach, the number of games won by each team, and the name of the losing team. Each table row should be stored in a single **Journey Step**.

You may notice that this isn't the first baseball example we've used. Baseball is an intricate game, rich with statistics, trivia and a long, storied history. It's perfect for practicing memorization.

This is definitely the most daunting **Memory Development** challenge you've faced yet. Three days have been put aside for this task, but please free to work on it for a few extra days if you need to. Most people will take longer at this point. Take planned breaks, but don't give up, as this type of difficult, tedious homework will train you to forge imaginative **Mnemonic Scenes** from less-than-ideal information.

Year	Winning Team	Coach	Games Won in Series	Losing Team
1970	Baltimore Orioles	Earl Weaver	4 to 1	The Cincinnati Reds
1971	Pittsburgh Pirates	Danny Murtaugh	4 to 3	The Baltimore Orioles
1972	Oakland Athletics	Dick Williams	4 to 3	The Cincinnati Reds
1973	Oakland Athletics	Dick Williams	4 to 3	The New York Mets

1974	Oakland Athletics	Alvin Dark	4 to 1	The Los Angeles Dodgers
1975	Cincinnati Reds	Sparky Anderson	4 to 3	The Boston Red Sox
1976	Cincinnati Reds	Sparky Anderson	4 to 0	The New York Yankees
1977	New York Yankees	Billy Martin	4 to 2	The Los Angeles Dodgers
1978	New York Yankees	Bob Lemon	4 to 2	The Los Angeles Dodgers
1979	Pittsburgh Pirates	Chuck Tanner	4 to 3	The Baltimore Orioles
1980	Philadelphia Phillies	Dallas Green	4 to 2	The Kansas City Royals
1981	Los Angeles Dodgers	Tom Lasorda	4 to 2	The New York Yankees
1982	St. Louis Cardinals	Whitey Herzog	4 to 3	The Milwaukee Brewers
1983	Baltimore Orioles	Joe Altobelli	4 to 1	The Philadelphia Phillies

1984	Detroit Tigers	Sparky Anderson	4 to 1	The San Diego Padres
1985	Kansas City Royals	Dick Howser	4 to 3	The St. Louis Cardinals
1986	New York Mets	Davey Johnson	4 to 3	The Boston Red Sox
1987	Minnesota Twins	Tom Kelly	4 to 3	The St. Louis Cardinals
1988	Los Angeles Dodgers	Tom Lasorda	4 to 1	The Oakland Athletics
1989	Oakland Athletics	Tony La Russa	4 to 0	The San Francisco Giants
1990	Cincinnati Reds	Lou Piniella	4 to 0	The Oakland Athletics
1991	Minnesota Twins	Tom Kelly	4 to 3	The Atlanta Braves
1992	Toronto Blue Jays	Cito Gaston	4 to 2	The Atlanta Braves
1993	Toronto Blue Jays	Cito Gaston	4 to 2	The Philadelphia Phillies
1994	(No Series)			

1995	Atlanta Braves	Bobby Cox	4 to 2	The Cleveland Indians
1996	New York Yankees	Joe Torre	4 to 2	The Atlanta Braves
1997	Florida Marlins	Jim Leyland	4 to 3	The Cleveland Indians
1998	New York Yankees	Joe Torre	4 to 0	The San Diego Padres
1999	New York Yankees	Joe Torre	4 to 0	The Atlanta Braves
2000	New York Yankees	Joe Torre	4 to 1	The New York Mets
2001	Arizona Diamondbacks	Bob Brenly	4 to 3	The New York Yankees
2002	Anaheim Angels	Mike Scioscia	4 to 3	The San Francisco Giants
2003	Florida Marlins	Jack McKeon	4 to 2	The New York Yankees
2004	Boston Red Sox	Terry Francona	4 to 0	The St. Louis Cardinals
2005	Chicago White Sox	Ozzie Guillen	4 to 0	The Houston Astros

2006	St. Louis Cardinals	Tony La Russa	4 to 1	The Detroit Tigers
2007	Boston Red Sox	Terry Francona	4 to 0	The Colorado Rockies
2008	Philadelphia Phillies	Charlie Manuel	4 to 1	The Tampa Bay Rays
2009	New York Yankees	Joe Girardi	4 to 2	The Philadelphia Phillies
2010	San Francisco Giants	Bruce Bochy	4 to 1	The Texas Rangers
2011	St. Louis Cardinals	Tony La Russa	4 to 3	The Texas Rangers
2012	San Francisco Giants	Bruce Bochy	4 to 0	Detroit Tigers
2013	Boston Red Socks	John Farrell	4 to 2	St. Louis Cardinals
2014	San Francisco Giants	Bruce Bochy	4 to 3	Kansas City Royals
2015	Kansas City Royals	Ned Yost	4 to 1	New York Mets
2016	Chicago Cubs	Joe Maddon	4 to 3	Cleveland Indians

2017	Houston Astros	A.J. Hinch	4 to 3	Lost Angeles Dodgers

Don't move on until you've memorized the list.

Days 6 - 7

By now, you should have mapped out your **Mnemonic Vocabulary** for the letters A through Z. Recite these **Letter Clues** in order as quickly as possible on at least ten separate occasions today, clocking yourself each time. You should become marginally faster with each attempt. Don't move on until you can recite your entire **Letter Clue Vocabulary** in under thirty seconds: "anteater, bear, cat, dog…"

Once you're confident with your **Letter Clue Vocabulary**, memorize the following arbitrary strings as quickly as possible. Don't worry about their order; you should be able to complete each string upon hearing only the first letter.

- EBFD
- MNERHD
- 238-CFJSD
- DS-OIH-JE44
- PQMEUIDCU
- 82HF899472BDS-332
- BJK3129C8F-10900019B
- SDFLKJ32908DFHFD823HDF7CHNWE0

Next, it' time to tackle *Advanced Memory Development*.

Section 4: Advanced Memory Development

Guess what, worm? You're in my world now. The Varsity Team. Special Forces. No excuses, no punches pulled. Shape up or ship out. You can't handle the truth. Today...is our Independence Day. You had me at "hello."

Sorry, I got carried away with the dramatic lines.

You're about to embark upon a journey that separates those with moderately trained memories from those whose memories fall into the top 0.01% worldwide. We're talking about people who pose a threat at international memory competitions. We're talking about those who can wow a crowd by speaking for hours without notes. Those for whom advanced mnemonic systems seem as natural as breathing. Those who have broken free of the shackles of digital reminders.

You should already be leaps and bounds ahead of your former self. You should be able to memorize and associate words, concepts, numbers, lists, alphanumeric strings and tasks with ease. You've poured the foundation, and now you're going to build upon it. Today, my friend, you venture into advanced territory.

In this section, you're going to extend your use of the **Journey Method**, then work on honing a powerful method for numerical memorization. You'll learn to use a single **Journey Step** to store two-, three-, four-, and even five-digit numbers. You could, for example, use this skill to memorize a sixteen-digit credit card number (along with the four-digit expiration date) in a **Journey** of only four **Steps**. You'll also be able to memorize a *one hundred* digit number—a previously insurmountable memorization challenge—within a mere twenty **Steps**. Soon after, you'll learn a few tips for easily memorizing numbers, followed by a lesson on memorizing names quickly (and permanently associating them with faces).

The following lessons will be challenging, so if you aren't in the right mental state, don't begin quite yet. If it starts to feel like a chore or something you dread, take a few days off and then return, refreshed and enthusiastic. As Ralph Waldo Emerson once said, "nothing great was ever achieved without enthusiasm."

Though you'll learn a few new tactics, many of these concepts are extensions of methods you've already mastered. Think of yourself as a mental athlete; you know how to run, but with conditioning, education, error correction, and the reinforcement of minute details that maximize positive habits, you can truly excel.

By the end of this section, you'll be so well versed in advanced **Memory Development** techniques that I'm going to ask you to memorize the Presidents of the United States (in order, including their first and last names and years in office) and the Periodic Table of Elements (including number, atomic weight, and symbol). Sound daunting? Right now, it should. By the time you have to perform these feats, though, I can promise they won't seem nearly as challenging.

Lesson 1: Taking the Journey to the Next Level

> *"A JOURNEY IS A PERSON IN ITSELF; NO TWO ARE ALIKE."*
> —JOHN STEINBECK, AUTHOR

As explained at length in *Basic Memory Development*, the **Journey** concept is instrumental to memorization. Here, you're going to expand your **Mega-Journey** so that you'll always have a **Journey** available when you need one.

Essentially, your goal is to prepare ahead of time so you can minimize the amount of "on the fly" **Journey** construction you need to perform. You already know you ideally want to begin each memorization endeavor with a **Contextual Journey** (one that's pertinent to the subject matter). Having a detailed **Mega-Journey** (a set of ordered **Journeys** with pre-defined **Steps**) on hand ensures quick access to a myriad of **Journeys** ; ideally one or more will fit the given context. A huge **Mega-Journey** also enables seamless continuance in case the information requires more than one **Journey**.

For instance, if you need to memorize **Permanent Information** about your friend Pete, you may begin at Pete's house. If the information requires more than the ten **Steps** you've defined in his home, you'll need to move on. By using a well-crafted **Mega-Journey**, you'll be able to move right from Pete's house to a subsequent **Journey** without giving it too much thought.

Let's get right to it. Your first task is to write out a 300-**Step Mega-Journey**. To review, a **Mega-Journey** is an array of independent **Journeys** (ideally containing ten **Steps** each), strung together with **Transitions** (imagined trips from one **Journey's** conclusion to the next **Journey's** beginning). 300 may sound like a daunting number, but really, you already have a database vastly larger than this in your head; it just isn't yet organized into distinct **Journeys** and **Steps**.

Begin by writing down the individual **Journey's** location (your house, your sister's house, your gym, etc.), and then break each **Journey** down into **Steps** (the *rooms* of your and your sister's houses, the *individual stations* at your gym, etc.). Determining the **Steps** in detail before you need to use them allows for more immediate application in a real-world setting. This is because you won't have to spend time establishing individual **Steps** as you're simultaneously trying to fill them with information.

Remember, traverse the rooms or areas in a logical, "walkable" order as you establish your **Steps**; don't jump randomly between locations (use the tip from *Basic Memorization*: go through the **Steps** as though you were a realtor showing the **Journeys** to prospective buyers). Connect **Journeys** together with interesting **Transitions**; for instance, when I make the **Transition** from my best friend's apartment to my family's former house, I imagine doing so by jet pack. While in the air, I imagine I encounter a hot air balloon, carefully guide myself into the balloon's basket, and ride it until I reach the airspace above my family's old house.

I jump out, crashing through the ceiling into the first **Step** of that **Journey**.

Including as much sensory detail as possible helps to ensure the **Transition** and first **Step** are memorable. While in the hot air balloon, I imagine the anxiety I'd feel when attempting to time my jump so I land in the correct spot. I imagine gusts of wind and birds flying by. I imagine the drywall dust I'd breathe and the pain I'd feel after crashing through the roof.

In addition, make sure your **Journeys** flow naturally. Imagine you're envisioning yourself at a friend's house; you could follow this **Journey** with a second **Journey** set somewhere you and your friend would likely visit together in reality. Likewise, you can place logical clues at the end of one **Journey** to trigger an idea about the next. I remember that my old gym is the **Journey** after my in-laws' house by imagining that, as I'm leaving the house, my father-in-law shakes my hand and gruffly comments that I'm "looking a bit scrawny." This is a clue to go to the gym, thus creating a logical connection between the two **Journeys**. If you usually go to the supermarket right after the laundromat, do the same in your mind.

Take some time to list some places (just the **Journeys**, not the individual **Steps**) you know well. You can ask a spouse, friend, or family member to help out (although the unprompted request, "Help me name places I know," may require further explanation). Often, thinking of one place will trigger a list of related places, and they'll come rushing into your consciousness all at once. If this happens, embrace it and quickly scribble them down. If you get stuck, take a look at the following list of suggestions.

- Your home and/or the home(s) you lived in while growing up (this could include apartment complexes, boarding schools, military housing, and dormitories)
- Your friends' current and former homes (I can still vividly picture my best friend's first apartment)
- Gyms, recreational areas, parks, studios, sports complexes, concert halls, and zoos
- Retail spaces you frequent, such as supermarkets, bookstores, department stores, malls, and shops
- Train and bus stations
- Airports
- Town centers
- Churches
- Restaurants, bars, and clubs
- Museums
- Current/former workplaces
- Current/former schools
- Vacation spots
- The offices of your doctor, dentist, therapist, lawyer, accountant, veterinarian, parole officer, bookie, psychic, or bookie's veterinary psychic

Once you've created a list of **Journeys**, begin putting it into a logical order. Once you've listed thirty places, it's time to break them down into **Steps**. Begin with ten **Steps** per **Journey**, but feel free to expand to twenty if doing so falls within your personal **Journey Standardization** rule set. Ten seems to work best for most people, however.

> *Tip*: Sometimes ***Journeys*** change. If you're considering using a clothing shop that you frequent, don't bypass it just because the layout changes each season. Locations are often dynamic, and your ***Journeys*** may need to be maintained and updated accordingly. Your mind is surprisingly good at keeping track of such things.

I would suggest using a spreadsheet program like Microsoft Excel to create this list. If you don't have Excel, Google offers free spreadsheet functionality through Google Drive (DRIVE.GOOGLE.COM). Regardless of the tool you use, create four columns; the first column is for the **Journey** name (Don's beach house, Acme Market…), the second for the **Step** number, the third for the actual **Step** (upstairs bathroom, Don's bedroom…), and the fourth for notes, reminders, creative additions, and comments about transitions between **Journeys**.

Here's an example of twenty possible **Steps**:

Journey	Step #	Step	Notes
Dad's House	1	Inside front door	
Dad's House	2	Living room	Remember: recently painted. Focus on new paint color.
Dad's House	3	Kitchen	
Dad's House	4	Laundry room	

Dad's House	5	Garage	
Dad's House	6	Small bathroom	
Dad's House	7	Hallway	
Dad's House	8	Dad's bedroom	
Dad's House	9	Spare bedroom	
Dad's House	10	Main Bathroom	Dad was hungry, as usual. Transition to supermarket on a motorcycle with Dad in the sidecar.
Acme Supermarket	1	Inside front doors	Always drafty.
Acme Supermarket	2	Register area	
Acme Supermarket	3	Between the deli and breads	
Acme Supermarket	4	Bakery aisle	Remember that this moved recently. This is the "new" bakery aisle, not the old one.

Acme Supermarket	5	Canned goods and ethnic foods aisle	
Acme Supermarket	6	Baking goods aisle	
Acme Supermarket	7	Cereal and bottled drinks aisle	
Acme Supermarket	8	Meat aisle	
Acme Supermarket	9	Dairy area	Imagine the cold of the refrigerators.
Acme Supermarket	10	Fruit and veggie area	You find a pineapple and place it into an oversized cannon; in doing so, you fall into the cannon as well. You (and the pineapple) are fired through the ceiling, fly through the air, and land in the parking lot of the Neptune Mall.

By the end of this exercise, you should have written down at least 300 **Steps**; that's a minimum of thirty **Journeys** at ten **Steps** each.

Large multi-**Journey** chunks of this **Mega-Journey** can be used to memorize longer lists, and individual **Journeys** can be used to memorize shorter lists. With so many options, you can avoid over-using the same short **Journeys** and running the risk of unnecessarily confusing the information you have stored in them.

> *Tip:* When dealing with structures like houses, stick to rooms or locations you would actually enter and can thus picture easily. This is vital for speedy recall. I can picture in detail a friend's parents' home since I was there almost every day growing up. However, I can't picture his older brother's room well because I only entered it a handful of times, so I skip over it in my **Journey**. Use your discretion.

Build the spreadsheet and create your 300-**Step Mega-Journey** now. Spend a few days memorizing it, and don't move on until you can recite it aloud and silently walk through it from beginning to end without problems. You should be able to start at any **Step** and move both forward and backward with ease. You'll test your familiarity by memorizing several long, daunting lists at the end of this section. The stronger your **Mega-Journey**, the easier this type of task will become.

Dedicate a specific chunk of time each day to memorizing your **Mega-Journey**. In addition, review it during any downtime you may encounter. Lastly, go through it a few times before bed. As you learned in *Learning and Revisitation Rhythms*, ingraining information right before you go to sleep helps to reinforce it, as it will be less likely to get discarded when your brain does its nightly "house cleaning."

As you build on this skill, be conscious about adding to your collection of **Journeys**; if you go somewhere new, simply add it to your collection. An added bonus when collecting fresh **Journeys**: their use—and continual reinforcement—strengthens your ability to recall details about these places in your day-to-day life. You'll find that your memories of new places you visit remain stronger for longer periods of time.

Once you're reasonably confident with your 300-**Step Mega-Journey**, move on to the next lesson.

Quick Review

1. Earlier in this book, you learned how to create and use **Journeys** to store information. Now that you're comfortable with the rules and constructs of the **Journey Method**, it's a good time to build on your lengthy **Mega-Journey** (collection of individual **Journeys** that link together through **Transitions**) for practical use in daily life. First compile the **Mega-Journey**, and then spend time memorizing it.

Lesson 2: The Mnemonic Character Library (Part 1)

> *"I HOPE THE NEXT TIME I MOVE I GET A REAL EASY PHONE NUMBER...SOMETHING LIKE TWO TWO TWO, TWO TWO TWO TWO. AND THEN PEOPLE WOULD SAY, 'MITCH, HOW DO I GET A HOLD OF YOU?' I'D SAY, 'JUST PRESS TWO FOR A WHILE AND WHEN I ANSWER, YOU WILL KNOW YOU HAVE PRESSED TWO ENOUGH.'"*
>
> —MITCH HEDBERG, COMEDIAN

Unfortunately, numbers are rarely as easy to memorize as 222-2222.

What you're about to learn could very well take a long time to master, but it's a valuable tool that's certainly worth the trouble.

In *Basic Memory Development*, you developed your first **Mnemonic Vocabulary** by creating **Single-Digit Mnemonic Clues** to represent the numbers zero through nine. That was a great start, but it was only the beginning. Expanding upon that skill, you're going to master the memorization of numerical information by creating a **Mnemonic Character Library**.

Mnemonic Characters: Using a Single Step to Represent a Two-Digit Number

This method for memorizing numerical information begins with the creation of a series of **Mnemonic Characters**. Each **Mnemonic Character** represents a unique two-digit number from zero (00) to ninety-nine (99). Early variations of this method date back hundreds of years, and many different versions have surfaced in the annals of mainstream mnemonic culture. It's been called the "people method," the "library method," and a slew of other names. Perhaps most recently, it has been promoted as the "DOMINIC System," a term coined by world-famous mnemonist and **Memory Development** coach Dominic O'Brien (O'Brien modestly claims that DOMINIC stands for <u>D</u>ecipherment <u>O</u>f <u>M</u>nemonically-<u>I</u>nterpreted <u>N</u>umbers <u>I</u>nto <u>C</u>haracters). We're going to discuss a vastly-expanded version of this I call the **Mnemonic Characters and Actions Method** (we'll address the "**Actions**" bit later).

Yes, creating **Mnemonic Characters** to represent ninety-nine unique numbers sounds difficult (and it surely is), but once established, their usefulness can't be overstated. One could argue that since two-digit numbers occur relatively often in everyday life (as opposed to, say, nine-digit numbers), this alone is an intrinsically useful skill. However, the real magic is how this method speeds memorization of longer numbers by grouping pairs of numbers together.

You can therefore think about a sixteen-digit number as eight groups of two digits. The practice of breaking longer numbers into series of smaller, more digestible numbers is called **Chunking**. For example, by **Chunking** a ten-digit identification number into five two-digit **Chunks**, memorization requirements can be reduced (in this case, from ten

Journey Steps to five). You can and will expand this to include three, four, and even five digits in a single **Step**.

That's right. Five digits in a single **Step**.

Over the course of the next few lessons, you'll learn the basics of this classical method as well as a suite of fantastic additions and adaptations unique to *Never Forget Again*. The end result is the most complete **Mnemonic Characters and Actions Method** available. Learning it will give you an incredible advantage when memorizing numbers.

The first step in creating a **Mnemonic Character Library** is to associate two-digit numbers with people from your personal life who remind you of these numbers. Choose as many of these "personal" **Mnemonic Characters** as possible. For example, if your son is an avid football player who always wears the jersey number 17, he would be a good choice for your **Mnemonic Character** for 17, because this number would probably naturally and automatically remind you of him. Only use the associate if it's immediate and works in either direction; in other words, just as your son immediately reminds you of 17, 17 should immediately remind you of your son. If your mother was born in 1940, and the number 40 immediately reminds you of her, use it. Just be sure never to force an unnatural or complex personal association.

After you've made as many personal connections as you can, you may next choose celebrities or fictitious characters who remind you of certain numbers, using personal associations that make sense to you. If your favorite hockey player was Eric Lindros, you could use him for the number 88 (his uniform number). If you're more of a movie buff, and Brad Pitt reminds you of the number 07 (because of his role in the film,

Seven), he may be a good fit. Again, only use immediate connections that work in both directions. Never force it.

Before continuing, memorize this small translation table. You'll understand why this is important in a few moments.

Number	Letter
1	A
2	B
3	C
4	D
5	E
6	S
7	G
8	H
9	N
0	O

Using this translation table, two-digit numbers can be converted to letter equivalents. AA equals 11, BC equals 23, and ON equals 09. Test yourself; what is OD? How about HA? BS? Going the other way, what about 89? 12? 37? When you're comfortable with the translation table, move ahead to continue learning the method.

After you've exhausted your roster of personal and celebrity associations, what about the dozens of other numbers for which you have no immediate **Character** associations? For these, turn again to celebrities or characters from fiction; but this time, use the alphabet translation table to convert their initials to numbers.

For example, "11" translates to "AA," and can stand for tennis great Andre Agassi. "54" translates to "ED" and could stand for comedian Ellen DeGeneres, and "78," which translates to "GH," can refer to late Beatles' guitarist George Harrison. For the number "53" (EC), you may choose to remember rocker Elvis Costello. For "43" (DC), you might think of comedian Drew Carey. "12" may be travelling gastrophile Anthony Bordaine, "00" could stand for rocker Ozzy Osbourne, and "81" may remind you of baseball Hall-of-Famer Hank Aaron.

You may ask, "if 'one = A' and 'two = B', why do we stray from the expected letter of the alphabet for six, nine, and zero?" The answer lies in the inner workings of the human mind. Most people can assess somewhat quickly that "A is the first letter of the alphabet, B is the second," etc., all the way up to "E is the fifth letter of the alphabet." Past that, it usually requires a tiny bit of thought; though not difficult by any stretch, the few seconds of thought required can interfere with the speed necessary to successfully employ this method.

In this system, six and nine start with S and N, respectively, and zero (often pronounced "oh") is pronounced the same (and looks the same) as the letter O. "Eight" and "H" sound a bit alike when said aloud, so only "G = seven" needs to be memorized through brute force. This exact set of letter-to-number pairings seems to have been constructed by the aforementioned memory guru Dominic O'Brien, years ago and is the most intuitive version I've come across in decades of study.

Let's recap one more time: it's optimal to use personal acquaintances for your **Mnemonic Characters**. Do this whenever possible, followed by personally significant celebrity/number associations as a second choice. When no one else comes to mind, use the translation table to translate celebrity initials into numbers.

You can also use the **Mnemonic Characters and Actions Method** to associate people with numbers in other creative ways, as long as they make sense to you. These associations are ultimately yours, so don't shy away from connections that feel natural. You'll never have to justify your choices to other people. Take, for example, an acquaintance's **Mnemonic Character** selection for "13": Donald Trump. Why? Though Donald Trump's initials are DT, he immediately reminds her of AC (Atlantic City, the site of a great many Trump properties and casinos). You can certainly use such freeform associations, but stick with what's natural; if the person doesn't immediately conjure up a numerical connection, don't force it. You'll need to access these associations quickly in the near future.

At the end of the day, the important thing is to create **Mnemonic Character** associations for the numbers 00 to 99 that can be *immediately and vividly imagined*.

You may be tempted to write these down as they come to you, but don't get caught up in the excitement yet; there's still much to learn about this method before settling upon your final **Mnemonic Character Library**.

Mnemonic Characters and Their Actions: Using a Single Step to represent a Four-Digit Number

When you decide upon **Characters** for the numbers 00 through 99, it's important that each individual you choose has a specific **Action** that he or she is always performing. For example, imagine that you chose "16" to represent comedian Adam Sandler (16 = AS = Adam Sandler). You could imagine Sandler angrily swinging a golf club, like his character in the film *Happy Gilmore*. "62" could be actress Sandra Bullock (62 = SB), gesturing as though steering a bus, a reference to her breakout role in the film *Speed*.

None of your **Mnemonic Characters** should perform characteristic **Actions** that might be confused with those of another **Character**. For example, it wouldn't be a good idea to choose Charles Barkley for "32" and then choose Shaquille O'Neil for "60," as both would likely be dribbling a basketball. This is important because you'll soon need to be able to recognize a **Mnemonic Character** based on either their face or their **Action**.

Here's how this works: by making sure that each **Character's Action** is unique, you can combine two **Characters** by pairing one's image with the other's **Action**. If I see the number 1662, I can imagine Adam Sandler (16) pretending to use a steering wheel, as this is Sandra Bullock (62)'s **Action**. The number 5494 conjures an image of Ellen DeGeneres (54) wearing a gaudy sequined jacket, which is Neil Diamond (94)'s **Action**. An **Action** can be any number of things; **Characters** can perform a motion or gesture, wear a certain garment, or possess a specific object.

This technique requires only one particular standard: whenever a **Mnemonic Character** is performing the **Action** of another, the

Character should always be used to represent the first two digits, and the **Action** should be used to represent the latter two; never reverse the order of this relationship. Holding steadfastly to this rule will provide consistency and avoid confusion down the road.

So, in using this novel method for merging two two-digit numbers, you can use a single **Mnemonic Scene** (and therefore a single **Journey Step**) to represent a four-digit number. Think of the applications! Using this method in conjunction with a single ten-**Step Journey** gives you the ability to memorize a forty-digit number. Your mind wants to be used creatively and visually, and by doing so you've unearthed a whole new world of technical possibilities.

Build Your Mnemonic Character Library

Get a piece of paper and a pen or create a spreadsheet. Write the numbers 00 through 99 in one column. You're going to fill a second column with a **Mnemonic Character** for each two-digit number.

Try to come up with personally significant individuals to represent each number from 00 to 99. Skip any that stump you for now. When you've done this, go back to each number for which you haven't decided upon a personally significant **Character**, and try to think of a celebrity who reminds you of each of those numbers. Finally, when these two reservoirs are exhausted, use the **Mnemonic Characters and Actions** translation table to choose a celebrity based on his or her initials. Remember to give each of these **Characters** a unique **Action**.

Though your **Mnemonic Character Library** should be as personal and customized as possible, here is a list of celebrity characters you can reference if you get stuck; I got stuck on quite a few numbers when I originally crafted my personal **Mnemonic Character Library** years ago. Hopefully these examples will help jump-start your imagination, as certain combinations of initials can be very elusive.

Number	Mnemonic Character Suggestions
00	Ozzy Osbourne, Olive Oyl
01	Ozzie Ardiles, Omar Al-Bashir, Omar Akram
02	Osama Bin Laden, Orlando Bloom
03	Oliver Cromwell, Ossie Clark
04	Oscar de la Hoya, Oscar de la Renta, Olivia de Havilland, Ossie Davis
05	Omar Epps, Oliver Ekman-Larsson
06	O.J. Simpson, Ozzie Smith, Oliver Stone, Omar Sharif, Oroku Saki, Oskar Schindler
07	Oscar the Grouch, Otto Graham
08	Oliver Hardy, Oliver Hudson, Oscar Hammerstein
09	Ollie North, Oscar Nunez
10	Ashley Olson, Annie Oakley, Apollo Ohno, Al Oerter, Aristotle Onassis

11	Andre Agassi, Arthur Ashe, Adam Ant, Abigail Adams, Adam Arkin, Alan Alda, Alan Autry, Amy Adams, Ansel Adams
12	Anthony Bordain, Al Bundy, Anne Bancroft, Aaron Burr, Alec Baldwin, Andrea Bocelli, Adrien Brody, Albert Brooks, Amanda Bynes, Angela Bassett, Annette Bening, Anthony Burgess, Antonio Banderas, Art Blakey
13	Alice Cooper, Al Capone, Agatha Christie, Alex Cross, Adam Carolla, Anderson Cooper, Andy Capp, Angela Cartwright, Art Carney, Arthur C. Clarke, Aaron Copeland, Aaron Carter
14	Angie Dickinson, Annie Duke, Adam Duritz, Alan Dershowitz
15	Albert Einstein, Amelia Earhart
16	Adam Sandler, Ashley Simpson, Alan Shepard, Alicia Silverstone, Amy Smart, Anna Nicole Smith, Anwar Sadat, Ariel Sharon, Arnold Schwarzenegger, Artie Shaw
17	Adrian Grenier, Al Green, Althea Gibson, Al Gore, Alan Greenspan, Alexander Graham Bell, Allen Ginsberg, Amy Grant, Andre the Giant, Andrew Greeley, Andy Griffith, Anthony Geary, Art Garfunkel, Astrud Gilberto, Ava Gardner
18	Anne Heche, Angelica Houston, Adolf Hitler, Alexander Hamilton, Alfred Hitchcock, Anthony Hopkins, Arsenio Hall, Audrey Hepburn

19	Aaron Neville, Anne Neville
20	Barack Obama, Bobby Orr
21	Bryan Adams, Ben Affleck, Bea Arthur, Benedict Arnold, Billie Joe Armstrong, Bud Abbott, Buzz Aldrin
22	"BB" King, Barbara Bush, Burt Bacharach, Big Bird, Bob Beamon, Bonnie Blair, Barry Bonds, Bertolt Brecht, Big Bopper, Bill Bradley, Bob Barker, Brigitte Bardot, Buffalo Bill
23	Bill Clinton, Barbara Cartland, Bob Cousy, Bruce Campbell, Bill Cosby, Billy Corgan, Billy Crystal, Billy Ray Cyrus, Bing Crosby, Butch Cassidy
24	Bo Diddley, Bo Derek, Bob Dylan, Bette Davis, Bob Denver, Bob Dole, Bobby Darin, Brian DePalma
25	Bill Engvall, Bob Eubanks
26	Bob Saget, Bart Simpson, Barbra Streisand, Barry Sanders, Britney Spears, Bruce Springsteen, B.F. Skinner, Barbara Stanwyck, Baxter Stockman, Ben Stiller, Bob Seger, Bram Stoker, Britney Spears, Brooke Shields
27	Billy Gibbons, Bear Grylls, Bill Gates, Bob Geldof, Brian Griffin, Bob Gibson, Benny Goodman, Billy Graham, Bob Guccione, Boy George, Buddy Guy
28	Ben Harper, Benny Hill, Bobby Hill, Ben Hur, Buddy Holly, Billie Holiday, Ben Hogan, Bobby Hull, "Wild" Bill

	Hickok, Bill Hicks, Bob Hope, Bret Hart, Brett Hull, Buddy Hackett
29	Bill Nye ("the science guy"), Bob Newhart, Bradley Nowell
30	Conan O'Brien, Chris O'Donnell
31	Christina Aguilera, Chris Angel, Christina Applegate, Charles Atlas, Chet Atkins
32	Charlie Brown, Chris Brown, Captain Beefheart, Candice Bergen, Carol Burnett, Charles Bronson, Charles Bukowski, Christian Bale, Christie Brinkley, Chuck Berry, Count Basie
33	Charlie Chaplin, Count Chocula, Chevy Chase, Christopher Columbus, Coco Chanel, Chelsea Clinton, Cab Calloway, Calvin Coolidge, Cesar Chavez, Chick Corea, Columbus, Chubby Checker, Cindy Crawford, Connie Chung
34	C.C. DeVille, Charles Darwin, Celine Dion, Cameron Diaz, Cecil B. DeMille, Charles Dickens, Claire Danes, Count Dracula
35	Clint Eastwood, Carmen Electra, Chris Evert, Cedric the Entertainer, Chris Elliott
36	Charlie Sheen, Carly Simon, Carl Sagan, Cat Stevens, Claudia Schiffer, Colonel Sanders, Cybill Shepherd
37	Christopher Guest, Che Guevara, Cary Grant, Catherine the Great, Cuba Gooding Jr.,

38	Chris Hanson, Chelsea Handler, Chris Hardwick, C. Thomas Howell, Charlton Heston, Clint Howard
39	Chuck Norris, Christopher Nolan, Captain Noah, Craig T. Nelson
40	Donnie Osmond, Daniel Ortega
41	Dan Aykroyd, Dave Attell, Danny Aiello, Desi Arnaz, Douglas Adams, Duane Allman
42	Drew Barrymore, Dave Barry, Danny Bonaduce, Dan Brown, David Beckham, Dick Butkus, Dickie Betts, Don Budge, Daniel Boone, Dave Brubeck, David Blaine, David Bowie
43	David Copperfield, David Cassidy, Dick Cheney, Drew Carey, Don Cheadle, Dale Carnegie, Dana Carvey, Dave Chappelle, Dave Coulier, David Carradine, David Caruso, David Crosby, Davy Crockett, Deepak Chopra, Dick Clark
44	Danny DeVito, Dr. Dre, David Duchovney, Dr. Drew, Donald Duck, Daniel Day-Lewis, Dom DeLuise, Doris Day, Dick Van Dyke
45	Dwight Eisenhower, Dennis Eckersley, Dale Earnhardt, Danny Elfman, Duke Ellington
46	David Schwimmer, Diana Spencer (Princess Di), Donna Summer, Dax Shepard, David Sedaris, Donald Sutherland, Danielle Steel, Deion Sanders, Dr. Seuss,

	Darryl Strawberry, David Spade, Dee Snider, Dick Smothers
47	Danny Glover, Donald Glover, David Gilmour, Debbie Gibson, Dizzy Gillespie
48	D.L. Hughley, Don Henley, David Hasslehoff, Don Hutson, Daryl Hannah, Deborah Harry, Dennis Hopper, Don Ho, Dustin Hoffman
49	Dave Navarro, Dan Naturman
50	Ed O'Neil, Eric Oliver
51	Ed Asner, Ellen Allien, Eddie Arcaro
52	Ed Burns, Elizabeth Berkley, Ed Begley Jr., Erin Brockovich, Elgin Baylor, Enid Blyton, Eric Bana, Ernest Borgnine
53	Eric Clapton, Eric Church, Eddie Cantor, Elvis Costello
54	Ellen Degeneres, Edgar Degas, Emily Dickinson
55	Eric Estrada, Emilio Estevez
56	Edward Scissorhands, Ebenezer Scrooge, Ed Sullivan, Eduardo Saverin, Ed Sullivan, Elisabeth Shue, Emmitt Smith
57	Eydie Gorme, Ed Gein, Elizabeth Gilbert, Eva Gabor, Edward Gorey

58	Elizabeth Hurley, Ed Harris, Ernest Hemingway, Eddie Van Halen
59	Ed Norton, Eric Northman
60	Shaquille O'Neal, Sandra Day O'Connor, Sharon Osbourne
61	Sam Adams, Spiro Agnew, Susan B. Anthony
62	"Wildman" Steve Brill, Steve Buscemi, Sandra Bullock, Stephen Baldwin, Sammy Baugh, Sandra Bernhard, Sonny Bono, Susan Boyle, Syd Barrett
63	Sean Connery, Santa Claus, Sarah Chalke, Sheryl Crow, Sidney Crosby, Simon Cowell, Steve Carell, Steve Carlton
64	Salvador Dali, Sandra Day O'Connor
65	Shannon Elizabeth, Sam Elliot
66	Stephen Spielberg, Steven Seagal, Sam Snead, Sidney Sheldon, Sammy Sosa, Sharon Stone, Sissy Spacek, Soupy Sales, Susan Sarandon, Suzanne Somers, Sylvester Stallone
67	Seth Green, Steve Guttenberg
68	Sammy Hagar, Sam Harris, Steve Harvey, Saddam Hussein, Salma Hayek, Sam Harris, Sherlock Holmes, Stephen Hawking
69	Stevie Nicks, Sam Neill, Steve Nash

70	Gary Oldman, George Orwell, Georgia O'Keeffe
71	"GG" Allin, Gillian Anderson, Greg Allman, Gene Autry
72	Garth Brooks, Gary Busey, Gerard Butler, George Burns, Glenn Beck, George Bush, George Benson, George Brett, Ginger Baker
73	George Clooney, Glen Campbell, George Clinton, Glenn Close, Gary Coleman, George Carlin, Grover Cleveland
74	Glenn Danzig, Geena Davis, Gerard Depardieu
75	Gloria Estefan, Greg Evigan
76	Gene Simmons, Gary Sinise, G.E. Smith, Georges St. Pierre, George Steinbrenner, Garry Shandling, Gene Siskel, George Stephanopoulos, George Strait, Gloria Steinem, Grace Slick, Gwen Stefani
77	Gilbert Gottfried, George Gershwin, Galileo Galilei, George Gobel, Gilbert Gottfried, Greta Garbo
78	George Harrison, Gregory House, Gordie Howe, Gene Hackman, Goldie Hawn
79	Graham Norton, Greg Norman
80	Haley Joel Osment, Harry Osborn
81	Hank Aaron, Henry Armstrong, Hank Azaria, Hans Christian Andersen

82	Halle Berry, Harry Belafonte, Helena Bonham Carter, Humphrey Bogart
83	Hillary Clinton, Ho Chi Minh, Harry Connick, Jr., Harry Chapin, Hayden Christensen, Harry Caray
84	Howard Dean, Howard the Duck, Hillary Duff
85	Harry Enfield, He-Man
86	Harry Shearer, Homer Simpson, Han Solo, Harriet Beecher Stowe, Hilary Swank, Horace Silver, Howard Stern
87	Hugh Grant, Happy Gilmore, H.R. Giger, Heather Graham
88	Hugh Hefner, Howard Hughes, Holly Hunter, Helen Hunt, Harry Hamlin, Harry (from Harry and the Hendersons), Harry Houdini, Herbert Hoover, Herbie Hancock, Hermann Hesse, Hulk Hogan
89	Harry Nilsson, Harry Newman
90	Nick Offerman, Nick Oliveri
91	Neil Armstrong, Nick Adams
92	Norman Bates, Ned Beatty, Norman Bridwell, Napoleon Bonaparte
93	Nicholas Cage, Nick Cannon, Nick Cave, Natalie Cole, Neve Campbell, Nick Carter

94	Neil Diamond, Nancy Drew, Napolean Dynamite
95	Ned Eisenberg, Nora Ephron
96	Norman Schwartzkopf, Nick Swardson, Neil Sedaka, Nicolette Sheridan, Nancy Sinatra, Neil Simon
97	Newt Gingrich, Neil Gaiman, Noel Gallagher
98	Neil Patrick Harris, Nathaniel Hawthorne
99	Nick Nolte, Nate Newton, Neil Nitin Mukesh

Hopefully this helps. Although I use personally significant individuals whenever possible, my own **Mnemonic Character Library** contains quite a few selections based on celebrity initials.

It can be difficult to choose a unique **Action** for certain **Characters**, but remaining creative and open-minded will drastically increase your options. For instance, my **Mnemonic Action** for 71—*X-Files* star Gillian Anderson—is "eating a cockroach." The reason for this revolves around a bit of *X-Files* trivia; while filming an episode called "Humbug" in the fall of 1995, Anderson was supposed to create the illusion that she was placing a cockroach in her mouth; apparently, the director had her practice "palming" the (real but dead) insect. According to lore, when it came time to film the scene, she actually ate the cockroach, to the shock and amusement of the film crew. Whether or not the story is true, this has always stood out to me as an **Action** for the actress.

Anderson is not the only **Character** performing a strange action. Nick Nolte (99) is having his mug shot taken (if you don't know why, Google

"Nick Nolte mug shot"). You *don't* want to know what shock rocker G.G. Allin is doing.

Let's review the rules one more time:

- Choose only one Mnemonic Character to represent each number. The list above contains multiple Characters per number only to provide some ideas.

- Each Mnemonic Character must be associated with an equally-recognizable Action.

- No two Actions should be similar enough to cause confusion. If you're using classic rockers Eric Clapton and Jimmy Page, for instance, and they're both playing guitar, you may run into problems (unless you're enough of a guitar geek to know that Eric typically plays a Stratocaster while Jimmy plays a Les Paul). The same goes for Jerry Rice and Eli Manning or Sam Kinison and George Carlin.

It's time to build and memorize your **Mnemonic Character Library**. Take as much time as you need. For some, this may only be a day or two, while for others this task may require upwards of two weeks. When you find you're able to recite the names of all one hundred **Mnemonic Characters** in order (while imagining their faces and **Actions**) in under four minutes, you may continue. Don't move on until you reach this point, as this skill will prove to be endlessly useful.

Once you hit the four-minute mark, you're probably comfortable enough to implement this concept in real-world scenarios, so it's time to practice.

Memorize the following numbers using **Mnemonic Characters** and **Actions**. When memorizing a two-digit number, simply imagine the **Mnemonic Character** performing his or her own **Action**. When memorizing a four-digit number, imagine the **Character** of the first two digits performing the **Action** associated with the last two digits.

- 44
- 82
- 39
- 71
- 83
- 8371
- 1234
- 1940
- 2380
- 1199

Mnemonic Characters and Single-Digit Mnemonic Clues: Using a Single Step to Represent Three-Digit Numbers

You now know how to use a single **Step** to store one-, two-, or four-digit numbers, but what about three? Three-digit numbers are incredibly common; they're used for telephone area codes, blood pressure levels, adult bodyweights (in lbs.), cooking temperatures and HTTP error codes. However, when memorizing three-digit numbers, you can't use a single **Mnemonic Character** (two digits) and you can't use an entire **Mnemonic Character/Action** pair (four digits).

In these cases, you can simply have your **Mnemonic Character** (the first two digits) use or interact with a **Single-Digit Mnemonic Clue**. Imagine that your **Mnemonic Character** for "55" is actor Eric Estrada, and your **Single-Digit Mnemonic Clue** for "7" is a boomerang. To memorize the number 557, picture Eric Estrada throwing and catching a boomerang. "849" would be represented by "84"'s **Character** interacting with the **Single-Digit Mnemonic Clue** for "9." It's easy once you get the hang of it.

Memorize the following numbers using this method:

- 873
- 101
- 378
- 676
- 320
- 872
- 555
- 207
- 999
- 844

We haven't fully explored **Mnemonic Characters and Actions** yet, but let's break here for a quick review. Next, we'll discuss odd cases and you'll learn how to memorize up to five digits in a single **Journey Step**.

Quick Review

1. By developing a **Mnemonic Character Library**, you can use a single **Journey Step** to store two, three, four, or even five digits (five-digit storage is covered in the next lesson). This **Mnemonic Character Library** should consist of one hundred **Mnemonic Characters** representing the numbers 00 through 99, and each **Character** should have a unique **Action** associated with it.

2. When building a **Mnemonic Character Library**, choose **Characters** based on the following hierarchy: 1.) Individuals you know personally, and who remind you of a specific number (ideal); 2.) Celebrities or characters from fiction who remind you of a specific number (when necessary); and finally, 3.) Celebrities or characters from fiction whose initials translate to a number using a translation table (last resort).

3. To store two digits in a single **Step**, imagine the appropriate **Mnemonic Character** performing his or her own unique **Action**.

4. To store three digits in a single **Step**, imagine a **Mnemonic Character** that represents the first two digits, and then a **Single-Digit Mnemonic Clue** (0 through 9) to represent the final digit. Imagine the **Mnemonic Character** holding, using, or interacting with the **Clue**.

5. To store four digits in a single **Step**, imagine a **Mnemonic Character** (representing the first two digits) performing the unique **Action** of another **Character** (representing the remaining two digits). Whenever a **Mnemonic Character** performs the **Action** of another, the **Character** itself should always be used to represent the first two digits, and the **Action**

of the second **Character** should be used to represent the latter two.

Lesson 3: The Mnemonic Character Library (Part 2)

> *"This is where the power lies!"*
> —Hulk Hogan, Pro Wrestling Icon

You just learned how to use **Mnemonic Characters and Actions** to memorize numbers. **Character**-based methods are popular among mnemonists, but now you'll set yourself apart by learning some innovative customizations.

Handling Specific Cases

You're going to learn about three types of numbers, called **Mirrored Numbers** (such as 1212 or 8686), **Negative Numbers** (such as -14), and **Decimal Numbers** (such as 1.196). There are specific ways to handle each.

Mirrored Numbers

You'll occasionally come across a four-digit number consisting of a repeated two-digit number (like 5454). As far as I can tell, no existing mnemonic system addresses how to memorize this without confusion. Using the method as you learned, memorizing the number 5454 would mean imagining 54's **Character** performing 54's **Action**. This poses a problem, as this is also what you'd imagine when memorizing the number 54 alone, as the **Character** for 54 would naturally appear to be performing his or her own **Action** if not performing someone else's.

The simple solution: imagine the **Character** holding a small vanity mirror instead of performing his or her normal **Action**. This is called a **Mirrored Number**.

If your **Mnemonic Character** for the number 20 is Barack Obama, you can memorize "2020" by picturing Obama looking at himself in a handheld mirror (perhaps combing his hair). This "looking in the mirror" **Action** is a **Shared Action**, or an **Action** performed by any **Mnemonic Character** to accommodate a special case.

If "looking in a mirror" is already assigned as one of your **Mnemonic Character's** native **Actions**, choose a different **Shared Action** to represent **Mirrored Numbers**; just be sure that it makes sense to you and that you can record and recall it instantaneously.

Negative Numbers

Negative Numbers (such as -22) come up fairly often. Whether referencing an accounting debt, Chicago's weather in the middle of February, or sports statistics, you need to be prepared to work these numbers into the framework of your preferred memorization methods.

Like **Mirrored Numbers**, you need to decide upon a way to recognize these types of numbers. This is called a **Negative Number Action**. What makes you think of **Negative Numbers**? You could imagine the **Journey's** first **Mnemonic Character** appearing upside down, or perhaps wearing pants on his or her head. It's really up to you, but an attribute (such as wearing a certain garment) is generally a better choice than a motion or gesture; movements are more likely to interfere with an **Action** the **Character** may need to perform.

The difference is subtle. While 4,521 would be represented by 45 (the **Character**) performing 21's **Action**, -4,521 would be 45 (the **Character**), with some sort of "negative number" indicator, performing 21's **Action**. This, too, is a sort of **Shared Action**.

When applying your **Negative Number Action** to **Single-Digit Mnemonic Clues** (such as in the case of -8), get creative; imagine how a bra or pair of sunglasses can perform such an **Action**.

Decimal Numbers

Decimal Numbers (numbers with a decimal place, such as 4.09) also occur frequently in the real world; considering currency alone, these come up nearly as often as integers. You should have already established a **Decimal Clue** when we covered decimals earlier in this book. However, using **Mnemonic Characters and Actions** presents a problem; previously, using only **Single-Digit Mnemonic Clues**, 4.5 would be represented by your **Single-Digit Mnemonic Clue** for 4, your **Decimal Clue**, and your **Single-Digit Mnemonic Clue** for 5. Now, if you were to use your **Mnemonic Character** for 45, there's no good way to "inject" your **Decimal Clue** into the **Scene**.

In such cases, revert back to using **Single-Digit Mnemonic Clues**. Like before, use your **Single-Digit Mnemonic Clue** for 4, your **Decimal Clue**, and your **Single-Digit Mnemonic Clue** for 5 to represent 4.5.

Here's a more complex example: 351.16. If this were a non-decimal number (35,116), you would cram as many digits as possible into the first **Step**—given what you know so far, this would mean 3511. Unfortunately, the decimal interrupts this; therefore, use your **Mnemonic Character** for 35 interacting with your **Single-Digit Mnemonic Clue** for 1, your **Decimal Clue**, and your **Mnemonic Character** for 16.

This example illustrates a straightforward rule: jam as many digits as possible into each **Step**, but think of **Decimal Clues** as disruptors you need to work around.

Take the number 1234 and consider how to store it using this rule when the decimal point shows up in different locations:

- 1234 – the Mnemonic Character for 12 performing 34's Action
- 1.234 – the Single-Digit Mnemonic Clue for 1, a Decimal Clue, and the Mnemonic Character for 23 interacting with the Single-Digit Mnemonic Clue for 4
- 12.34 – the Mnemonic Character for 12, a Decimal Clue, and the Mnemonic Character for 34
- 123.4 – the Mnemonic Character for 12 interacting with the Single-Digit Mnemonic Clue for 3, a Decimal Clue, and the Single-Digit Mnemonic Clue for 4

Using all three "special case" methods you just learned, describe the best way to memorize each of the following numbers:

1. -16
2. 4848
3. 1.6849
4. -12.28
5. -59.5

Answers:

1. Your Mnemonic Character for 16 performing your Negative Number Action

2. Your Mnemonic Character for 48 performing your Mirrored Number Action

3. Your Single-Digit Mnemonic Clue for 1, a Decimal Clue, and your Mnemonic Character for 68 performing 49's Action

4. Your Mnemonic Character for 12 performing your Negative Number Action, a Decimal Clue, and your Mnemonic Character for 28

5. Your Mnemonic Character for 59 performing your Negative Number Action, a Decimal Clue, and your Single-Digit Mnemonic Clue for 5

Creating Interactions Between Mnemonic Characters

You already know it's important to create **Transitions** between **Mnemonic Scenes** and the **Steps** of **Journeys**. Now you'll learn how **Mnemonic Characters** can get involved in the action.

Imagine this: Rocker Rod Stewart sits on a throne at the first **Step** of a **Journey**. He begins to disintegrate rapidly into a green cloud of smoke, which drifts off to the left. The smoke leads us to the second **Step**, where actor Gary Busey applies red lipstick. He kisses an envelope, folds it into a paper airplane, and throws it to the next **Step**, where it lands at the feet of our third **Character**. On and on it goes.

In this example, **Characters** (Rod Stewart, Gary Busey) perform other **Character's Actions** (sitting on a throne, applying lipstick); the smoke and the envelope/paper airplane are simply there to provide strong **Transitions** and interactions between the **Steps**. As you know by now, creating logical—if absurd—connections between **Steps** is vital, and involving **Characters** in these **Transitions** will help to strengthen the artificial memory.

Consider a **Contextual Journey**: I arrive at a hotel where I'm enrolled in a frequent customer rewards program. During check-in, I need to give the receptionist my customer account number, 26722235. My **Contextual Journey** takes place in the hotel itself and begins in the front lobby. There, Bob Saget (26) greets me, but instead of the blue blazer he often wore when hosting *America's Funniest Home Videos*, he wears a red cape and swings a sword at me (Gerard Butler's action, 72). I dodge the blade and sprawl upon the lobby's carpet; I can smell it, feel it, and even note minor details in the pattern.

When I look up, Saget walks away, heading toward the second **Step** in the **Journey**, which is occupied by blues legend B.B. King (22). King sits on a stool, next to which Saget dramatically thrusts his sword into the ground. The sword's handle sticks straight up in the air; I see it wobble for a moment.

B.B. King is visibly startled. Rather than playing his trusty guitar, Lucille (his native **Action**), B.B. points a large revolver at me (Clint Eastwood's **Action**, 35). This **Transition**—the interaction between Bob and B.B.—is useful for creating a flowing, cohesive narrative within the **Journey**; this will be drastically easier to remember than isolated **Characters** performing isolated tasks within isolated **Steps**.

Using a Single Step to Represent Five Digits

That's right. Five digits.

Right now, you can store four digits in a single **Step** (the first two digits represented by a **Mnemonic Character** and the last two coming from another **Mnemonic Character's Action**). Let's kick it up a notch and add a fifth and final digit.

To put this in perspective, five digits in a single **Step** means you can memorize a one-hundred-digit number in twenty **Steps**, which you should have at your immediate disposal; that's only two ten-**Step Journeys**, which, at this point, should be mere child's play. In fact, assuming you've developed at least 300 **Steps** in your **Mega-Journey**, you should have enough available storage to memorize a random 1,500 digit number.

The fifth and final digit will come from the initial **Mnemonic Vocabulary** you created in *Section 1* for **Single-Digit Mnemonic Clues**. There's nothing more to learn; simply stick one of these **Clues** into the end of a four-digit **Scene**.

Consider the number 20,961.

This number would be represented by the **Mnemonic Character** for 20 performing 96's **Action**, and interacting with or utilizing the **Single-Digit Mnemonic Clue** for 1. This **Scene** is easily fit into a single **Step**. How the **Scene** looks will depend on your **Mnemonic Characters** and their **Actions**, of course—for you, this could mean Barack Obama (20 = BO), driving a tank (96 = Norman Schwarzkopf's **Action**), while holding an oversized pencil in the air (pencil = 1)

Try one yourself: 11,092. Who is your 11? What is 09's **Action**? Picture 11 performing 09's **Action**. Then add your **Single-Digit Mnemonic Clue** for 2.

11, performing 09's **Action**, involving 2. It's that easy.

Consider how this affects **Step** usage; memorizing a seven-digit number, such as 8,154,291, can be accomplished in just two **Steps**: 81542 (a **Character**, **Action**, and **Single-Digit Mnemonic Clue**) and 91 (a **Character**). In fact, a nine-digit number like 918,257,432 could also be stored in two **Steps**: 91825 (a **Character**, **Action**, and **Single-Digit Mnemonic Clue**) and 7432 (a **Character** and **Action**).

Take a crack at this quick exercise. Think of the last car you were in; you're going to use it as an improvised two-**Step Journey**, where the front seat is the first **Step** and the rear seat is the second. Using this two-**Step Journey**, memorize the following number: 4,967,810,185.

You just memorized ten digits in two **Steps**.

A Quick Note on Standards

There's a lot to this method, so it's important to establish some rules to maintain order.

Fill Each Step Before Moving On

Let's take a six-digit number: 545,211. This number has more than five digits, so you'll need two **Journey Steps** to memorize it. You may think it makes sense to store this as 5452 (a **Character** and **Action**) and 11 (a **Character**), because storing it as 54521 (a **Character, Action**, and **Single-Digit Mnemonic Clue**) and 1 (a **Single-Digit Mnemonic Clue**) seems "wasteful."

Sure, it may feel strange to use an entire **Step** for a single digit, but I strongly recommend doing so. Stuff as many digits into each **Step** as possible (unless decimals are involved), even if it results in a seemingly-underutilized final **Step**. The space is not "wasted," and sticking with one standard method reduces confusion.

The only potential exception to this rule should be **Template Chunking** situations, which we'll discuss next.

Treat Chunks as Individual Numbers

Due to the nature of the human mind, we don't often think of a longer number as a single, continuous unit; rather, it's usually split into a few smaller, more manageable **Chunks** (example: 18002221222 becomes 1-800-222-1222).

Phone numbers, bank account numbers, and social security numbers are prime examples of **Template Chunks**; the **Template**, or the expected format of the numbers, is familiar and feels natural. Phone numbers fit into an *(nnn) nnn-nnnn* **Template**. Social security numbers fit into an *nnn-nn-nnnn* **Template**.

Out of an instinctive courtesy to others, people will usually **Chunk** continuous numbers when conveying them verbally. The speaker leaves a brief pause between the **Chunks** to allow the person recording the number to catch up.

In most cases, you should fill each **Step** with as many digits as possible, as you learned. However, once you're reasonably experienced with mnemonic techniques for memorizing numbers, you have the option of memorizing **Chunked** numbers in **Chunks**.

> *Tip*: *You also have the option of creating a* **Shared Clue** *or* **Action** *for* **Chunked** *numbers, like you did for* **Negative** *or* **Mirrored** *numbers.*

If you do indeed decide to **Chunk** memorized numbers, the idea is simple: you can split a number such that each **Chunk** fills a **Step**. With a phone number, the first **Chunk** (three-digit area code) could be broken up so the first two digits are a **Mnemonic Character** and the third digit is a **Single-Digit Mnemonic Clue**; these would all occupy a single **Step**. The same goes for the next three digits (the second **Step**). In the third and final **Step**, you'd translate the remaining four digits into a **Mnemonic Character** (first two digits) and an **Action** (final two digits).

Practice this by memorizing the following **Chunked** information using one **Step** per **Chunk**. You should, of course, create vivid, clear **Mnemonic Scenes** that leave very little room for interpretation.

1. 38-1921
2. 655-12-388
3. 48929-2893

You should have memorized the above information in the following manner:

1. 38 (Character); 19 (Character), 21 (Action) : [Two Steps]
2. 65 (Character), 5 (Single-Digit Clue); 12 (Character); 38 (Character), 8 (Single-Digit Clue) : [Three Steps]
3. 48 (Character), 92 (Action), 9 (Single-Digit Clue); 28 (Character), 93 (Action) : [Two Steps]

Since none of the **Chunks** exceeded five digits (your upper limit for storing information in a single **Step**), you shouldn't have had to split any individual **Chunk**. You would be hard pressed to find **Chunked** information containing any single **Chunk** that exceeds five digits; the human mind doesn't like to deal with such long, uninterrupted strings of digits, and so numerical formats (**Templates**) have evolved to avoid them.

Extended Character/Action Methods

If you research **Character**-based **Mnemonic** methods, you may find certain permutations in which each **Character** is associated with an object as well as an **Action**. This lets you store six digits in a single **Journey Step**.

This practice can be summed up in three words: not worth it.

For the sake of practicality and mitigating complexity, we will skip this addition. Unless you're dedicating yourself wholly to **Memory Development** for the sake of competition, the "up front" work involved in becoming accustomed to this system far outweighs any benefits it produces. To put it in perspective, this would mean that for each **Mnemonic Character**, you would have to decide upon, associate, and memorize not just a unique **Action**, but also an **Object**; Charlie Brown (**Character**), attempting to kick a football (**Action**), wearing a yellow shirt with a black stripe (**Object**). Chuck Norris (**Character**) performing a flying kick (**Action**) while wearing a cowboy hat (**Object**). The number 123456 would be represented by 12's **Character** performing 34's **Action** while interacting with 56's **Object**. As great as that sounds, it's a lot to piece together in a high-pressure moment.

For most people, five digits per **Step** is the upper threshold of manageable complexity, and trying to cram more information in leads to diminishing returns. That said, if you wish to introduce **Objects** (or anything else) into your personal interpretation of the **Mnemonic Characters and Actions Method**, you're certainly free to do so.

Behold the Power

Using a combination of **Contextual Journeys**, **Meta-Information**, and your newfound ability to jam more information into a single **Journey Step**, memory storage will slowly become easier with practice.

You're learning this not to hoard information, but rather to improve the process of memorizing information you encounter naturally. Just because you can impress your nerdy neighbor by memorizing Pi to the thousandth digit doesn't mean you should. The real victory here is in practical applications. You're used to scrambling to write things down, since storing complex information in your mind was never an option before. With time, you'll be more self-reliant and less often tethered to third-party tools. As it becomes more natural to trust your mind, you'll do so more often. With practice, your imagination will grow. With a stronger imagination, your confidence will grow. With more confidence, you'll feel comfortable using these methods more often, and the cycle will feed itself. You'll come off drastically more capable, and reliable, and in many ways, you *will* be drastically more capable, and reliable.

Quick Review

1. To use a single **Step** to store five digits, simply use a **Character/Action Combination**, and then add a **Single-Digit Mnemonic Clue** to the **Scene**.

2. To handle **Decimal Numbers** (example: 91.22), **Negative Numbers** (example: -119), and **Mirrored Numbers** (example: 6767), construct a standard **Shared Action** or **Clue** for each and use it consistently each time you encounter that type of number.

3. When a number is **Chunked** (especially when it conforms to a recognizable format or **Template**, such as a phone number), it's acceptable to use one **Journey Step** per **Chunk**. Otherwise, fill each **Step** with as many digits as possible (up to five, your maximum).

Lesson 4: Memorizing People (Names and Faces)

> *"I KNOW THAT DUDE!"*
> —SPICOLI, FAST TIMES AT RIDGEMONT HIGH

How many times have you uttered Spicoli's iconic exclamation and yet been unable to match a name to said dude's face? As you may imagine, there's a method that makes this common task much easier.

In *How to Win Friends and Influence People*, Dale Carnegie wrote, "I once interviewed [Postmaster General and chairman of the Democratic National Committee] Jim Farley...he asked me what I thought was the reason for his success. I replied: 'I understand you can call ten thousand people by their first names.' 'No. You are wrong,' he said, 'I can call *fifty* thousand people by their first names.'"

Exaggerated or not (who truly knows fifty thousand people?), this is absolutely achievable. But how do you even begin to work toward such an astounding level of memorization prowess?

The World is Full of Incomplete Solutions

Name-to-face memorization may be discussed more in our culture than any other topic found in this book. Since it's an important skill for businesspeople, salespeople, administrative assistants, and so on, hundreds—if not thousands—have profited from sharing their secrets and tips. However, in years of research, I've failed to find a single name-to-face memorization method that both works well and covers a wide range of reasonable, practical cases.

Many years ago, at a former job, I noticed a CD audio course sitting on a shelf in a break area. I don't recall the exact title, but it promised to teach the listener to categorically and precisely remember names. After walking past it for several weeks, curiosity got the best of me, and I listened to the entire course during my commute.

I was expecting to have my mind blown by some sort of ingenious technique for filing away distinct personal details in a sophisticated mental database. Instead, the course claimed the best way to memorize a name is to pick a funny attribute about the person, and then come up with a catchy name followed by a trailing rhyme (even if the rhyme doesn't make sense). For example, if you met Bob, who has big ears, you would say to yourself, "Big Ear Bob with the corn on the cob."

The course—which, as it turned out, was sold at a shockingly high price—didn't even touch on last names or foreign names. Though it did tap into the basic concept of mnemonics and the need to apply a fundamental level of creativity to memorization endeavors, it was a "waste of time like a mic for a mime."

Very few experts agree about the best way to memorize names and faces. Though many popular methods involve variations of the ideas explored here, most are largely incomplete; as with the CD course found at my former job, surnames and difficult or foreign names are rarely discussed. This failure maximizes the "wow" factor, and one walks away feeling successful; that is, until he or she attempts to use these methods in a practical context. For most Westerners, the "Bobs" and "Janes" are easy to remember; the "Yasemins," "Hui Zhongs," and "Marinelas" are not.

The EFL Method

You'll now learn to memorize names and faces using a technique I call the **EFL** (**E**xaggerate, **F**irst Name Location, **L**ast Name Clue) **Method**.

Let's walk through it using a fictional name: Ashley McCann.

1. **E: Exaggerate.** Look at the individual you just met. Note distinguishing characteristics—large nose, pronounced brow, pointy ears, etc.—and exaggerate them in your mind. Picture the person becoming a caricature before your eyes. Imagine that our example, Ashley McCann, has a somewhat pronounced overbite; so, picture Ashley with an extreme, cartoonish overbite.

2. **F: First Name Location.** Take the first name and think of a location that reminds you of someone you already know who shares this same name. Picture Ashley McCann standing in this location. Be sure to include the exaggerated physical features mentioned above. For many people, the name Ashley should create an instant connection to a place (for me, it is my friend

Vinnie's old car; I recall talking to his ex-girlfriend Ashley in his car years ago).

3. **L: Last Name Clue.** Finally, add **Mnemonic Clues** about the person's last name to the **Scene**. Make sure you can decipher these later. I'd imagine Ashley McCann holding a green can in her lap. The can has a white four-leaf clover painted on it (Irish can = McCann). As you did with the **Memorization of Unfamiliar Entities**, liven up the image with distinct and quirky visuals. I picture Ashley McCann—with a giant overbite—in my friend Vinnie's car, eating glowing potatoes out of the can. The potatoes further reinforce the "Irishness" of the can. Ashley is eating messily, and the potatoes are spilling all over her. Just like any other **Mnemonic Scene**, adding humor and absurdity will help to solidify the image.

Many people ask why exaggeration is so important, and in order to understand why, you must first consider a principle known as the **Caricature Effect**. You most likely think of caricature as the comical, exaggerated portraits found at carnivals, fairs, and amusement parks, but there's more to them than this. Facial recognition is a core function of the mind; research performed by psychologist Chiara Turati shows that even newborns appear to possess rudimentary facial recognition skills. Especially when we're young, caricature-like exaggeration sits at the heart of our ability to remember facial features and tell individuals apart from one another. In the modern age, these concepts (under the moniker **Caricature Effect**) are used to drive facial recognition software. This phenomenon can be harnessed to your advantage; exaggerating a face in your mind establishes a more solid, well-rooted mental image of that face.

Let's discuss some common problems that people experience when implementing the **EFL Method**.

Common Problems and Solutions

E: Exaggerate. What if you have trouble identifying and exaggerating distinct characteristics? What if someone doesn't seem to have an outstanding feature? No overbite, no big ears?

The fact is, everyone has *some* characteristic that stands out, whether negative or positive; try to imagine what feature the person may be self-conscious about, or how you'd describe the individual to someone else. Exaggerate whatever you can, and don't be subtle; give them pointy elf ears, a thick, pronounced, caterpillar-like "uni-brow," or an elongated nose, like Steve Martin's in the film *Roxanne*.

Even if the person is incredibly good looking, take the exaggeration in a different direction; make their teeth sparkle and their skin glow.

It's vital that you locate and exploit *some* aspect of their look, as skipping this step can negatively impact the quality of the memory in a drastic way; it essentially stops the **EFL Method** from working.

F: First Name Location. What if you experience difficulty matching first names to people you know (and their respective places)? It's easy if you meet a Mary and can imagine her at your Aunt Mary's house, but what if you've never met a Mary before this one?

If you come upon a first name that doesn't conjure up any personal associations for you, try celebrities, and transport the person you've met to a setting that instantly reminds you of the celebrity (perhaps a memorable scene from a film or television show). If you met someone named Owen, and Owen reminds you of actor Owen Wilson as his character in *Zoolander*, you could imagine that person strutting down a runway.

When it comes to foreign first names, like the three I mentioned (Yasemin, Hui Zhong and Marinela), it will probably be difficult to find a suitable first name location. These names (which are common Turkish, Chinese, and Romanian names, respectively) may necessitate using a **Clue** about the individual's first name instead of a first name location.

Imagine that you met Bulgarian scientist/author Klara Obretenova and you have never met a Klara or Clara before, and so the first name location option is out. In this case, you can instead create a **Clue** about the name at the place where you first met her. Form a **Clue** about the name (Klara) just as you do for last names; perhaps it could be a clear piece of glass (or some other reference to clarity). If you only saw her name and photo in an article, imagine the **Clue** in the room you were in when you saw the article; the association will be stronger than you may think.

You may ask, "What if I meet three or four people named Tom?" There's no reason they can't all share your "Tom" location; they'll each interact with different last name **Clues**, so their respective **Scenes** should be very different. If you like, differentiate them further by using different spaces within your "Tom" location; if your "Tom" location is a home or other building, you can store the different Toms you meet (and their respective **Scenes**) in the different rooms or areas of your "Tom" location.

L: Last Name Clue. What if you have trouble creating **Clues** about last names? There is no sure solution except to "think outside the box."

Lassiter can translate to "laughs at her," Donovan can translate to "donut on a van," and Kasparov can translate to "cat spears Hof" (as in "a feline stabbing David Hasslehoff"). With time and practice (and your increasingly flexible imagination), these types of images will come to you faster.

If you use a first name **Clue**, ensure you don't confuse the first and last names by using a **Linear Scene**.

Let's Practice

Let's work through an example together: James Lyons.

First, exaggerate something about James. Perhaps he has crooked teeth and a receding hairline. Imagine bright lights reflecting obnoxiously off of his shiny forehead, and a mouth full of missing teeth like a 1970s NHL forward (**Exaggerate**).

Now, where does the name "James" take you? Follow the first lead your mind puts forward. Do you have a friend or relative named James? If so, picture his home, office, or whatever location you instinctively associate with him. Seeing this place in your mind should instantly bring the name "James" to mind, so it shouldn't be a shared location that could just as easily remind you of other people (**First Name Location**).

Finally, imagine James Lyons in this place (be sure to include the shiny forehead and missing teeth), sitting on a throne, looking cocky and regal. Now, imagine him stroking the manes of two pet lions, which are lazily stretched out on either side of him.

When you see Mr. Lyons next, you'll imagine your "James" location, and know his first name is James. Then, imagining the pet lions, you'll quickly piece together that his last name sounds like "lions."

This <u>Sounds</u> Easy, But Do You Really Know a John Smith?

Many last names instantly provide colorful **Mnemonic Clues**, such as Frank Underwood (trapped under a log), Annie Fisher (fishing pole), or Dale Lipshchitz (a lip that...never mind). Not every name is so easy to picture, however; some last names are downright tricky.

By now, you have flexed your creative muscles quite a bit, so you should be somewhat comfortable breaking complex names down into familiar, manageable images. To illustrate this point, I asked a few people to suggest the most difficult (real) surnames they've come across. Some submissions are listed here. The last name **Clues** I would personally use to memorize them are included to provide examples of how these could be broken down. Before reading my solutions, try to work them out on your own.

The names: Szczyporski, Bhatnagar, Balasubramaniam.

My Last Name Clues:

Szczyporski: This Polish name is pronounced, "suh-POOR-ski." I'd picture the individual skiing, using two giant "sporks" in place of ski poles. To reinforce the memory, I would make the sporks hot pink. When I picture the **Scene**, I'll think, "sporks...ski?" and the name will easily come to me.

Bhatnagar: Indian last names can be tricky for Westerners. This name would immediately make me think of a "bat in a car." I'd imagine this person holding a toy car (about the size of a brick), with (real) bat wings poking out from the side windows, indicating that a live bat is stuck inside. The wings of the panicked, trapped mammal flap wildly, and Bhatnagar's arms are extended, holding the shaking contraption as far away from his or her face as possible.

Speaking of Indian names, behold my favorite submission...

Balasubramaniam: For this name—pronounced "ball-a-sub-RAMIN-yom"—a vague **Clue** may not help with pronouncing it correctly, so it must be broken down carefully and literally.

I imagine a hard ball of dry Ramen noodles making SONAR-like audio emissions. This individual is holding the ball, rubbing his tummy, and grinning ear to ear. Deciphering the **Scene** later, I'd say, "It's a...ball of Ramen. SONAR? Submarine? Ball of Submarine Ramen? That sounds a bit familiar. Why is the person holding his stomach and smiling? Tasty? Delicious? No, that's not it. What else would one say? Yummy? Yum? Ball of Sub Ramen...Yum?"

These **Clues** may not work for you, but something will, and you'll find your own unique style only through practice.

Try memorizing a few name/face pairs. Go online and find a series of unfamiliar individuals, making sure both their faces and names are displayed. This could be a company's board of directors, a bunch of musicians, an unfamiliar sports team, or a distant relative's Facebook friends. Try to stick with groups within your country, as you'll need to practice with simpler, more familiar names before attempting more difficult ones.

Remember: notice and exaggerate their most prominent features. Transport each individual to a location that his or her first name brings to mind, and leave the **Scenes** littered with **Mnemonic Clues** about their last names. Shut your eyes and make each **Scene** as vivid as possible. What do you hear? What do you smell?

How did that exercise go? Were your attempts to use this method successful? If not, figure out what went wrong and try again. Did you use weak last name **Clues**? Was it difficult for you to exaggerate physical attributes?

This lesson began with an excerpt from Dale Carnegie's classic book, so it seems appropriate to end with one.

"The average person is more interested in his or her own name than in all the other names on earth put together. Remember that name and call it easily, and you have paid a subtle and very effective compliment. But forget it or misspell it, and you have placed yourself at a sharp disadvantage."

Quick Review

1. The best way to memorize someone's name and associate it with his or her face is the **EFL (Exaggerate, First Name Location, Last Name Clue) Method**. First, exaggerate some of the individual's prominent physical features, and then imagine them in a setting that reminds you of their first name (usually the home of someone you know with the same first name). Finally, in this imagined setting, leave yourself a **Mnemonic Clue** (or

series of **Mnemonic Clues**) you can later decipher to remember the individual's last name.

Review and Development: Section 4

Doesn't time fly when you're having fun? In this section, you expanded your use of the **Journey Method**, developed a dynamic **Mnemonic Character Library** for the numbers 00 through 99, learned to store up to five numerical digits in a single **Step**, and discovered a powerful method for remembering names and faces.

Review

Let's take a moment and review what you learned in *Section 4: Advanced Memory Development*.

1. **Take the Journey to the Next Level**: Earlier in this book, you learned how to create and use **Journeys** to store information. Next, you must build on your **Mega-Journey** (collection of individual **Journeys** that link together through **Transitions**) for practical use in daily life.

2. **Mnemonic Character Library**: By developing a **Mnemonic Character Library**, you can use a single **Journey Step** to store two, three, four, or even five digits. This **Mnemonic Character Library** should consist of one hundred **Mnemonic Characters** representing the numbers 00 through 99, and each **Character** should have a unique **Action** associated with it.

3. **How to Choose Mnemonic Characters**: When building a **Mnemonic Character Library**, choose **Characters** based on the following hierarchy: 1.) Individuals you know personally, and who remind you of a specific number (ideal); 2.) Celebrities or

characters from fiction who remind you of a specific number (when necessary); and finally, 3.) Celebrities or characters from fiction whose initials translate to a number using a translation table (last resort).

4. **One Step - Two Digits**: To store two digits in a single **Step**, imagine the appropriate **Mnemonic Character** performing his or her own unique **Action**.

5. **One Step - Three Digits**: To store three digits in a single **Step**, imagine a **Mnemonic Character** that represents the first two digits, and then a **Single-Digit Mnemonic Clue** (0 through 9) to represent the final digit. Imagine the **Mnemonic Character** holding, using, or interacting with the **Clue**.

6. **One Step - Four Digits**: To store four digits in a single **Step**, imagine a **Mnemonic Character** (representing the first two digits) performing the unique **Action** of another **Character** (representing the remaining two digits). Whenever a **Mnemonic Character** performs the **Action** of another, the **Character** itself should always be used to represent the first two digits, and the **Action** of the second **Character** should be used to represent the latter two.

7. **One Step - Five Digits**: To use a single Step to store five digits, simply use a **Character/Action** Combination, and then add a **Single-Digit Mnemonic Clue** to the **Scene**.

8. To handle **Decimal Numbers** (example: 91.22), **Negative Numbers** (example: -119), and **Mirrored Numbers** (example: 6767), construct a standard **Shared Action** or **Clue** for each and use it consistently each time you encounter that type of number.

9. **Filling Each Step**: When a number is **Chunked** (especially when it conforms to a recognizable format or **Template**, such as a

phone number), it's acceptable to use one **Journey Step** per **Chunk**. Otherwise, fill each **Step** with as many digits as possible (up to five, your maximum).

10. **Remembering Names and Faces**: The best way to memorize someone's name and associate it with his or her face is the **EFL (Exaggerate, First Name Location, Last Name Clue) Method**. First, exaggerate some of the individual's prominent physical features, and then imagine them in a setting that reminds you of their first name (usually the home of someone you know with the same first name). Finally, in this imagined setting, leave yourself a **Mnemonic Clue** (or series of **Mnemonic Clues**) you can later decipher to remember the individual's last name.

Development

You'll spend a minimum of seven days developing the skills you learned in *Section 4*.

At this point, you've worked your way through three sections' worth of development exercises. You may be asking yourself, "Is all this practice really necessary?" You may have absolutely no interest in memorizing the Presidents of the United States or the Periodic Table of Elements (which you'll do soon); in fact, you may downright despise history or chemistry.

Keep in mind that these are exercises in the truest sense of the word. Like physical exercises, they aren't always fun, and you may prefer to spend your time doing something different; however, they're a means by which to condition your mind, strengthen your skills, and pursue expertise. As

Albert Einstein said, "the only source of knowledge is experience." Gaining experience is not always easy, and requires discipline, dedication, and maturity; the value is in the long-term reward.

Days 1 - 2

During *Day 1*, quickly review the entire section to make sure you're comfortable with the material. If any topic seems confusing, spend extra time with it.

Throughout *Days 1* and *2*, work on perfecting your personal **Mnemonic Character Library**. You should have already selected **Characters** to represent each number from 00 to 99, and you should be able to recite your entire list in under four minutes. During these days, review it as often as possible; picture each **Character** and imagine his or her unique **Action**.

If you're having a particularly difficult time remembering certain **Characters**, put a mark next to their names and ask yourself if there might be better choices for these numbers; clearly, they're not as memorable as they need to be. These associations need to be immediate. With practice, "translation" will no longer be necessary; you should be able to see the number 4207 and instantly store it as something like "Danny Bonaduce popping out of a garbage can." Make any final changes to the list.

Remembering what you learned in *Learning and Revisitation Rhythms*, review the list several times (including just before bed each night), and quiz yourself often. Practice memorizing numbers you encounter throughout the day.

By the end of *Day 2*, you should be able to recite your list of **Mnemonic Characters** in under three and a half minutes. If you can't, stop here and keep practicing until you can. Don't cheat and skip ahead—you'll only be cheating yourself.

Day 3

Review your **Mnemonic Character** list as soon as possible after waking on *Day 3*.

The focus of *Day 3* is going to be an exercise. Memorize the following numbers at your own pace, using **Contextual Journeys** and your newly developed **Mnemonic Character/Action Library**. Keep in mind everything you learned about **Mirrored, Decimal,** and **Negative Numbers, Chunking,** and how to use **Single-Digit Mnemonic Clues** to help store three- or five-digit numbers.

- 8.537: The number (in millions) of NYC residents (according to a 2016 census)
- 713: The number of minutes of daylight on March 14, 2001
- (800) 222-1222: The U.S. Poison Control hotline (a good number to have handy)
- 466.164: The standard frequency (in hertz) of the musical note, A#
- 0, 1, 1, 2, 3, 5, 8, 13, 21, 34: The first ten numbers in the Fibonacci sequence
- 2,075: The melting point (in degrees Celsius) of boron under normal conditions
- -114: The freezing point (in degrees Celsius) of pure ethanol under normal conditions

- 07/20/1969; 20:17: The date and time of the first lunar landing (UTC)
- 649,740: The odds (649,740 to 1) of getting a royal flush in a game of poker
- 1,409,517,397: The population of China (according to a 2017 census)
- 5,778: The temperature (in Kelvin) of the surface of the sun
- 238,855: The average distance (in miles) from the earth to the moon
- 453.59237: The number of grams in a pound

Day 4

By now, all your **Mnemonic Characters** (and their distinct **Actions**) should be immediately available for at-will recall, so you can move on to other skills.

Spend at least an hour reciting your current **Mega-Journey** and each **Journey's** individual **Steps** as quickly as you can. Do this aloud if your surroundings permit it. You should be able to stop at any point during your recital, and—with only a moment or two of thought—become aware of exactly what **Step** you're on (i.e., **Step** 194, 61, or 211). This is achieved through familiarity with nearby **Steps** that represent the beginnings of smaller individual **Journeys** (10, 20, 50, 100...1000). Of course, this assumes that you complied with the suggested standard of ten **Steps** for each **Journey**.

If you still need help recalling your **Mega-Journey**, reference the spreadsheet you made. Print it out or send it to your smartphone if you have one that can display spreadsheets. Go over it whenever possible, taking special care to review it a few times each night immediately before you go to sleep. Continue to review your **Mega-Journey** even after you feel you've mastered it.

Day 5

You'll spend *Day 5* working on a wide range of skills.

First, spend at least an hour combining your **Entity Memorization** and **Association** skills with your newfound **Mnemonic Character** abilities. For example, you can arbitrarily create a name, assign an arbitrary phone number to this fictional person, and then quiz yourself after ten such combinations.

You're also going to work on memorizing names and faces by finding a high school yearbook full of strangers (a spouse's, friend's, or even one from your local library) and memorizing the names and faces of the entire faculty. Your memorization should work in two directions, meaning you should be able to imagine their faces after seeing only their names and recall their names after seeing only their faces.

Begin slowly and work your way toward creating an immediate mental record. Once mastered, this skill allows you to instantly memorize the names and faces of an entire group of people after only briefly meeting each individual. The applications of this skill are numerous, and its usefulness can't be overstated.

Lastly, now that you're comfortable with your **Mega-Journey**, you'll use it to memorize one or two "impressive" things (often requiring a good deal of **Meta-Information**). Some suggestions (which you can easily find on the web):

- A list of every song ever recorded by a band you don't know very well. Include the album name, year, and record label
- Pi, to the 100th digit
- Every front-page top headline from last year's New York Times
- Every single actor in your favorite movie, down to the least important characters
- The birthdays of a few of your friends, converted to UNIX timestamps (a specific type of computer-readable format). Convert the dates at EPOCHCONVERTER.COM

If the things you choose to memorize take more than a day, feel free to extend this exercise a bit. It's far more important to memorize correctly than quickly; speed will come with time.

Days 6 - 7

During your last days of development, you'll journey back to elementary school to tackle some things you were probably supposed to learn but never did. This may very well take you more than two days; as usual, you're encouraged to take as long as you need.

You're going to memorize two lists that include intense, difficult **Meta-Information** (both text-based and numerical).

First, tackle the Presidents of the United States, in order, including their years in office. How you approach this is up to you; you have all the tools you need, and you're free to use these tools to memorize this information in a way that seems natural to you. For instance, you may want to begin each **Mnemonic Scene** with a **Clue** about the President's last name (Monroe = actress Marilyn Monroe; Pierce = actor Pierce Bronson), interacting with (or exhibiting the **Action** of) your **Mnemonic**

Character for the last two digits of their inaugural year. "John Tyler, 1841" could be represented by Aerosmith singer Steven Tyler (name **Clue**) performing 41's (the year **Clue's**) **Action** in the **Journey's** tenth **Step**; if necessary, work a **Clue** in about the President's first name (John).

As there are no gaps between presidents, you only need to memorize their inauguration years; you can determine the year of each president's departure from the inauguration year of his successor. Additionally, it's relatively easy to determine the century of a President's service, so you probably only need to memorize the last two digits of the inauguration year. For example, if James Buchanan's year **Clue** is "57," you can determine from context that this refers to 1857, and then can determine that his presidency ended in 1861, because that's when his successor (Lincoln) was sworn in.

1. George Washington, 1789-1797
2. John Adams, 1797-1801
3. Thomas Jefferson, 1801-1809
4. James Madison, 1809-1817
5. James Monroe, 1817-1825
6. John Quincy Adams, 1825-1829
7. Andrew Jackson, 1829-1837
8. Martin Van Buren, 1837-1841
9. William Henry Harrison, 1841
10. John Tyler, 1841-1845
11. James Knox Polk, 1845-1849
12. Zachary Taylor, 1849-1850
13. Millard Fillmore, 1850-1853
14. Franklin Pierce, 1853-1857
15. James Buchanan, 1857-1861
16. Abraham Lincoln, 1861-1865

17. Andrew Johnson, 1865-1869
18. Ulysses S. Grant, 1869-1877
19. Rutherford B. Hayes, 1877-1881
20. James Abram Garfield, 1881
21. Chester Alan Arthur, 1881-1885
22. Grover Cleveland, 1885-1889
23. Benjamin Harrison, 1889-1893
24. Grover Cleveland, 1893-1897
25. William McKinley, 1897-1901
26. Theodore Roosevelt, 1901-1909
27. William Howard Taft, 1909-1913
28. Woodrow Wilson, 1913-1921
29. Warren Harding, 1921-1923
30. Calvin Coolidge, 1923-1929
31. Herbert Hoover, 1929-1933
32. Franklin Delano Roosevelt, 1933-1945
33. Harry S. Truman, 1945-1953
34. Dwight Eisenhower 1953-1961
35. John Fitzgerald Kennedy, 1961-1963
36. Lyndon Johnson, 1963-1969
37. Richard Milhous Nixon, 1969-1974
38. Gerald Ford, 1974-1977
39. James Carter, Jr., 1977-1981
40. Ronald Reagan, 1981-1989
41. George H. Bush, 1989-1993
42. William Jefferson Clinton, 1993-2001
43. George Walker Bush, 2001-2009
44. Barack Obama, 2009-2017
45. Donald Trump, 2017-

When you're finished, not only will you be able to list the presidents and their years in office, you'll be able to quickly tell who served before and after each.

Next, it's time for a more daunting challenge. You'll memorize the Periodic Table of Elements (the atomic number, atomic weight, name, and symbol of each element). Don't just dive in; come up with a plan first. What will be your **Core Information**? How will you remember all the included **Meta-Information**?

Though you're free to approach this however you like, I'll outline one possible method in case you need inspiration.

If you think you can figure out which **Step** you're on relatively quickly, you can use the **Step** number to represent each element's atomic number, since they start at 1 and continue in order. If you'd like to store that information, however, you can do so using **Mnemonic Characters** for two-digit numbers or **Mnemonic Characters** coupled with **Single-Digit Mnemonic Clues** for three-digit numbers. This number can be followed by a name **Clue** (for instance, Hydrogen could be represented by a hydra or hydrant and Selenium could be Celine Dion). This will be your **Core Information**. The *atomic weight* could come next, followed by the *symbol*.

As a bit of a shortcut, you could skip the symbol if it's simply the first two letters of the element's name (e.g., Lithium/Li). Otherwise, use **Letter Clues** to recall them if they're either single-letter symbols (e.g., Fluorine/F), or two letters that stray from the first actual letters of the name (e.g. Magnesium/Mg). In other words, consider the first two letters of the name to be the default symbol, and only bother to store information if the default doesn't apply.

Using this system, hydrogen could be represented by the following **Scene**: your **Mnemonic Character** for 01 being eaten by a hydra, and then the number 1.0079, followed by a **Letter Clue** for H ("H" isn't the exact first two letters of Hydrogen—"Hy"—so we need to encode it separately). Once that's stored in a **Mnemonic Scene**, utilize a creative **Transition** to go on to the next **Step**.

At this stage of **Memory Development**, most people take far more than a day to store this much information. As usual, please feel free to take your time and work on this exercise for an additional day or two. However, it shouldn't take you more than five days of reasonably dedicated study; if it does, you may want to reassess the way you're trying to memorize it.

Atomic #	Atomic Weight	Name	Symbol
1	1.0079	Hydrogen	H
2	4.0026	Helium	He
3	6.941	Lithium	Li
4	9.0122	Beryllium	Be
5	10.811	Boron	B
6	12.0107	Carbon	C
7	14.0067	Nitrogen	N
8	15.9994	Oxygen	O
9	18.9984	Fluorine	F

10	20.1797	Neon	Ne
11	22.9897	Sodium	Na
12	24.305	Magnesium	Mg
13	26.9815	Aluminum	Al
14	28.0855	Silicon	Si
15	30.9738	Phosphorus	P
16	32.065	Sulfur	S
17	35.453	Chlorine	Cl
18	39.948	Argon	Ar
19	39.0983	Potassium	K
20	40.078	Calcium	Ca
21	44.9559	Scandium	Sc
22	47.867	Titanium	Ti
23	50.9415	Vanadium	V
24	51.9961	Chromium	Cr
25	54.938	Manganese	Mn
26	55.845	Iron	Fe
27	58.9332	Cobalt	Co

28	58.6934	Nickel	Ni
29	63.546	Copper	Cu
30	65.39	Zinc	Zn
31	69.723	Gallium	Ga
32	72.64	Germanium	Ge
33	74.9216	Arsenic	As
34	78.96	Selenium	Se
35	79.904	Bromine	Br
36	83.8	Krypton	Kr
37	85.4678	Rubidium	Rb
38	87.62	Strontium	Sr
39	88.9059	Yttrium	Y
40	91.224	Zirconium	Zr
41	92.9064	Niobium	Nb
42	95.94	Molybdenum	Mo
43	98	Technetium	Tc
44	101.07	Ruthenium	Ru
45	102.9055	Rhodium	Rh

46	106.42	Palladium	Pd
47	107.8682	Silver	Ag
48	112.411	Cadmium	Cd
49	114.818	Indium	In
50	118.71	Tin	Sn
51	121.76	Antimony	Sb
52	127.6	Tellurium	Te
53	126.9045	Iodine	I
54	131.293	Xenon	Xe
55	132.9055	Cesium	Cs
56	137.327	Barium	Ba
57	138.9055	Lanthanum	La
58	140.116	Cerium	Ce
59	140.9077	Praseodymium	Pr
60	144.24	Neodymium	Nd
61	145	Promethium	Pm
62	150.36	Samarium	Sm
63	151.964	Europium	Eu

64	157.25	Gadolinium	Gd
65	158.9253	Terbium	Tb
66	162.5	Dysprosium	Dy
67	164.9303	Holmium	Ho
68	167.259	Erbium	Er
69	168.9342	Thulium	Tm
70	173.04	Ytterbium	Yb
71	174.967	Lutetium	Lu
72	178.49	Hafnium	Hf
73	180.9479	Tantalum	Ta
74	183.84	Tungsten	W
75	186.207	Rhenium	Re
76	190.23	Osmium	Os
77	192.217	Iridium	Ir
78	195.078	Platinum	Pt
79	196.9665	Gold	Au
80	200.59	Mercury	Hg
81	204.3833	Thallium	Tl

82	207.2	Lead	Pb
83	208.9804	Bismuth	Bi
84	209	Polonium	Po
85	210	Astatine	At
86	222	Radon	Rn
87	223	Francium	Fr
88	226	Radium	Ra
89	227	Actinium	Ac
90	232.0381	Thorium	Th
91	231.0359	Protactinium	Pa
92	238.0289	Uranium	U
93	237	Neptunium	Np
94	244	Plutonium	Pu
95	243	Americium	Am
96	247	Curium	Cm
97	247	Berkelium	Bk
98	251	Californium	Cf
99	252	Einsteinium	Es

100	257	Fermium	Fm
101	258	Mendelevium	Md
102	259	Nobelium	No
103	262	Lawrencium	Lr
104	261	Rutherfordium	Rf
105	262	Dubnium	Db
106	266	Seaborgium	Sg
107	264	Bohrium	Bh
108	277	Hassium	Hs
109	268	Meitnerium	Mt

The Never-Ending Journey

Get ready for an M. Knight Shyamalan-style twist: you're going to add five ten-**Step Journeys** to your **Mega-Journey** every week for the rest of your life. This may seem daunting now, but it isn't so bad if you truly think about it; even if you've barely traveled beyond the confines of your hometown—unless you're reading this inside an iron lung or hypoallergenic bubble—you've likely been to thousands upon thousands of unique places.

Put a recurring reminder in your calendar to add five ten-**Step Journeys** to your **Mega-Journey** each week. Perhaps you can schedule this for a time during your workweek that tends to be a bit slow. (What do your Thursdays at noon look like?) Perhaps you can do it before you go to sleep on Sunday night, or even while commercials play during your favorite TV show.

Setting aside a specific time doesn't mean you should work on your **Mega-Journey** only during that time. With experience, you'll become more cognizant of your **Mega-Journey** in general. If you happen to think of (or physically stumble upon) a good **Journey** throughout the week, write it down.

Once you've been working with the **Journey Method** for a while, you'll become aware of the great many places you've seen, and you'll be amazed at how well you can recall them. Many experienced mnemonists can record the intricacies of a building's interior in great detail and use it as a **Journey** for years after only a single visit to the physical location.

At this point, you've developed your memory far beyond the capabilities of the average person. Next, in *Bonus Material—Extreme Memory Development*, you'll go even further, taking these skills to a level that will seem to border on the supernatural.

Section 5: Bonus Material—Extreme Memory Development

This is where I challenge your very perception of human limitations. Where the obsessed leave the hobbyists behind. Where you cross the line from the practical into the incredible.

Section 5 seeks to accomplish three tasks.

First, you're going to learn a few tips and tricks reserved for experienced **Journey** architects. You'll learn how to make sure you're not losing your place within your **Journeys**, as well as ways to become considerably more confident about the accuracy of any important numerical information you memorize.

Second, you're going to learn how to index your entire life from this day forward so you can always pinpoint the details and timeline of a specific memory. It's prohibitively difficult and relatively impractical to do so, but if you love challenging yourself and improving your abilities, you'll learn how.

Lastly, you'll learn about memory care and some of the science behind this strange gift. We'll discuss sleep and nutrition, and how these factors affect memory.

Let's get started.

Lesson 1: Additional Numerical Mnemonic Skills

> *"THE TWO OFFICES OF MEMORY ARE COLLECTION AND DISTRIBUTION."*
> —SAMUEL JOHNSON, AUTHOR

At this point, you should be a master of the **Journey Method**, able to quickly access and use parts of your **Mega-Journey** in order to store mnemonic information. In this lesson, you'll learn about two small additions that will save time and improve your ability to navigate your **Journeys**.

Repeating Numbers

First, here's a simple, useful shortcut for handling **Repeating Numbers** (numbers that are more than two digits long but consist only of a single repeating digit). Examples would be $5.55, (888) 888-8888, and $99.99.

Before you can use this shortcut, you must decide on a **Mnemonic Clue** you'll forever associate with **Repeating Numbers**, such as a skipping record player, a large pink plastic "infinity" symbol, or something similar that makes sense to you. This will be your **Repeating Number Clue**.

Recall that we chose similar **Clues** related to **Negative** and **Decimal Numbers**. Working this **Clue** into a single **Scene**, along with your **Single-Digit Mnemonic Clue** for the repeated digit, you can quickly and easily deduce the intended number.

This plan has a glaring flaw; how will you know when to terminate the number? Isn't there a risk of confusing 555, 5,555, and 55,555? Due to this restriction, you can only use this shortcut in cases where the context allows you to infer the length of the number. If you're considering purchasing a lunch special at a Chinese restaurant in a major U.S. city and discover the price is $9.99, you can use this method; when referencing this **Mnemonic Scene** as a reminder of the price, it's safe to assume you didn't intend to memorize $0.99 (unrealistically inexpensive) or $99.99 (unrealistically expensive). A two-terabyte external computer hard drive is more likely to be $88.88 than $888.88 or $8.88. A very small townhome in an average neighborhood near a large U.S. city would more likely cost $111,111 than $11,111 or $1,111,111.

Take that last example and work it out. How would you remember $111,111?

For me, the repeating 1s would be represented by an oversized pencil (a **Single-Digit Mnemonic Clue** for the number 1) stabbed through a record player (my **Repeating Number Clue**). Adding details to reinforce the image, I imagine the record player sparking and attempting to spin despite the pencil; it's making a terrible, looping racket. If possible, this **Scene** should take place within a **Contextual Journey**, such as on the front stoop of the $111,111 home in question.

Try another on your own: imagine a friend takes up jogging and completes her first 5k race with a time of 22:22. Given the context, it's likely she didn't run it in 2:22 (physically impossible) or 2:22:22 (*really* slowly), so this is a prime candidate for such a shortcut. Work through this example. How would you remember this?

"Checkpoints" on Every Fifth Step

Before sharing the next addition, allow me to illustrate its usefulness with an example: the process of making a loaf of bread.

1. Gather your ingredients and equipment.
2. With a wire whisk, mix sugar, salt, rapid yeast, and some flour.
3. In a saucepan, bring liquids and butter to 120 to 130 degrees (F) or until small bubbles form around edge of pan.
4. Gradually, add warm liquid mixture to the flour mixture. Combine it with an electric mixer for 2 minutes on medium.
5. With a wooden spoon, gradually add enough flour to form a soft dough.
6. On a lightly floured breadboard, knead the dough until smooth and elastic (about 8 to 10 minutes).
7. Cover the dough with lightly greased plastic wrap and let it rest for 10 minutes.
8. Roll the dough into a rectangle and again cover it with lightly greased plastic wrap.
9. Let the dough rise in pan(s) for an hour in a warm, draft-free place.
10. Bake dough for 30 minutes.

Imagine you spent a few minutes memorizing this using the **Journey Method**. Once memorized, you'd probably be able to answer the following two questions without trouble:

- What was the first **Step**?
- What was the final **Step**?

Now, answer this question:

- What was **Step** seven?

The last question took you longer to answer. Why? The first **Step** was presented first, and the last was presented last, and so it's easy to know exactly where to look for each. However, locating the seventh **Step** required you to traverse the **Journey** from the beginning. Though you may be able to recall the second step as the "**Step** after the first," or the ninth as the "**Step** before the last," you tend to lose track of the **Steps** that fall in between. This can be fixed to help you navigate your **Journeys** more quickly.

You should already be using **Journeys** that naturally feature ten **Steps**. A **Checkpoint** is a static object, theme, or reminder that you can work into the fifth **Step** of any **Journey**; there, it will serve as an indicator that you've reached the **Journey's** halfway point. These fifth-**Step Checkpoints** allow you to find the third, fourth, fifth, sixth, and seventh **Steps** more quickly. If you wanted to locate **Step** 6 in a **Journey**, you no longer have to begin at **Step** 1 and climb to 6 (or begin at 10 and retreat back to 6); instead, you can simply begin at **Step** 5 (since you'll know where it is) and climb by one **Step** to arrive at **Step** 6.

Never use a person or object as your **Checkpoint** that could be confused with an established **Mnemonic Character** or **Single-Digit Mnemonic**

Clue. Ideally, it should be a unique setting attribute (such as a golden glow or bright green wall), or elemental attribute (such as a strong wind). Avoid objects (such as a genie's lamp) as much as possible; your **Checkpoint Clue** should be an element of the **Journey Step**, not of the **Mnemonic Scene** it hosts. Additionally, while a **Checkpoint Clue** can subtly interact with the actions or activities that are taking place within a **Step**, it should never interfere or become intrusive.

Imagine you're tasked with remembering a series of ten numbers, and you're using a friend's house as a **Journey**. Say your fifth **Step** in this **Journey** is a bathroom, and you have to use this step to store a 5-digit number (88220).

As you learned, you would use the **Mnemonic Character** for 88 performing the **Action** of 22 and utilizing the **Single-Digit Mnemonic Clue** for 0. You may have imagined a soccer ball bobbing up and down in the toilet bowl to represent the final digit (0). Now, inject into this location a **Checkpoint Clue** that will let you know this is your fifth **Step**. If your **Checkpoint Clue** was "golden light," you could imagine that you can hardly see the floating soccer ball due to a blinding, golden light radiating from the toilet bowl.

As a bonus, if you find yourself facing your **Checkpoint Clue** after only four **Steps**, you'll know you have skipped a **Step** somewhere.

Regardless of your choice of **Checkpoint Clue**, the important thing is that you place something in every fifth **Step** that will inform you instantly that you're at the fifth **Step** of your **Journey**.

Performing a Precision Check on Important Numbers

Here, you'll learn how to store important numerical information "safely;" that is, how to lessen the risk of making mistakes when storing or retrieving numbers more than four digits long.

When digital data is transferred from one place to another over a network or stored on a device, it's usually subject to some sort of data integrity check. The data is often processed through a system that adds a piece of meta-data to the original data. This meta-data is checked upon receipt, confirming the critical data has likely arrived intact. If the meta-data is compromised, it indicates that the real data may have also been compromised.

There are many different ways to accomplish this, and most are difficult to understand if you don't have a computer science background (if you're interested, begin by looking up the term, "cyclic redundancy check"). Simplified implementations of these principles can be employed to enhance the **Journey Method**.

To better understand this, imagine that I have a bit of information ("my dog has fleas"), and I must pass this information to *Person F* through word of mouth. To get to *Person F*, however, it must pass through a few others (*Persons A* through *E*), like the children's game, "telephone" or "whisper down the lane." If I say only, "my dog has fleas," to *Person A*, and they pass it on to *Person B*, and so on, neither I nor the intended recipient (*Person F*) can be certain they received the message I passed along originally.

However, imagine that *Person F* and I previously made an agreement that any information passed between us would have attached to it two additional pieces of information: the number of words and number of characters in my message. I could then pass along the message, "my dog has fleas 4 13." Once received, Person F can check the raw message ("my dog has fleas") against the number of words (4) and number of characters (13), and enjoy a higher degree of confidence that the message wasn't corrupted in transit.

Obviously, this is a simple example, as it only confirms the number of words and characters, not the message content itself; nonetheless, this hopefully illustrates the integrity check concept. You'll be using a specific method to ensure your message (your **Journey**) reaches its intended recipient (your future self) intact.

As you'll see, by "overlapping" two two-digit numbers (a **Mnemonic Action** and a **Character**), you can perform a makeshift "check" on each grouping of four numbers. Unfortunately, doing this to any given **Journey Step** will decrease your memorization speed and prevent you from implementing a fifth digit using **Single-Digit Mnemonic Clues**; nonetheless, this "check" all but ensures precision, and so it's an invaluable tool for memorizing numbers that absolutely must not be forgotten or confused.

Step 1: Rawwwr! Find your Precision Check Monster

It's important to remember that you're using a **Precision Check**, or your **Mnemonic Characters** will translate to inaccurate numerical information. To do so, begin your **Journey** with a preemptive "zero'th **Step**," where there lives a vivid, flamboyant monster. This will be your **Precision Check Monster**.

My personal **Monster** is purposely over-the-top, akin to the creature depicted on the cover art of Terry Gilliam's film *Jabberwocky*; it's dragon-like, and yet a bit cartoonish and awkward. Your **Precision Check Monster** should be able to shrink and expand in size based on the needs of the particular **Journey**. Over the course of your life, your **Precision Check Monster** may be called upon to participate in a variety of **Scenes**; it may begin one **Journey** lounging lazily in a recliner and the next stomping an entire city a fit of rage.

Choose your own **Precision Check Monster**, keeping in mind that you'll be placing this creature at the onset of any **Precision-Checked Journey**.

Step 2: Learn to Overlap

The following method may be a bit confusing at first, but it makes sense once you get used to it. Imagine you have to record the number 1621. You would usually memorize this within a single **Journey Step**. Since my own **Mnemonic Characters** for 16 and 21 are Adam Sandler (1=A, 6=S) and Ben Affleck (2=B, 1=A), respectively, I would normally picture Adam Sandler acting like Ben Affleck (dressed as his very forgettable character from his very forgettable film, *Daredevil*). Note that there is no **Precision Check** involved.

This is fine in most cases, as vivid images and **Mnemonic Scenes** can be very powerful and memorable. It'll work for the address you're trying to find for the party. It's your decision whether it's adequate for the combination to your gym locker. But if you're trying to remember that 1621 is the "code to the safe where the antidote is stored," or the "code to the disarming mechanism for the missile," there's no shame in wanting some extra insurance, no matter how experienced a mnemonist you may be. Let's memorize that number again (1621), but this time we'll have the digits overlap one another.

Take the first three digits (162) and break them up into two separate numbers that share the middle digit (6). This gives us 1**6** and **6**2. Next, put these numbers together and memorize them; 1662 = the **Mnemonic Character** 16 performing 62's **Action** (in my case, Adam Sandler performing Sandra Bullock's **Action** = Adam Sandler turning a disembodied steering wheel, emulating Bullock's signature action from the film, *Speed*).

Next, shift your attention one digit to the right (from 1621 to 1621) and employ the same method. From this, you end up with 62 and 21, which you memorize: The **Mnemonic Character** 62 performing 21's **Action** (6221 = Sandra Bullock performing Ben Affleck's **Action** = Sandra Bullock dressed as *Daredevil*). You've now memorized 1662 and 6221 using two **Steps**, with each **Step** containing four digits.

Step 3: Tie It Together

Assuming you remember that you began your **Journey** with your **Monster** and haven't made an error in your memorization as outlined above, a **Precision Check** is in place.

Here's why it works: The **Character** whose **Action** you used in the memorization of the *first* four-digit group should be the same as the actual **Character** used in the memorization of the *second* four-digit group. With 1621, you have memorized 16**62** and **62**21; in my case, Sandra Bullock was the **Action** of the first **Step** and the **Character** of the second.

If the first **Step's** second two digits (62, the **Action**) fail to match the second **Step's** first two digits (62, the **Character**), it serves as an alert that a mistake has been made. Hence, using this method helps ensure you've memorized each individual **Mnemonic Scene** (and thus the entire number) with precision. The first two digits and final two digits of the overall number are the only ones that aren't repeated in this manner; however, you can solve this by:

taking the **Action** associated with the number's first two digits and having your **Monster** perform it in the zero'th **Step**; and
adding a **Step** to the end of your **Journey** containing only the **Character** that represents final two digits.

Let's practice one; imagine it's vital that you memorize the fact that there are 31,556,926 seconds in a year. Memorize this number, using a **Precision Check**. Work it out on your own, and then check it below.

You should have memorized the following sets of digits, requiring a total of eight **Steps**:

1. 31 (**Action** only)
2. 3115
3. 1555
4. 5556
5. 5669
6. 6992
7. 9226
8. 26 (**Character** only)

Note that this number could have been memorized without a **Precision Check** in only two **Steps**. This illustrates an important point: The **Precision Check** method drastically slows down memorization and introduces additional complexity, so you should use it sparingly and only when dealing with truly crucial or sensitive information.

Quick Review

1. **Repeating Numbers** can be memorized quickly by filling a single **Journey Step** with a **Single-Digit Mnemonic Clue** representing the repeating digit, accompanied by a predetermined **Repeating Number Clue**.

2. By implementing a **Checkpoint** within the fifth **Step** of each ten-**Step Journey** you create, you can more quickly navigate your **Journeys**. Additionally, this will help you to ensure that you haven't missed **Steps**; if you find yourself facing your **Checkpoint Clue** after only four **Steps**, you'll know that you skipped a **Step** somewhere.

3. When memorizing important or sensitive numerical information, you can implement a **Precision Check** to help ensure you don't forget or confuse any digits. **Precision Checks** are performed by first reminding yourself that a **Precision Check** has been put into place (using a **Precision Check Monster**), and then using a method that requires that each **Step** serves as a "check" of the previous **Step's** information.

Lesson 2: Memorizing Strings of Letters: Advanced Practices

> *"It is half man, half bear, half pig."*
> —(Parody of) Former United States Vice President Al Gore, South Park (Season 10, Episode 6)

By the end of this lesson, you may very well find yourself imagining a man-bear-pig (or something equally ungodly and absurd).

Earlier in *Never Forget Again*, you learned how to memorize strings of letters or alphanumerics by using the **Journey Method** to store **Clues** about each letter. Now that you're experienced in this practice, it's time to explore ways to make it more efficient.

To stuff more than one **Letter Clue** into a single **Journey Step**, decide on a standard interaction protocol that the **Clues** must follow when sharing a **Step**. You've done this before; when filling a single **Journey Step** with four numerical digits, your standard ensures the first two digits are represented by a **Mnemonic Character**, and the final two by an **Action**. It's never done the other way around. This reduces the risk of **Clues** being transposed and minimizes confusion.

As mentioned in *Memorizing Strings of Letters*, it's a good idea to use animals or living things as your **Letter Clues**. There are several ways to combine two animals into one hybrid creature, such as "the first letter is represented by the hybrid animal's head, and the second letter by its body" (example: LE = Lion Elephant = a lion's head on an elephant's body). If you didn't adhere to the suggested standard of using animals/living things for your **Letter Clue Mnemonic Vocabulary**, this method can work with non-animal **Clues** as long as you anthropomorphize them (example: AC = Apple Car = a car with an apple for a head). It may be a bit more difficult, but it can be done; you just need to think creatively. Think like a child; many cartoons, comics, stories, and art feature humanized versions of animals or simple objects.

The "head of x with the body of y" method isn't your only option for a standard. Another method could be to keep both animals/objects intact, but to have them interact in a specific manner. You could envision the first letter's **Clue** riding on a saddle placed upon the back of the second letter's **Clue**. Obviously, the shrinking or expanding of the **Clues'** scales may be required, such as in the case of a whale riding a hamster (WH) or a car riding an apple (CA).

Try not to exceed three **Letter Clues** per **Step**, and don't attempt three until you've soundly mastered two. The more you use, the more laborious they'll be to memorize.

If you do decide to move beyond two letters in a single **Step**, your standard will have to adapt accordingly; it would be confusing to imagine three letters as an animal in a saddle on an animal in a saddle on an animal; you'd quickly lose track of your **Scene** in the repeated imagery. You could choose to imagine **Clue** x holding a bucket in which **Clue** y is sitting. **Clue** *z* can follow closely behind, frantically trying to climb onto *x*'s back.

Though the "head of *x* with the body of *y*" and "*x* riding *y*" standards have been explored here, these are merely examples, and your choice of standardization is totally up to you. You should know yourself (and your memory) well enough by now to come up with the method that will work best for you.

Decide upon a standard now.

Push the limits of your imagination, have fun, and practice memorizing the following strings, connecting all two-letter groupings into a single **Scene**:

- ADVOHI
- OIJEFB
- 2JV09
- 3G902
- 8FK28DJ2

Quick Review

1. To store more than one **Letter Clue** in a single **Journey Step**, devise a standard that dictates how the individual **Letter Clues** interact; doing so will help to prevent confusion about the order of the letters.

Lesson 3: Indexing Your Life and Remembering Each Day Forever

> *"MEMORY IS THE TREASURY AND GUARDIAN OF ALL THINGS."*
> —MARCUS TULLIUS CICERO, PHILOSOPHER

Though a beautiful and poetic observation, Cicero failed to mention that this guardian is far from perfect, often allowing the contents of this treasury to escape.

The *Discovery Health* program *The Fantastic Plastic Brain* once aired an episode called "Total Recall and the Spotless Mind," which profiled a gentleman who can remember everything. Really. Everything. He can recite any conversation he's ever had verbatim and can take you through any day of his life (going back to adolescence), step by step, seemingly without missing a single detail.

Although some people with superior autobiographical memories utilize some of the same faculties we've developed throughout this book (visualization, imagination, creative association, etc.), this man wasn't taught these skills. He possesses a natural predisposition we can only dream of. Recent research by Aurora LePort at the University of California Irvine has shown that people with this type of natural ability tend to have measurable differences in as many as nine separate brain structures.

However, unlike those with trained memories, this man lacks the numerous benefits of selectivity; to hear him explain it, his ability is more of a burden than a gift.

People who have a **Photographic Memory** (technically called an **Eidetic Memory**) are able to quickly store an observed visual scene in the mind and then recall it in astounding detail at a later time. Although it has been commonly believed by the mainstream that this gift comes from rare and unique wiring in the brain, many scientists now believe that **Eidetic Memories** are a myth, and that most individuals who exhibit these abilities are doing something much simpler, yet equally interesting: naturally utilizing some of the same associative skills you've developed artificially through this book.

Regardless of how it's done, the abilities demonstrated by those who claim to possess this gift are impressive to behold.

Unless you're born with one (and again, the very possibility of this is heartily debated), you're never going to have an **Eidetic Memory**. That's a shame, because—despite the many hardships it may cause you—the ability to remember everything you see and learn could come in very handy. Should you witness a crime, lose a possession, or have to explain driving directions to a stranger, having an **Eidetic Memory** would certainly be useful. It could also be useful for the memorization of text-based information, as the presentation medium could theoretically be more easily retained than the information it contains. Why memorize the facts on a page if you can memorize the page itself?

In reality, we have a love-hate relationship with memory. Our memories are our sole personal link to our pasts. Even when accessing the past through third-party means (such as books, videos, photographs, or the reminiscence of others), our own memories alone provide the context through which these narratives come alive. It's through memory that we can reference our understanding of love, pain, trust, and joy. In this way, our memories are a cherished and celebrated part of who we are. They define us, and this is why the loss of memory that often accompanies aging or illness is regarded as one of the most painful tragedies of life. To lose one's memory is, in many ways, to lose oneself.

However, our memories are far from perfect. We put a great deal of trust in them, and yet they constantly lead us astray. Our memories are inconsistent, fickle, and devoid of detail. Our emotions and the passage of time bias and color remembrances of events and the order in which they occurred. As such, we don't so much remember events as they truly happened, but rather as we interpreted them either at the time or after the fact. Recent research shows that each time we access an episodic memory, it is essentially being erased and rewritten, colored by our thoughts and mood at the time of recollection. After time, the past becomes a soup of vague memories tainted with opinions, misinformation, and implanted desires.

If you think about it, humans are terrible at remembering events in their pasts. Even seemingly memorable events become blurred with other like events. "Remember that weekend when we went snow tubing in 2000, when Josh's tube went off-course and he fell halfway down the mountain? Oh, that wasn't in 2000? Wait, we went snow-tubing twice? When was the second time? Ohhh—you're right. So when was that second time? 2002? 2005? I thought it was earlier, because I could swear that Dale was still in college at the time..."

The fact is, we forget for a reason; it's an important part of being human and vital to the maintenance of a healthy mind. To lose one's ability to forget—as did the gentleman featured in the documentary—is arguably to suffer an affliction nearly as tragic as the loss of one's memory.

What you're about to learn doesn't claim to emulate an **Eidetic Memory**, nor does it claim the ability to salvage lost or corrupted memories. It does, however, claim to drastically lessen the likelihood of forgetting details about the days on which you employ this method.

This is the most advanced skill taught in this book (as it relies on the amalgamation of many independent skills you've learned); however, it's fascinating, useful (though arguably *impractical*), and—once worked into your routine—relatively non-intrusive to practice and perform.

Make no mistake, however; what you're about to learn is truly extreme **Memory Development**. In order to master this skill, you'll need immense dedication, discipline, and honed imaginative abilities.

Leveraging Association

The premise behind this is relatively simple. The recollection of memories (especially distant memories) tends to ripple out from a single remembered detail. For example, you may not initially be able to recall what you ate for dinner three Mondays ago or what item you purchased at the store on April 21st, 2016. However, if you were fed a **Trigger Memory**—such as a particular detail about another activity that took place on these nights—you may find you're better able to place yourself in the respective scenes, and details would begin to emerge one by one until they facilitate the desired recall.

You're going to learn to record specific details about each day (including the date), and then associate this information with **Trigger Memories** based on events that occur on that day. By accessing this information, you can begin to make associations about other events of the day, and your memories can ripple outward from a single semi-artificial starting point.

In order to accomplish this, you'll build a **Daily Index** (a collection of information about a given day), consisting of two parts. The first is called the **Daily String** (encoded numerical information about the day), and the second is a **Trigger Memory**. After learning about both, you'll see how they tie together.

The Daily String

A **Daily String** is a unique series of integers in which to encode detailed information about a given day, essentially creating a "serial number" that can be used to identify the day. You should already be fantastic at memorizing long numbers, so the memorization aspect of this process should be a cinch.

Let's build a **Daily String** together.

Part 1: The Day and Date

The **Daily String** begins with the two-digit day of the month, followed by the two-digit month itself. Together, this will result in the format *DDMM*; for example, March 7th would be 0703. Next, add the two-digit year. Most people aren't likely to need more than ninety-nine years, so don't worry about the first two digits of the year. You want to keep this as simple as possible.

So far we have *DDMMYY*. March 7, 2012 = 070312.

Finally, add the day of the week (1 through 7, where 1 is Sunday and 7 is Saturday).

All said and done, we're looking at *DDMMYYd* for the date portion of our **Daily String**. Wednesday, March 7, 2012 = 0703124.

Using this format, what would the date portion of a **Daily String** be for Monday, September 16, 1991?

Answer: it would be 1609912.

There's a good reason why the day of the month precedes the month itself; doing so allows for more diversity between the **Mnemonic Scenes** used in the first **Journey Steps** of adjacent days. For example, consider Monday, September 16, 1991 and the next day, Tuesday, September 17, 1991. When starting with the day of the month, as we learned to do, Monday, September 16, 1991 would be 1609912, and Tuesday, September 17, 1991, would be 1709913. These both begin with different **Mnemonic Characters**, and we will therefore be less likely to confuse them.

So far, your **Daily Strings** contain seven digits. Given everything you've learned so far, you would most likely assume you should "jam as many digits as possible" into each **Step**, and should therefore record this information as five digits followed by two digits (a **Mnemonic Character, Action**, and **Single-Digit Mnemonic Clue** in the first **Step**, and a **Mnemonic Character** in the second). However, we want to record this information as a **Mnemonic Character** and **Action** in the first **Step**, followed by a **Mnemonic Character** and **Single-Digit Mnemonic Clue** in the second. Though this may seem counter-intuitive, it's important. The reason will be explained in detail when you learn about recall.

Before moving on, let's reinforce this by working through another quick example: the daily string for Tuesday, March 02, 2010 begins with 0203103; Wednesday, March 03, 2010 begins with 0303104; and Thursday, March 04, 2010 begins with 0403105. Build **Mnemonic Scenes** for the **Steps** involved in each of these dates, according to the format discussed.

Part 2: Additional Information

Feel free to add additional information to your **Daily String**, as long as you consistently include this information for each individual day's **Daily String** without fail. Including it only some of the time or changing it will cause this method to break down. Honestly, I don't even suggest doing this part, but I want you to understand how to go about doing so should you find it valuable.

Depending on your interests, lifestyle, or line of work, you may want to add specific incidental information to the **Daily String**. Some examples of the types of information you may wish to include are:

- The Temperature. You may choose to record information about the temperature in your Daily String. For example, you could include the minimum (low) and maximum (high) temperature in your area; this would total four digits, as any three-digit temperature would be self-explanatory (if the low on a July day is 88 and the high is 01, you should realize that this means 101 without having to explicitly remind yourself). Alternatively, you could simply store the average temperature (this would require only two digits, and would be enough information in most cases to provide a sense of whether or not it was uncharacteristically warm or cool). If you wanted even more simplicity, you could record only first digit of the average temperature ("7" = "it was in the 70's").

- The Weather: If this is particularly interesting or important to you, you could indicate a rain/snow free day with a 0, cloudiness/moderate precipitation with a 1, significant precipitation with a 2, and a downpour with a 3.

- Your Personal Health Status: If you suffer from an ongoing physical ailment or acute health problems, you could devise a 0-9 scale by which to track your level of discomfort, the presentation of symptoms, etc. in order to determine patterns. Though this may be data better suited for recording via some sort of external medium, this could prove useful to include in your Daily String so you always have quick access to it.

- Almanac Information: If you work in agriculture, for example, you could note the times of sunrises and sunsets.

- Financial Information: If you work in finance, you could store the closing prices of NASDAQ, the Dow Jones Industrial Average, or the value of your personal stock portfolio.

- Sports/Entertainment: If you're a sports buff, you could record information about your favorite sports team; this will require some creativity on your part when it comes to organizing this information (scores, opposing teams' scores, etc.).

If attempting to record non-numerical information, you could include **Mnemonic Clues** or **Letter Clues** if you'd like, though I strongly suggest you stick with integers when it comes to your **Daily String**.

Make it a point not to include trivial, useless, "Rain Man" data (such as the color of shirt you were wearing) just for the sake of pseudo-impressive thoroughness. Trust me, no one will be impressed enough to make it worthwhile. **Daily Strings** should ultimately be—to quote Albert Einstein again—"as simple as possible, but not simpler." They should be useful, practical, and well thought-out. For most people, this means only recording information about the date and day of the week, and foregoing the inclusion of any additional information.

Before moving forward, decide what type of information—if any—you'd like to add to your **Daily String**, and how you'd like to encode it.

Trigger Memories

A **Trigger Memory** is a featured memory from a given day you'll use as a reference point to begin recall of that day.

Choosing a stand-out memory from each day can be quite challenging, as similar or repeated events tend to blur together as time passes. Indexing a day relies on your ability to identify a unique attribute about the day, and then use mnemonic association to "attach" the day's **Daily String** to this **Trigger Memory**. Even on an utterly typical day, you can usually pick out some sort of unique identifying characteristic, even if that characteristic seems insignificant or superficial.

What Makes a Good Trigger Memory?

If you saw a bear run down the center of a highway, your spouse asked for a divorce out of the blue, or your hometown baseball team won the World Series, you've been handed an easy **Trigger Memory**. But unless you're a professional adventurer, many days can prove to be relatively uneventful. On such days, you may struggle to decide upon a unique or memorable **Trigger Memory**; when this happens, try to select a **Trigger Memory** that allows you to recall the highest volume of overall information. That is to say, a good **Trigger Memory** doesn't have to be the most obvious thing that occurred during the day. The most important aspect of a quality **Trigger Memory** is that it lies at the epicenter of a ripple of other memories. When presented with such a memory, you should be able to chronologically work your way backward (to events earlier in the day) and forward (to events later in the day).

Let's illustrate this with an example. Say on October 2, 2007, you recorded a **Trigger Memory** involving watching your son's soccer game, which the team lost by a considerable margin. You could probably take this memory and travel backward and forward into other parts of the day. However, this poses a problem: you could easily confuse this soccer game with other similar games (they didn't do very well that year).

Instead, what if the selected **Trigger Memory** was a strange or humorous conversation your family had in the car on the way home from the game? Using this as your **Trigger Memory** would record the memory of this conversation (which may have been lost had you simply recorded the game) and would also trigger the memory of the game, as you would be contextually aware that this conversation took place on the way back from a soccer game. By using this less-significant event (the conversation), you get two memories (the conversation and the fact that you were at a soccer game) for the price of one. In this case, the conversation—which took place during a transitional event (the trip home from the game)—has more rippling power than the soccer game.

Consider the following fictitious associative ripple: "I was in the department store at the mall, and I was talking with the woman at the counter for a while." Imagine that this is a **Trigger Memory**. You can take it from there: "I wasn't at the normal checkout counter, so I wasn't buying something. Hmm. I must have been returning something. Ah! We were returning the fishing reel we bought for Sam, because when he opened the box, he found it was broken. Given the **Daily String**, I know that this occurred on June 18th, so it was a birthday present, since that's right after his birthday. We ran into John and Tina at the mall that night, remember? Is that when they told us they were moving? Anyway, I remember being in the living room earlier that day when Sam opened the gift and found that it was broken..."

In the above example, a simple discussion at a department store has a good deal of rippling potential, as it provides context for events that occurred before and after the event (including the gift-opening itself). This illustrates that even "bear running down the highway"-style events may turn out to be poor **Trigger Memories** if they're isolated, whereas seemingly innocuous events can be effective if they have enough rippling power.

Though uneventful days make it difficult to find a suitable **Trigger Memory**, you may sometimes find yourself facing the opposite problem: a day with several memorable events. Imagine a Saturday in late December on which you went to visit a relative (aunt Millie) in the morning and then attended a holiday party at your job that same night. In such a case, you may be tempted to use either of the two events as your

Trigger Memory. If you think you can make the connection between the two events, then by all means do so. However, if you're uncertain whether or not you'd be able to recall one from the memory of the other, you may want to use a transitional event (such as an early departure from the family visit) as the **Trigger Memory**. This departure (and perhaps some conversations you had during the departure) may have more rippling power than either of the two events on their own, as it could—like the soccer example—tip you off to *both* the relative visit and the party; "Why did we leave aunt Millie's so early that day?" you may ask yourself, "Was there something else we had to do that night?"

This advice only pertains to those who want to take this method to the extreme and remember as much as possible about each day. If you don't care about the events of typical days and your goal is to simply date-stamp significant events ("I went to the hospital for a broken ankle on June 23, 2005"), then you can certainly use only the most obvious **Trigger Memories**.

Can I use more than one Trigger Memory?

In cases such as the example we just explored (visiting relatives and the holiday party), can't you just use more than one **Trigger Memory**?

You could, but it's not a suggested practice until you're incredibly comfortable using a single **Trigger Memory**.

In order to store two **Trigger Memories**, you would create a hybrid memory by injecting clues from one **Trigger Memory** into the other. In the above example (visiting relatives and the holiday party), you may choose to recall the family visit, but imagine everyone present dressed in formalwear, like the people at the holiday party. This will trigger recall about both events, as you'll ask yourself why you're imagining everyone dressed up at your aunt Millie's when no one really was, and decode this clue into information about the holiday party.

Alternately, you could inject your aunt Millie into the holiday party. "Why am I imagining my aunt Millie at my work holiday party? Oh, right, we visited her earlier that day."

With a good deal of practice, feel free to merge up to three **Trigger Memories** into your **Daily Index**. Never include more than three, even after years of practice; not only is it rare to experience more than three noteworthy events or distinct partitions in a day, but each additional **Trigger Memory** used increases the potential for confusion when attempting to recall the day quickly at a later time.

Do I need a Trigger Memory at all?

Yes. A **Daily String** without a **Trigger Memory** is like water without a glass, lacking any practical delivery method.

Consider a day—a Tuesday—in which you wake up, eat the same breakfast you normally do, go to work (which is uneventful), come home, eat dinner, ask your kids about their days (their responses are, as usual, dismissive and cryptic), hang out with your family, go for a jog, watch a rerun of a television show, and go to bed—or imagine the equivalent of this that would fit your specific life.

On such a day, you may very well feel as though you haven't experienced an event worth remembering; however, if you'd still like to record a **Daily String** for this day, you're going to need a **Trigger Memory** to store it.

If you think hard enough, *something* unique usually stands out about each day, even if it's just a passing conversation.

Tying It All Together

In order to record a **Daily Index** for a given day, imagine a **Mnemonic Scene** that features your encoded **Daily String** for that day set against the backdrop of said day's **Trigger Memory**. The location of the **Trigger Memory** essentially becomes your **Daily String's Journey**. Later, you'll learn to recall and decode the **Daily Index**.

Recording the Daily Index

Let's take a look at my **Daily Indexes** from two random adjacent days in 2011. To begin each, I came up with my **Daily String** for the day, including all the information I personally deemed useful. I then attached this information to the appropriate **Trigger Memory**.

The first of the two days was a relatively uneventful Thursday. I woke up, worked for a bit, ate lunch, went to the gym, and worked some more. Later, I watched a movie at home and ate dinner with my wife and two of our friends (my oldest child hadn't yet been born). I worked late into the night, played guitar for a few minutes, and went to bed.

The next day was a Friday. I awoke early in the morning, exercised, tended to some personal errands, and then worked. I met a friend for lunch, and on the way home, witnessed the aftermath of a minor automobile accident; two SUV's had collided, and the owners were trading information on the side of the road. I had to swerve in order to avoid driving over some debris. After lunch, I worked some more and later drove from my home in Philadelphia to New York City, where a friend was celebrating his birthday at a Japanese restaurant. When I got home, I read a bit before heading off to bed.

Thursday was relatively uneventful, while Friday was very eventful.

There were no great transitional events on Thursday, so I decided to make my **Trigger Memory** a particularly memorable moment in the film, when a jarring plot point caused those present to react. Remembering this moment and everyone's reaction reminds me that I watched it at home with these specific friends. In my opinion, no other events of the day seemed particularly worthy of recall.

Friday is different; since there were two distinct stand-out parts of the day (lunch with my friend and the trip to NYC), I chose to create two **Trigger Memories**. Since I chose two, I had to combine them into one aggregate, hybrid **Trigger Memory**. In this case, I imagine my lunch friend sitting with me at the table at the NYC restaurant. To ensure I don't accidentally think he was actually present in New York with me (though he wouldn't be, as he doesn't know my friend from New York), I imagine him in a bizarre way: dressed in an all-red jumpsuit and sitting on the table as opposed to in a chair. When I recall the **Scene**, I'll realize that my lunch friend was part of the day, but not part of that actual memory. After some mnemonic detective work, I'll be able to stitch the details of the day together.

So, how do you connect the **Daily String** to the **Trigger Memory**?

The **Mnemonic Scene** created by your **Daily String** should fit seamlessly into your **Trigger Memory**. That is to say, the **Mnemonic Characters**, **Actions**, and **Single-Digit Mnemonic Clues** brought to life by your

Daily String should interact within in the context of the **Journey** setting provided by your **Trigger Memory**.

In my case, this means bizarre **Scenes** and interactions unfold in my living room while my friends and I react to the film and while at the restaurant in NYC. The real memories are punctuated by intense artificial narrative, complete with dancing tigers, sobbing actors, flying car tires, and talking seagulls.

Recalling the Daily Index

Once you've combined a day's **Daily String** and **Trigger Memory** into a neatly packaged **Daily Index** and recorded it in your memory, you can recall the details of the day in either of two directions.

If you were given a memory ("Remember that time Maude choked on a bun during that hamburger eating contest?") and can remember its setting, you should be able to find your way to that day's **Trigger Memory**. From there, you should be able to figure out what **Mnemonic Scene** you've placed within it. The **Mnemonic Scene** can then be deciphered into the individual numbers of the **Daily String** ("Oh yeah, that was January 18, 2008. It was 38 degrees that day and the real estate market took a dive.")

The most difficult part of this process is finding your way to your **Trigger Memory**. If Maude's choking incident isn't your **Trigger Memory** for that day, you should be able to find your **Trigger Memory** as long as it is "ripply" enough to lead you to the referenced memory (in this case, Maude's choking incident).

For instance, if your **Trigger Memory** was a five-hour traffic jam on the way home from the hamburger eating contest, you'd be able to link the two events somewhat easily.

That's how you locate a **Daily Index** based on a memory, but you can also approach this from the opposite side; begin with a date and translate it to the date portion of a **Daily String**. From there, connect it to its **Trigger Memory** so you recall what you experienced on that day.

You may recall that a somewhat counter-intuitive format was suggested for recording the date portion of **Daily Strings** (a **Mnemonic Character** and **Action** at the first **Step** and a **Mnemonic Character** and **Single-Digit Mnemonic Clue** at the second). Here's why: imagine you were presented with a date ("where were you on January 18, 2008?"); you would translate this number (180108) to two **Mnemonic Scenes** (18's **Character** performing 01's **Action**, followed by 08's **Character**). From there, you can determine all but the final **Action**. If you had instead recorded this information using five digits in the first **Step** (maximizing the **Step's** storage potential), you'd need to know the day of the week in order to make sense of the second **Step** (a two-digit **Mnemonic Character**) and gain access to the date's memory. As you don't often have the luxury of knowing the day of the week, it's best to be sure you can access this memory without it.

If you're given a date, as in the above example (numerical date, month, and year), you can imagine a **Mnemonic Scene** involving these **Characters** and **Actions**. You can then ask yourself where you've seen this **Scene** before. What was the setting? Once you've placed it (i.e., located the **Trigger Memory**), you should be able to both:

- travel either backward or forward to figure out the details of the day ("Yeah, that was the same day that Maude choked on a bun at that hamburger eating contest"), and
- determine the day of the week and the remainder of the Daily String (additional information) through further exploration of the Mnemonic Scene ("after the alligator dances on a stripper pole, ending the date portion of the Daily String…").

To recap:

If given a date: Translate the date first into a series of integers (the beginning of the **Daily String**) and then into a **Mnemonic Scene**. Attempt to place the **Scene** within your memory and tie it to a **Trigger Memory**. From there, work through the day, and if necessary, determine the remainder of the **Daily String**.

If given a memory: Attempt to locate the memory. If it is not a **Trigger Memory**, attempt to connect it to a **Trigger Memory** from the same day. Once you've pinpointed a **Trigger Memory**, try to recall the **Mnemonic Scene** you've placed within it. From there, decode the **Mnemonic Scene** into a **Daily String** to determine the date, etc., and imagine traveling chronologically through the day, beginning with your **Trigger Memory**.

What About the Past?

As mentioned, the point of this skill isn't to recover lost memories, but rather to minimize the loss of new ones moving forward; however, there are several things you can do to jog memories from the past and create **Retroactive Indexes**.

Becoming a Memory Detective

Although you may sound a bit odd when making the request, try to get together with some old friends or family members for the purpose of some focused, directed reminiscing. During the session, take notes about memorable past days and events as though trying to piece together missing parts of a diary. Then, using your notes, you can create **Retroactive Indexes** by using select uncovered memories as **Trigger Memories**. If you need to fill in missing information pertaining to the non-date portions of your **Daily Strings**, a wealth of information is available online (such as historical weather, financial, and sports information), and you can very easily determine which day of the week a specific date fell upon using a digital calendar.

As a side note, this practice can be a wonderful and emotionally fulfilling experience; many of us have fast-paced lives and rarely get together for the sole purpose of reminiscing. It's also strangely rewarding to figure out the exact date of a distant memory. Pieces of your past will start to knit together as the rippling effects of the memories you discuss uncover moments long forgotten.

Practice and Repetition

Once you've constructed a **Daily Index** for a given day, it may be easy to let the detail fade with time. It's therefore important to engage this skill in two distinct ways.

First, you must commit to dedicated practice. Spend time purposely reviewing the **Daily Indexes** that you've built. This can be time-consuming, but if you're serious about adopting this practice, you must perform the necessary maintenance. For instance, you can spend a few minutes each morning reviewing the **Daily Indexes** for the same month and day of every previous indexed year.

The second way to practice is by forcing yourself to walk through a given day's **Daily Index** whenever you're prompted to refer to that day for any reason whatsoever. Imagine your mother asks you, "About how long ago did you last see the dentist?" and you knew (just offhand, without using this new skill) that you had gone approximately five months ago. Given the nature of the question, a rough approximation of "about five months ago" seems an appropriate response. Once you've answered, however, you should take a moment to privately pinpoint the day, some details of the day, and the **Daily String** associated with it. Let life dictate chances for recall; opportunities are more abundant than you may realize.

You'd be surprised how much this practice can improve your memory in general. It's challenging to attach specific information (such as a **Daily String**) to a date, and it's even more challenging to allow **Trigger Memories** to ripple outward and unearth other memories. Working through these challenges strengthens your overall powers of association, which—as you learned—form the foundation of functional human memory.

If your situation permits, it is best to develop your **Daily Index** at night, just before going to sleep. Not only will the act of sleeping reinforce the memory (we'll explore why in *The Profound Effects of Sleep on Memory*), but it isn't until you're about to go to sleep that all of the day's events have been revealed to you. You don't want to select your day's **Trigger Memory** in the afternoon only to experience something dramatic and noteworthy at 10PM.

Our memories are constantly being altered and compromised. It's part of life and a symptom of the way the mind works. Those of us who are troubled by this finally have an option, albeit a somewhat extreme one. Adopting this practice is one of the most striking preventative measures you can take to battle this constant corruption and loss. If you commit yourself to this skill, you can come away looking like a memory superhero: "Oh, December 2, 2003? Yeah, that was a Tuesday. The kids were both sick. It was 44 degrees, and..."

As mentioned in the introduction, I actually have a friend who—to some extent—possesses this skill naturally. Years spent observing the way he searches through his memories contributed to the development of the method discussed here. I'd always been impressed by his ability. Someone would mention an event—perhaps a concert—and I'd watch as he'd shut his eyes and begin to mumble. He'd say something like, "I remember that concert. Afterward, we stopped at a 7-11 next to a strip mall. It was late. I was drinking a raspberry *Snapple*. You were wearing a hooded sweatshirt, so it must have been cool outside. Spring or fall. It was fall. October. My sister was there, so it must have been while she was on break from work, so it had to be late October. And given the location of the concert, it was an all-day trip, so it was probably a Saturday or Sunday. Most likely a Saturday." I'd then stare in amazement as he'd casually pull out his mobile phone, check his calendar, and figure out the exact date based on the context clues he'd uncovered.

His system—like ours—relies almost entirely on association, and it's vital for you to understand that embracing association is the only reasonable way to develop such a complex skill.

Quick Review

1. Using **Daily Indexes**, you can record information about each day of your life that you can then retrieve at a later date.

2. A **Daily Index** has two parts: a **Daily String** (which stores raw numerical data about the day itself), and one, two, or three **Trigger Memories** (relevant personal events that occurred during the day, or transitional events that will remind you of several of the day's events).

3. The **Daily String** and **Trigger Memories** can be connected to each other through creative association.

4. While **Daily Indexes** are primarily useful for current and future dates, past dates can often be salvaged and memories recovered through the creation and use of **Retroactive Indexes**.

Lesson 4: Memory Health

> *"To keep the body in good health is a duty...otherwise we shall not be able to keep our mind strong and clear."*
> —Buddha

Though the statues in Chinese restaurants depict him as a bit portly to be doling out health advice, the Buddha was on to something. Memory is a function of the brain, and as much as it's surrounded by a mystical aura (as the sole regulator of the seemingly-inconceivable complexities of consciousness), the brain is a physical organ. Like any organ, the brain suffers from the strain you place upon it and is directly and measurably affected by the quality of the nutrition you provide it. It's an amazing structure that comprises many different interacting divisions. I strongly suggest you do some independent research on the brain; having at least a superficial understanding of the underlying neuroscience will help you to appreciate everything it does for you.

You don't have just one type of memory. Memories are born in one part of the brain and stored long-term in another part entirely. Each memory goes through a life cycle (Encoding, Consolidation, Association/Integration, Recall/Recognition, Reconsolidation, and

Erasure), and can be categorized as one of two different types (**Declarative** or **Non-Declarative**).

A **Declarative** memory—put simply—is one that can be explained to someone else. This is further broken down into Episodic memories, which pertain to specific events, and Semantic memories, which pertain to timeless information, such as remembering that the capital of Nebraska is Lincoln. **Non-Declarative** memories include emotions, thoughts, feelings, and ideas that can't necessarily be put into words. These memory types can also be broken down into sub-types, such as **Procedural Memories** (as in "procedures," like knowing how to jump rope, place a telephone call, start a car, or mail a postcard).

It's all incredibly fascinating, but far too complex to explore in detail here. Instead, let's discuss some ways to maintain and enjoy optimal memory health.

Before continuing, note that supplementation for the sake of optimizing memory or cognitive ability can be considered somewhat extreme. Among other factors, supplementation (whether for cognitive or physical reasons) involves dedication to a regular intake schedule and can be a burden on your budget; moreover, due to manufacturing complexities, the safety and purity of even the most tested supplements can't always be guaranteed. In addition, supplement laws are in many cases flexible; just because something is on the market and readily available to the public doesn't mean it's been tested by a reputable or governmental regulatory entity.

There are relatively few supplements that have been conclusively proven to target memory health directly; however, since memory is a function of a collection of cognitive processes spread across an array of interconnected subsystems, it can be argued that to improve one's brain health overall can have positive effects on memory. Collectively, drugs or supplements that address cognition or memory are called nootropics. Consult your doctor before beginning any supplement regimen.

When the first edition of this book was released in 2013, I went through great lengths to research and present the latest science available on memory supplementation. I wrote about Omega 3 Fatty Acids and the suggested dosages of both EPA and DHA. I wrote about B6, B12, and B9. I wrote about Ginkgo Biloba, and how its effects at the time were believed to be almost immediate and usually peak within two and a half hours of ingestion. I wrote about Creatine Monohydrate, citing a 2003 study by Caroline Rae from the Biochemistry school of the Royal Society that showed Creatine Monohydrate's effect on cognitive performance.

By 2017—when I began working on the second edition of *Never Forget Again*—almost everything I had suggested needed to be updated. While every supplement mentioned was still proven to provide benefits, dosage suggestions changed, ingestion timing changed, etc. New science has emerged about the effects of time-restricted eating, gut flora, epigenetics, and inflammation on cognitive function and memory, and by the time you read this, suggestions will most likely have changed yet again; frankly, scientific discovery occurs at a pace that doesn't work well with the printed word. As a result, I'll refrain from offering specific suggestions and will instead encourage you to perform your own research. Avoid marketing websites and advice that lacks empirical rigor; use tools like Google Scholar to find academic articles, and be sure your sources cite recent, peer-reviewed studies with large sample sizes. Once you've settled on supplements you'd like to try—if any—choose brands based on objective safety, label accuracy, and purity ratings. Certain services (like Labdoor) offer a good amount of such information to the public for free.

Quick Review

1. To improve and maintain the exceptional memory you've cultivated, you can ingest nutritional supplements that have been shown to positively affect cognitive function. As these recommendations are constantly changing, spend some time researching the latest science on your own, if this interests you.

Lesson 5: The Profound Effects of Sleep on Memory

> "OH BOY! SLEEP! THAT'S WHERE I'M A VIKING!"
> —RALPH WIGGUM, THE SIMPSONS (SEASON 7, EPISODE 5)

Unlike most lessons found in this book, you're hereby presented with two options: a.) read ahead to find a full, detailed explanation of why sleep is vital for memory, or b.) simply take the following sentence to heart and move on:

Failure to sleep soundly for at least seven hours per day will in many cases result in a measurable negative impact on your ability to retain new memories.

Mothers have been saying this—perhaps in a less verbose manner—for millennia, and if you're like me, you've shrugged their advice off for most of your life. As it turns out, there exists a great wealth of information pertaining to sleep and its relationship with memory. In years of study, I've yet to encounter even one reputable empirical study claiming that proper sleep is non-essential for the consolidation of new memories.

Earlier in this book, I mentioned an engaging talk by Berkeley's Matt Walker entitled *Secrets of the Sleeping Brain*. In it, Walker outlines the technical relationship between sleep and memory, citing a series of experiments he and his research team have performed. These experiments show that sleep plays a vital role in the retention and maturation of new memories.

It turns out Mom was right.

In case you don't feel like watching the hour-plus talk (though I promise you it's worthwhile), some of the key points are:

Sleep after learning consolidates memories: Consolidation is an iterative process wherein a memory ultimately becomes better anchored in the mind than when it was first formed. Research shows that failure to sleep within twenty-four hours after learning something new will almost entirely rob you of the chance to consolidate that memory. Using fMRI technology, Walker shows that while "fresh" memories are stored in one part of the brain, they are relocated to an entirely different part after sleeping. This is an obscenely simplified version of what's actually happening; these memories are actually distributed among several individual parts of the brain both before and after consolidation takes place. Simplification aside, the takeaway is that the first significant post-learning instance of sleep shifts the "location" of a memory from temporary to permanent storage.

Sleep after learning integrates memories: Relational memory refers to the ability to combine two related ideas in order to produce a third idea; for instance, it's relational memory that allows you to deduce such things as, "I enjoy eating popcorn and I enjoy walking through the park, so I'd probably enjoy eating popcorn while walking through the park." Walker demonstrates that sleep is vital for keeping your relational abilities sharp. Some experts suggest that the often-absurd nature of dreams is the mind's way of testing potential associations between new information (often extracted from the day's experiences) and existing information. Expanding upon this concept, Walker suggests that dreams convert knowledge (facts) into wisdom (applicable, complex ideas). This is known as integration.

Sleep before learning is critical to initial memory formation: There are several different stages of sleep (REM and NREM stages 1 through 4), and you cycle through these stages each night, achieving some of them multiple times. As discussed earlier, there are several different types of memory, which are either **Declarative** (Episodic, Semantic) or **Non-Declarative** (Procedural, Implicit, Non-Associative, Conditioning). As it turns out, your ability to store each of these different types of memories relies on your success in achieving the different types of sleep mentioned above. For example, missing out on Stage 2 NREM may inhibit your ability to store one specific type of memory, while missing out on Stage 3 NREM may inhibit another.

Sleep deprivation negatively affects the function of the hippocampus: The hippocampus may sound like a place where semi-aquatic mammals go to college, but it's actually the part of the brain that initially processes new working memories. Research shows that sleep deprivation can directly cause measurable hippocampal problems not unlike physical damage to that region of the brain.

Realistically, this is just the tip of the iceberg, but you get the idea; if you want to develop your memory, it's crucial to get adequate sleep on a regular basis. You can't skimp on it, and you can't make up for lost sleep (a concept known as "sleep debt") at a later time.

Quick Review

1. Failure to sleep soundly for at least seven hours per day will in many cases result in a measurable negative impact on your ability to retain new memories.

Review and Development: Section 5

By the time you began *Section 5*, you were already an elite memory warrior. You carried with you an intense arsenal of mnemonic weapons that distinguished you from the average person in a profound and measurable way. You're an entirely different person from the one who decided to embark on the *Never Forget Again* adventure some time ago.

Section 5 accomplished three tasks. First, it provided you with some suggestions for minor alterations and additions to existing methods that have the potential to increase efficiency or precision. Next, through **Daily Indexes**, you learned to take your skills to another (arguably obsessive) level, if you're inclined to do so. Lastly, you learned a bit about the science behind proper memory care.

Let's review what you learned.

Review

1. **Repeating Numbers**: **Repeating Numbers** can be memorized quickly by filling a single **Journey Step** with a **Single-Digit Mnemonic Clue** representing the repeating digit, accompanied by a predetermined **Repeating Number Clue**.

2. **Checkpoints on Fifth Steps**: By implementing a **Checkpoint** within the fifth **Step** of each ten-**Step Journey** you create, you can more quickly navigate your **Journeys**. Additionally, this will help you to ensure that you haven't missed **Steps**; if you find yourself facing your **Checkpoint Clue** after only four **Steps**, you'll know that you skipped a **Step** somewhere.

3. **Precision Checks**: When memorizing important or sensitive numerical information, you can implement a **Precision Check** to help ensure you don't forget or confuse any digits. **Precision Checks** are performed by first reminding yourself that a **Precision Check** has been put into place (using a **Precision Check Monster**), and then using a method that requires that each **Step** serves as a "check" of the previous **Step's** information.

4. **Advanced Letter Clues**: To store more than one **Letter Clue** in a single **Journey Step**, devise a standard that dictates how the individual **Letter Clues** interact; doing so will help to prevent confusion about the order of the letters.

5. **Daily Indexes**: Using **Daily Indexes**, you can record information about each day that you can then retrieve at a later date. A **Daily Index** has two parts: a **Daily String** (which stores raw numerical data about the day itself), and one, two, or three **Trigger Memories** (relevant personal events that occurred during the day, or transitional events that will remind you of several of the day's events). The **Daily String** and **Trigger Memories** can be connected to each other through creative association.

6. **Retroactive Indexes**: While **Daily Indexes** are primarily useful for current and future dates, past dates can often be salvaged and memories recovered through the creation and use of **Retroactive Indexes**.

7. **Memory Supplementation**: To improve and maintain the exceptional memory you've cultivated, you can ingest nutritional supplements that have been shown to positively affect cognitive function. As these recommendations are constantly changing, spend some time researching the latest science on your own, if this interests you.

8. **The Profound Effects of Sleep on Memory**: Failure to sleep soundly for at least seven hours per day will in many cases result in a measurable negative impact on your ability to retain new memories.

Development

You're going to spend a few extra days ingraining these concepts before wrapping up.

Days 1 - 4

On *Day 1*, review the entire section. If any lessons seem particularly difficult or confusing, spend some extra time with them.

Spend four days focusing on the skills covered in *Indexing Your Life and Remembering Each Day Forever*. If you haven't already, decide upon a final format for your **Daily String**. Spend time reviewing your past and trying to piece fading memories together with the goal of identifying the dates of two or three foggy past events. Begin creating a **Daily Index** each night and continue to do so moving forward.

Day 5

During *Day 5*, begin aggressively memorizing strings of letters or alphanumerics using a method that combines multiple **Letter Clues** into a single **Mnemonic Scene**.

Days 6 - 7

During *Days* 6 and 7, focus on memorizing numerical information using your new **Checkpoints** for every fifth **Journey Step**. Using your **Precision Check Monster**, construct a few **Journeys** around legitimately sensitive information, such as credit card or social security numbers.

By now, you should be memorizing obsessively. The more you embrace structured memorization as a fully-integrated facet of your lifestyle, the more practice you'll get; the more practice you get, the better you'll become. The power of human memory is truly staggering, but you get out of it only what you put in. Hard work and constant practice pay off.

Well done. On to the conclusion of Never Forget Again.

Conclusion

You've graduated!

You started as a forgetful, excuse-making, smartphone-reliant disgrace, and now—assuming you actually went through the process and didn't simply skip ahead—you're a shining example of what one can achieve with a little hard work and determination.

Congratulations are in order, as you've endured a mentally taxing, sometimes-frustrating voyage. In the process, you drastically improved your ability to procure, process, retain, and apply information for the rest of your life.

What you've learned here will affect all types of skill acquisition and development moving forward, from solving puzzles and playing video games to cooking meals and navigating the streets of your city or town. I would argue that no other single skill has the potential to benefit you so broadly.

Let's wrap up with troubleshooting, tips for continuing your personal education, and some reflection and introspection.

Why Isn't This Taught in School?

> *"THE WORDS PRINTED HERE ARE CONCEPTS. YOU MUST GO THROUGH THE EXPERIENCES."*
>
> —ST. AUGUSTINE, THEOLOGIAN

Had you known the techniques you've learned in *Never Forget Again*, school would have been much, much easier. Do you remember poring over lists of dates and battles before a history test? Trying to memorize Spanish words and their English equivalents? For most of us, it was agonizing.

You can now memorize the battles of the Korean war in mere minutes. You can use creative mnemonic images and **Scenes** to tie the Spanish words for left and right (izquierda and derecha) to their English equivalents ("to the left is a key—duh!"/ "right is where the wrench is").

So why isn't this taught in school?

You Can't Teach Creativity

Methods for using your imagination can be organized and somewhat standardized (as evidenced by this very book); however, the creativity required can only be encouraged, not taught. Children mature at different rates, and so do their imaginations and propensities for creativity. Children often lack the attention span or capacity for abstraction and association necessary to successfully execute some of the methods covered in *Never Forget Again*.

Despite common misconceptions, our imaginations are in many ways much more highly developed and sophisticated as adults than they were as children. The ability to construct complex, absurd, memorable images comes more easily now, due to intellectual growth and the comparably vast data set from which to draw concepts for imaginative **Scenes**. If you think about it, much of our context for humor and irony can be attributed to clever, sexual, violent, absurd, or subtle ideas that couldn't have been grasped in youth.

Of course, this doesn't mean kids aren't thinking creatively. As memorization skills are mostly left out of curricula, children are left to develop isolated mnemonic devices on their own. You'll notice that mnemonics such as songs and acronyms seem to be the method most often used by self-taught memorizers. Attending Catholic school in 1986, I remember learning the "corporal works of mercy," a list of ideals intended to guide the behavior of all good little Catholic children. I learned them once, way back then, and distinctly remember them to this day. They are:

1. Feed the hungry.
2. Give drink to the thirsty.
3. Welcome the stranger.
4. Clothe the naked.
5. Visit the sick.
6. Visit those in prison.
7. Bury the dead.

How do I remember them so clearly? After struggling for several minutes to memorize them via brute force, I came up with a little melody for them that sounded a bit like the oldies tune, *Poison Ivy*.

I also had trouble remembering which part of the day was AM and which was PM. I simply began to imagine that "AM" stood for "After Midnight," and "PM" for "Pefore Midnight." To some extent, most people naturally use mnemonics to remember things, and kids are no exception.

Not all mnemonics rely upon one's personal likelihood to construct such tools; there are also mnemonics that have informally permeated mainstream society, such as this one for remembering the planets of the solar system: "My very earnest mother just sent us nectarines" = "Mercury Venus Earth Mars Jupiter Saturn Uranus Neptune." Another famous example is the order of operations for arithmetic: "Please excuse my dear Aunt Sally" = "Parentheses exponents multiplication/division addition/subtraction."

Kids can certainly grasp the concept of mnemonic devices, and their minds thrive on creative associations much like adult minds; however, unlike adults, it can prove difficult to teach a group of children to harness their imaginations in any uniform way.

Children Lack Raw Context

St. Augustine's quote at the beginning of this chapter is appropriate; though they may be able to read words and understand concepts, most children don't have the wealth of experience required to build and maintain a substantial referential database.

You can't tell a group of third graders to shut their eyes and create forty ten-**Step Journeys**; many of them literally haven't been to that many places yet. You can't expect them to have enough personal or celebrity references on-hand to construct a full hundred-character **Mnemonic Characters** and **Actions** library. You certainly can't expect them to strengthen **Mnemonic Scenes** with bizarre, cultural, historical, or violent imagery, as they lack the life experience to have any real understanding of these things. You can't expect them to use the **EFL Method** for associating names with faces; to implement this skill properly, one should ideally know individuals with the same first names as the strangers he or she meets. How many people have most young children met? They lack the sheer volume of context to apply this method appropriately.

Lack of Educational System Integration

Teaching fundamental **Memory Development** concepts in school would essentially require an overhaul of the current educational system. Any country would have a difficult time justifying a slow-down of early childhood education in order to teach such "learning skills" as these. It's an interesting circle; imagine if learning about the branches of government was delayed in order to first master **Memory Development** tools that would both decrease learning time and increase retention. Though this makes sense in theory, it's a hard sell. Unless this practice was adopted globally, it would put the adopting country's youth at an initial disadvantage in a competitive global educational landscape (not to mention an increasingly globalizing workforce).

It will be a long time before any such changes are made, if they're *ever* made. So, for now, it's your responsibility and right to educate yourself (and if you're so inclined, your children, once they reach an appropriate age).

Troubleshooting Memory

> *"'TIS NOT ENOUGH TO HELP THE FEEBLE UP, BUT TO SUPPORT THEM AFTER."*
>
> —WILLIAM SHAKESPEARE, PLAYWRIGHT

Don't worry; you won't be left high and dry. If you've gone through this book in its entirety and still don't quite "get it," that's okay. There's nothing wrong with you; this is a very complex, brand new way of thinking for most of us. We're all different, so naturally—as with everything from basketball to trigonometry—some of us will pick it up quickly, and some of us will have to exert a bit more effort.

Common Concerns and Issues

Let's tackle some common concerns and issues encountered when learning the **Memory Development** methods taught in *Never Forget Again*.

I'm Not Smart Enough

False. Although some of us may be able to easily comprehend differential equations and others may not, "natural intelligence" has less to do with

Memory Development than you may think. According to Daniel H. Pink's acclaimed book, *A Whole New Mind: Why Right-Brained People Will Rule the World*, being predominantly "right-brained" (a "creative type") will benefit you in memorization more than a natural ability to solve complex technical problems will. The methods for developing a powerful memory leverage creativity and imagination, which are in many ways separate from what's typically thought of as core intellect. Even a slight appreciation for humor, irony, and sarcasm shows you have a sense of creativity. As long as you can form comparative opinions about creative works—for example, that you like some music more than other music, or some art more than other art—you have a sense of imagination, which is required to interpret these things; you can exercise your creativity like a muscle and force it to grow.

I'm Not Creative Enough

Maybe, but we can fix you. This one is a bit trickier, as creativity *is* key to developing a powerful, disciplined memory. If you're having problems coming up with interesting, creative, absurd imagery and associations when constructing **Mnemonic Scenes**, you should try to "work your imagination out" a bit more.

Improvisational acting (also known as "improv") is a skill that actors and comedians develop that allows them to instantly "riff" on a cue. For example, if a well-trained and experienced improvisational actor is given the cue "balloon," he or she will immediately find humorous, interesting, clever ways to use "balloon" as the focal point of a skit or presentation. When improv actors are training, they often practice by immediately exclaiming the images and ideas that come to mind when presented with a concept (this is called "word association"). When practicing word-association for the cue, "balloon," one might rapidly exclaim, "um...air, string, blue, clown, party, birthday, candles..." The idea is to give your brain total freedom to roam with an idea.

Practicing rapid word association on your own may help to loosen your brain up and allow you to explore less obvious associations; this, in turn, will help you to develop your imagination and become more comfortable with your creative self. Spend some time looking around and noticing objects; begin making mental associations as quickly as possible. Let your brain run away with creative impunity.

Another great way to work out your creative muscles is to write out **Mind Maps**. Popularized by author and personal development guru Tony Buzan, **Mind Maps** are a way to leverage your mind's natural tendency to create associations. The idea is that by taking notes or exploring ideas in a visual, object-oriented manner, you can unlock innate creativity in ways that are limited by more linear idea exploration methods.

Unlike word association, **Mind Maps** are written/drawn. To create a **Mind Map**, first write down the central theme or idea in a circle, which sits in the center of a piece of paper, and then create connections/associations that branch out from this theme. A very basic **Mind Map** version of the "balloon" example may begin like this:

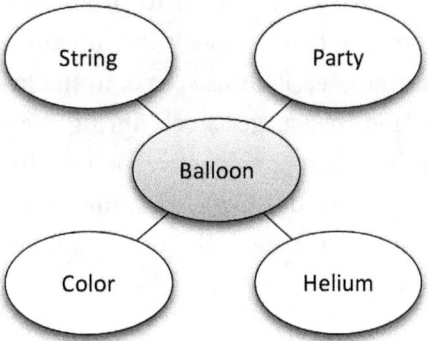

From here, you would create deeper connections that branch off of the secondary concepts. It may look something like this:

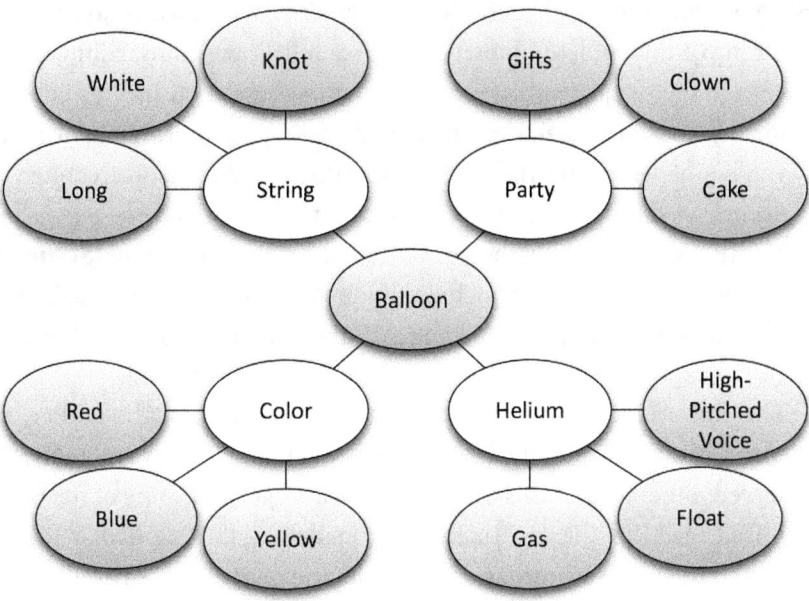

305

Mind Map creation has been shown to promote creativity and help people conquer writer's block, unlock lost memories, and even solve crossword puzzles more easily; this speaks to the human mind's sheer powers of association. If you get stuck during the process of reading *Never Forget Again* due to imaginative or creative blockages, **Mind Mapping** can help you unlock associations you might otherwise overlook, and thus, over time, help you develop a more agile and powerful imagination.

I Keep Forgetting Images/Clues/Scenes and Journey Steps

<u>Get weirder</u>. If you have trouble retaining your **Clues** or are losing track of what happened in which **Scene**, you're probably "half-assing" your **Scene** construction. This could mean you're going too quickly, choosing boring or incomplete **Clues**, developing dull **Transitions**, failing to truly engage the setting, or any combination of these. You may be choosing images that are foreign or meaningless to you, or **Journey** locations you're not very comfortable with. Slow down and work on creating vivid **Scenes** at your own pace. It's paramount that you become *good* at this before worrying about being *fast* at it. Ensure that your **Scenes** are detailed, developed, and include unique flourishes. Clothe the **Entities** in your **Scenes** in odd attire and make them say and do odd things.

The importance of creativity can't be stressed enough. Earlier, you memorized, in order, the Presidents of the United States and their years served. I memorized this information years ago, and some of the **Scenes** I used read like the nightmares of a madman. This particular **Journey** featured grisly axe-murders, people slipping in rivers of horse excrement, and human-sized cats smashing cars with baseball bats. There are cartoon characters performing sex acts, vacuum cleaners in lab coats, accordions being thrown through movie theater screens, elevators filled to the brim with tears, and an ex-coworker retrieving a drum stick from a giant starfish and passing it to Marilyn Monroe, who magically transforms it into a microphone to be used by a puppet made of wet napkins. At one point, an ex-girlfriend is working out in a mall food court while a Viking in drag heckles her. Wooden buildings are set on fire by people with surgically implanted helicopter blades jutting from their skulls.

Get crazy, throw out every rule, and let your imagination run free.

I Can't Concentrate

A legitimate concern. Many people have problems with focus and con— oh man, did you see that red bird?

Modern culture has wrecked our ability to focus. If this is the case for you—as it is for many—there are opportunities for rehabilitation through practices such as breath awareness and mindfulness meditation. Regardless of how it's accomplished, a proper attention span is vital for effectively implementing **Memory Development** methods.

Do some independent research and find some concentration techniques that work for you. Additionally, limit your caffeine intake to under 120mg/day and—when possible—work on mnemonic techniques in a dark room (with limited noise and stimulation) until you're comfortable enough to venture out into more distracting environments.

I Keep Forgetting the Methods

You aren't practicing enough. In order for these newfound memory methods to stop seeming like interference, they need to become a lifestyle, integrated into the framework of your every action.

You'll never achieve an incredible memory if you only use the methods taught in this book on special occasions. They must be worked into the construct of your minute-by-minute consciousness and used in place of the old methods that have failed you your entire life.

The words of your native tongue are symbols that represent discrete concepts, and, in a way, translating a word or phrase from a foreign language into a meaningful concept is a process that requires two separate steps. For example, in Spanish, "el libro" is translated to "book" (step 1). This word ("book") in turn means "a collection of text, printed on pieces of paper, bound as a single unit" (step 2). Many experts agree that you learn languages most effectively when you focus on comprehending the meaning of the words themselves, rather than first translating them into your preferred language. This means that instead of the two-step process described above, "el libro" would simply mean, "a collection of text, printed on pieces of paper, bound as a single unit." To the fluent, the translation-to-native-tongue step disappears.

Similarly, only with practice will you learn to cease translating concepts to mnemonics in your head. With time, as you encounter numbers throughout your daily life, you'll begin to see them instinctively as **Mnemonic Characters/Actions**, **Single-Digit Mnemonic Clues**, etc. In this way, **Mnemonic Vocabularies** are much like foreign languages. You'll be able to instantly scatter these **Characters**, **Actions**, and **Clues** along the path of a familiar **Journey** without having to think very much;

your **Journeys**, used constantly, will be at your immediate beck and call. You'll be able to paint vivid imaginative **Scenes** in your mind with stunning speed, as the more you use your creative assets, the stronger and quicker they'll become.

None of the world's top chess players, pole-vaulters, or sharpshooters rely on natural ability alone; they all study and practice every day to be at the top of their respective games. Anyone can gain expertise in **Memory Development**. Regardless of any natural predispositions you may have for the skills in this book, and regardless of your overall intellect, you'll need to work hard to maintain what you've acquired. All worthwhile endeavors require effort.

Additionally, if you find yourself forgetting the methods taught in *Never Forget Again*, you may be moving too quickly from one lesson to the next. This isn't a race, and your memory won't improve overnight; you need to work to become comfortable with each method before moving on, taking care to increase your speed incrementally.

So be patient but persistent. If you have faith in yourself, have faith in the methods, and learn to enjoy the challenge, you're well on your way to mnemonic greatness.

Beyond This Book

> *"INPUT. INPUT."*
> —JOHNNY 5, SHORT CIRCUIT

You've read and absorbed many difficult and challenging subjects; where do you go from here? Let's discuss how to continue developing and applying the skills you've worked so hard to cultivate.

Finding Information to Memorize

Finding and memorizing information (especially challenging information and lists) sharpens your skills and helps to unlock your powers of imagination. In order to stay sane and invested, it's important to practice—especially when first starting out—by memorizing practical, applicable, personally interesting information. Fascinated by social studies? Memorize points of the United States Constitution, or data about the individual states of the union (population and demographic information, establishment years, capitals, etc.). Interested in science? Memorize the plant and animal classes of Linnaean taxonomy.

If you'd rather just have some fun practicing your newfound skills, you may prefer to start with a book of trivia, such as *Jeopardy* champ Ken

Jennings' *Trivia Almanac*. As the subtitle boasts, this book contains 8,888 bits of trivia; it would be a daunting undertaking for most, but with your newfound knowledge, such a challenge is far from impossible.

Once you become more comfortable and experienced, you may want to move on to something more challenging. In my opinion, the single best non-web resource is a small gem of a book called *The Order of Things: Hierarchies, Structures, and Pecking Order*, by Barbara Ann Kipfer. This simple book contains a wealth of listed, ordered information, ranging from the types of highway interchanges to the dynasties of ancient China; from a tabular explanation of the EPA air quality index to the world's major deserts (arranged in descending order by size). It's incredibly inclusive; if you read it in its entirety, you'll know the names of the past kings of England, which cuts of beef come from which parts of the cow, and the names and defining attributes of bridge types and bird beaks. This holy grail of nerdy memorization is the closest thing to *Wikipedia* in physical book form, and is an inexpensive must-have for anyone interested in developing imaginative memory (or kicking ass at *Trivial Pursuit*).

There are many other books out there, but you can't go wrong with Wikipedia. Look up anything that interests you, follow links, and get lost in a veritable world of information. Fall willingly down the rabbit hole.

If you graduate to a "Rain Man" level of phone-book-memorizing insanity, consider Thomas J. Glover's *Pocket Ref*, a small, intimidating little black book of numbers. It contains information such as the density of different gasses at specific temperatures, German degrees of hardness, and extension cord current capacities. If you were stranded on a desert island with this book, you would have in hand the knowledge required to both construct a home and have it pass all applicable building codes in your current neighborhood. It's pretty hardcore, however, so don't consider this book a starting point.

Education on a Budget

Since the dawn of the information age, educational resources have been leaking out of the classroom and into our homes and devices. Much information that was once only available for hundreds of dollars in an encyclopedia or tens of thousands of dollars from a university is now available for free online.

Coursera (COURSERA.COM) and OpenCulture (OPENCULTURE.COM/FREEONLINECOURSES) contain links to hundreds of free courses from top universities. MIT has offered a number of their courses for free to the online community through their Open Courseware program (OCW.MIT.EDU). Stanford's Engineering Program has released major portions of its computer science curriculum for free online through their Stanford Engineering Everywhere (SEE) program (SEE.STANFORD.EDU/). You can also find a wide range of educational resources at Wikiversity (EN.WIKIVERSITY.ORG). These are just a few examples; thousands of similar resources on a variety of subjects exist on the web. With a little searching, you'll be surprised how much is out there.

If you prefer videos to the written word, nothing beats Khan Academy (KHANACADEMY.COM). The website provides simple, short, engaging educational videos on almost any imaginable subject. It's great for both adults and children, and is organized such that you can track your progress. Khan received funding from the Bill and Melinda Gates foundation and has been helping to educate the world since.

Speaking of video, you can learn almost anything through the magic of YouTube. I've used YouTube to educate myself in topics as diverse as real estate law, video editing software, robotics, and blackjack. I can thank YouTube (and the video contributors) for teaching me everything from the mechanics of a proper high-barbell squat to how to properly hold a newborn.

What Does the Future Hold for Memory?

> *"THE FUTURE AIN'T WHAT IT USED TO BE."*
> —YOGI BERA, BASEBALL LEGEND

It happens all the time: you're unable to remember something—the name of a historical figure, perhaps—and you whip out your mobile phone to look it up. Whereas in decades past, one would be forced to research such a mystery in a book or encyclopedia (or, unthinkably, go on living without finding the information at all), most of us now have the answers to billions of questions at our fingertips. For the first time in history, we have the technology to supplement our knowledge and memories in real-time.

With intuitive gesture recognition and the development of accurate voice-command technology, we interact with these devices—and therefore the information that they can access—in more natural ways with each passing year. Eyewear exists that overlays information atop actual settings, creating a "heads up display" that allows users to perform many tasks historically left to mobile phones, such as checking email, updating social media feeds, taking photos, and performing web searches. These devices can accurately recognize faces, objects, places, and products, and offer immediate supplemental information about them.

The applications of such technologies are becoming more numerous and practical; with time, many experts agree that these devices will eventually make their way out of our eyewear and into our actual eyes. In fact, many agree that information supplementation devices will eventually be created to interact directly with our brains. The transition will be slow, and it will take time for the mainstream public to trust this technology and stop associating visible assistive prosthesis with infirmary or disability.

Regardless of what the future holds, we live at a very exciting time for memory, as we've already witnessed the first true artificial memory upgrades; through mobile technology, we connect every day to the collective memory repository known as the Internet.

We've only seen the beginning, and it will be fascinating to see how these advances change the way we memorize and share information.

Final Thoughts: Some Words of Caution

> *"FEW THINGS ARE HARDER TO PUT UP WITH THAN A GOOD EXAMPLE."*
> —MARK TWAIN, AUTHOR

Like a kitten learning the purpose of its claws, you need to come to understand the best uses of the tools you now carry with you at all times. There are many possible applications for the **Memory Development** methods taught in *Never Forget Again* beyond those suggested in the book, but I encourage you to use your discretion when you're first implementing them.

Don't Overdo It (Especially at First)

Some **Memory Development** systems suggest using your mind as a calendar. In popular incarnations of this method, you reserve a unique thirty-one **Step Journey**, with each **Step** representing a different day of the current month. You then store information and **Meta-Information** about appointments, plans, and the like in the individual **Steps**. This "calendar" practice works surprisingly well once your memory is properly trained, and it's something you can certainly adopt if it would be beneficial for you. As mentioned earlier, with time, you may well begin to resent your reliance on technology and third-party tools, considering them a bother. At that point, practices like this mental calendar can become valuable.

However, especially given the sheer amount of information in most of our calendars and to-do lists, this is an example of one function that may be best suited for an external tool, especially while you're still learning. As your memory develops, practicality should define the extent to which you use the skills you've developed.

If you do decide to implement methods like the mental calendar, ease your way in. If you quit calendars cold turkey and the exclusive use of mnemonic methods results in a mistake, you may become soured on the practice and give up prematurely. Wean yourself off of such tools slowly. For instance, you can begin by keeping two parallel calendars; one in your mind and one in a third-party tool. Once you have managed to reconcile them without error for quite some time, you may feel more comfortable making the transition.

Don't Be a Smart-Ass

The most notable difference between well-liked and wholly disliked intelligent individuals is how desperately they want everyone around them to know they're intelligent. If you've memorized a vast amount of trivia, realize that your newfound knowledge isn't a license to offer unsolicited information about every subject that comes up. As difficult as it can be to keep "interesting" information to yourself, it's usually best to do so in social settings. What's interesting to you isn't interesting for everyone, and becoming a walking *Trivial Pursuit* card is a quick way to become very lonely.

Now that you've finished *Never Forget Again*, you'll be able to absorb and retain vast amounts of information more quickly and successfully than most people you know. Unfortunately, people dislike know-it-alls (they don't particularly like being corrected, either). Once you're proficient in the skills discussed in this book, you'll possess a newfound power, and as Spiderman/Peter Parker's Uncle Ben once said, "with great power comes great responsibility."

Wield it wisely.

Glossary

Action See Mnemonic Action.

Alphanumeric String A group of characters containing both numbers and letters.

Associated Entities Two or more **Entities** that are connected in some way, forming a single unit for memorization.

Associated Familiar Entities Two or more **Familiar Entities** that are connected in some way, forming a single unit for memorization.

Associated Unfamiliar Entities Two or more **Unfamiliar Entities** that are connected in some way, forming a single unit for memorization.

Asynchronous Scene An imaginative **Mnemonic Scene** (set within a **Journey Step**) that does not rely on cause and effect.

Brain Plasticity — See **Neuroplasticity**.

Caricature Effect — The tendency for the mind to exaggerate facial features in order to make them more memorable.

Character — See **Mnemonic Character**.

Checkpoint — A place within a **Journey** where you become aware of the current **Step** number.

Checkpoint Clue — A **Mnemonic Clue** that lets you know that you're at a specific **Step** within a **Journey**.

Chunk / Chunking — The act of breaking long numbers or **Alphanumeric Strings** into several parts so as to more easily memorize them.

Clue — See **Mnemonic Clue**.

Consolidation   An iterative process through which a memory becomes better anchored in the mind.

Contextual Journey   A **Journey** that's somehow associated with the particular individual or thing you're attempting to remember.

Core Information   The primary information being memorized; the information to which **Meta-Information** applies. For instance, a country's name could be **Core Information**, while its population, crime rate and climate data could be **Meta-Information**.

Daily Index   A means by which to record information about a specific day. A **Daily Index** is comprised of two parts: a **Daily String** and one or more **Trigger Memories**. The **Daily String** and **Trigger Memories** are connected to one another via creative association.

Daily String	A numerical (or alphanumeric) representation of a given date, containing the day of the week as well as other information. Part of a **Daily Index**.
Decimal Clue	A **Mnemonic Clue** that represents a decimal, allowing you to place a decimal inline within a number when storing it using the **Journey Method**.
Decimal Number	A number that contains a decimal.
Declarative Memory	A memory that can be explained to someone else. **Declarative Memories** are further broken down into Episodic memories, which pertain to events, and Semantic memories, which pertain to time-agnostic information.
EFL Method	A system by which to remember names and associate them with faces or individuals. It stands for e̲xaggerate, f̲irst name location, l̲ast name clue.

Eidetic Memory	The ability to recall visual information in incredible detail (often referred to as a **Photographic Memory**). Experts disagree about whether or not **Eidetic Memories** truly exist.
Entity	A noun (person, place, thing or idea) that can be memorized using **Mnemonic Techniques**.
Exaggerate	The first step of the **EFL Method** for memorizing names and faces. In this step, you exaggerate details about the individual's physical appearance.
Familiar Entity	A noun (person, place, thing, or idea) for which you have some sort of frame of reference; you've come into contact with this **Entity** in the past, and can thus immediately either imagine it or imagine **Clues** about it.
Finality Indicator	A **Clue** placed within a **Journey** that alerts you that you've reached

the end of a certain piece of information.

First Name Location   The second step of the **EFL Method** for memorizing names and faces. In this step, you imagine the individual in a location associated with someone you know who shares a similar first name.

Index   See **Daily Index**.

Journey   An imagined location, featuring multiple **Steps** or stops.

Journey Method   A method of storing information by imagining it distributed throughout the **Steps** of a **Journey**.

Journey Standardization   A set of personal standards about the construction of **Journeys**, such as rules about the maximum number of **Steps**, etc.

Last Name Clue   The third and final step of the **EFL Method** for memorizing names and faces. In this step, you record the individual's last name by remembering **Clues** that remind you about the way it sounds.

Learning Rhythms The patterns of study you utilize when initially developing skills or learning new information.

Letter Clues / Letter Clue Vocabulary **Mnemonic Clues** that represent the letters A through Z.

Linear Scene An imaginative **Mnemonic Scene** (set within a **Journey Step**) that relies upon cause and effect.

Mega-Journey An ordered array of adjacent **Journeys**.

Memory Development The act of assessing and altering the methods by which you store memories. Any process by which to improve the efficiency and usefulness of your memory as a whole.

Meta-Clue	A **Mnemonic Clue** that provides information about a specific piece of **Meta-Information**.
Meta-Information	Secondary information meant to be applied to **Core Information**. For instance, a country's name could be **Core Information**, and its population, crime rate, and climate data could be **Meta-Information**.
Mind Map	An established method by which to record free associations between interrelated concepts.
Mirrored Number	A four-digit number that consists of repeated two-digit numbers (e.g., 5656 or 9191).
Mirrored Number Action	A **Shared Action** used by a single two-digit **Mnemonic Character** to indicate that it's being repeated.
Mnemonic Action	An action performed by a **Mnemonic Character** and used to represent a specific two-digit number from 00 to 99.

Mnemonic Character	A fictional or real person used to represent a specific two-digit number from 00 to 99.
Mnemonic Character / Action Pair	A mnemonic representation of a four-digit number. In such a pair, a **Mnemonic Character** represents the first two digits and a **Mnemonic Action** represents the final two.
Mnemonic Character Library	A customized list of one hundred **Mnemonic Characters** to be used with the **Mnemonic Characters and Actions Method**.
Mnemonic Characters and Actions Method	A tool through which you can use a single **Journey Step** to store between two and four digits using **Mnemonic Characters** and **Actions**.
Mnemonic Clue	A creative concept or image that represents a distinct piece of information.

Mnemonic Scene	An imagined narrative that takes place in a **Journey Step**.
Mnemonic Technique	The use of a creative concept or image to memorize information that would otherwise be difficult to retain.
Mnemonic Vocabulary	A personalized set of **Mnemonic Clues** used to represent a specific type of information.
Name Memorization	The act of memorizing an individual's name and associating it with his or her face for an extended period of time.
Negative Number Action	A **Shared Action** that represents a **Negative Number**, allowing you to store such a number using the **Journey Method**.
Negative Number	A number with a value less than zero.

Neuroplasticity	The brain's ability to recover, forge new physical pathways, and alter itself.
Non-Associated Entities	Two or more **Entities** that are not connected in any way.
Non-Declarative Memory	Memories relating to emotions, thoughts, feelings and ideas that can't be put into words easily.
Permanent Information	Information that doesn't change or changes infrequently.
Photographic Memory	See **Eidetic Memory**.
Plasticity	See **Neuroplasticity**.
Precision Check	A tool for ensuring you don't accidentally skip or confuse any digits when recalling sensitive numerical information. A **Precision Check** forces you to memorize pairs of digits twice, allowing you to check adjoining

	Mnemonic Clues and **Actions** against each other.
Precision Check Monster	A **Mnemonic Clue** that indicates that a number has been memorized using a **Precision Check**.
Projected Treasure Map	A set of **Mnemonic Clues** placed within a real-world setting at which you're reasonably certain you'll arrive in the near future. By vividly imagining such a hybrid real/fictitious scene, you'll be forced to recall the meanings of the **Clues** when you arrive there.
Reflective Treasure Map	A set of **Mnemonic Clues** placed within a real-world setting you're currently observing in real time. Later, when the information is necessary, you can transport your awareness back to the point at which you recorded the information, recall the setting, extract the imaginary **Clues**, and derive their meaning.

Repeating Number	A number that consists of only one repeated digit, such as 444 or $99.99.
Repeating Number Clue	A **Mnemonic Clue** that indicates that a single memorized digit represents a **Repeating Number**.
Retroactive Index	A **Daily Index** for a date that predates your regular use of **Daily Indexes**.
Revisitation	The act of reviewing a piece of memorized information.
Revisitation Rhythms	The patterns of study you utilize when revisiting information after you've initially learned it.
Scene	See **Mnemonic Scene**.
Shared Action	A **Mnemonic Action** that can be performed by any **Mnemonic Character** in order to convey specific information.

Single-Digit Mnemonic Clue An object or entity that represents a single number from zero to nine.

Step A single location or point within a **Journey**.

Template The format to which specific numbers or **Alphanumeric Strings** are expected to conform. For instance, phone numbers fit into an *(nnn) nnn-nnnn* **Template** and social security numbers fit into an *nnn-nn-nnnn* **Template**.

Temporary Information Information that may change or that will only be pertinent for a short while (such as an individual's flight number, hotel room, or raffle ticket number).

Transition An imagined occurrence that takes place in order to bridge adjacent **Journeys** or **Journey Steps**.

Treasure Map / Treasure Map Method A short-term memorization method that involves placing imaginary **Mnemonic Clues** within the context of real-world settings.

	There are two methods for doing so: **Reflective Treasure Mapping** and **Projected Treasure Mapping**.
Trigger Memory	A memorable occurrence that acts as a point from which other memories may be uncovered when creating a **Daily Index**.
Unfamiliar Entity	A noun (person, place, thing or idea) for which you have no frame of reference. You've never come into contact with this **Entity** in the past, and thus cannot immediately imagine it or imagine **Clues** about it.
Vocabulary	See **Mnemonic Vocabulary**.

Works Referenced

Brown, Derren. *Tricks of the Mind*. London: Channel 4/Transworld Publishers, 2007. Print.

Carlson, J.J., et al. "Safety and Efficacy of a Ginkgo Biloba-Containing Dietary Supplement on Cognitive Function, Quality of Life, and Platelet Function in Healthy, Cognitively Intact Older Adults." *Journal of the American Dietetic Association* 107.3:422-32 (2007). Print.

Carnegie, Dale, *How to Win Friends and Influence People*. New York: Pocket Books, 1990. Print.

Foer, Joshua. *Moonwalking with Einstein: The Art and Science of Remembering Everything*. New York: Penguin Books, 2012. Print.

"How Food Affects The Brain: Omega 3 Especially Important." *ScienceDaily*. 11 July. 2008. Web. 17 May. 2012. ‹ WWW.SCIENCEDAILY.COM/RELEASES/2008/07/080709161922.HTM ›

LePort, Aurora K.R., et al. "Behavioral and Neuroanatomical Investigation of Highly Superior Autobiographical Memory (HSAM)." *Neurobiology of Learning and Memory* 98.1: 78-92 (2012). Print.

O'Brien, Dominic. *Quantum Memory Power*. New York: Simon & Schuster, 2003. Print/Audio.

Pashler, Harold, Mark McDaniel, Doug Rohrer, and Robert Bjork. "Learning Styles: Concepts and Evidence." *Psychological Science in the Public Interest* 9.3 (2008). Print.

Pink, Daniel H., A Whole New Mind: Why Right-Brained People Will Rule the World. New York: Riverhead Trade, 2006. Print.

Rae, C, A.L. Digney, S.R. McEwan, and T.C. Bates. "Oral Creatine Monohydrate Supplementation Improves Brain Performance: a Double-Blind, Placebo-Controlled, Cross-Over Trial." *Proceedings of the Royal Society B: Biological Sciences* 270.1529: 2147-50 (2003). Print.

"Secrets of the Sleeping Brain." *Fora.tv*. 11 Aug. 2009. Web. 13 Aug. 2012. ‹ fORA.TV/2009/08/11/MATT WALKER SECRETS OF THE SLEEPING BRAIN ›

Simons, Daniel J., and Christopher F. Chabris. "What People Believe about How Memory Works: A Representative Survey of the U.S. Population." PLoS ONE 6.8 (2011). Print.

Sur, Mriganka, Laurie von Melchner, and Sarah L. Pallas. "Visual Behavior Mediated by Retinal Projections Directed to the Auditory Pathway." *Nature* 404.20: 871-876 (2000). Print.

Taleb, Nassim Nicholas. *The Black Swan: The Impact of the Highly Improbable*. New York: Random House, 2007. Print.

Turati, Chiara, Viola Macchi Cassia, Francesca Simion and Irene Leo. "Newborns' Face Recognition: Role of Inner and Outer Facial Features" *Child Development* 77.2: 297-311 (2006). Print.

Yates, Frances. *The Art of Memory*. London: Random House UK, 1992. Print.

www.ingramcontent.com/pod-product-compliance
Lightning Source LLC
LaVergne TN
LVHW051357080426
835508LV00022B/2863